Islamic Ethics of Life

Studies in Comparative Religion
Frederick M. Denny, Series Editor

Islamic Ethics of Life

ABORTION, WAR, and EUTHANASIA

Edited by

JONATHAN E. BROCKOPP

with a foreword by Gene Outka

UNIVERSITY OF SOUTH CAROLINA PRESS

Published in Columbia, South Carolina, by the
University of South Carolina Press

Manufactured in the United States of America

07 06 05 04 03 5 4 3 2 1

Library of Congress Cataloging-in-Publication Data

Islamic ethics of life : abortion, war, and euthanasia / edited by Jonathan E. Brockopp ; with a foreword by Gene Outka.
p. cm.—(Studies in comparative religion)
Includes bibliographical references and index.
ISBN 1-57003-471-0 (pbk. : alk. paper)
1. Life in the Koran. 2. Life—Religious aspects—Islam. 3. Abortion—Religious aspects—Islam. 4. War—Religious aspects—Islam. 5. Euthansia—Religious aspects—Islam. 6. Life and death, Power over—Religious aspects—Islam. I. Brockopp, Jonathan E., 1962– II. Series: Studies in comparative religion (Columbia, S.C.)
BP134.L54 I85 2003
297.5'697—dc21 2002015449

Portions of chapters 4, 5, and 6 originally appeared in *The Muslim World*, Volume 89, No. 2 (April 1999). Used with permission of the publisher, the Duncan Black Macdonald Center at Hartford Seminary.

Contents

Foreword

This volume focuses on one tradition and on three problems. Islam is the subject of scrutiny, from beginning to end. And abortion, war, and euthanasia are selected under the rubric of "killing and saving." What the authors consider, then, is how, within Islam, these problems have been and are addressed. The reasons Muslims have for engaging in the disputes, and reaching the verdicts they do, remain the center of gravity. External vantage points that stipulate the terms and determine the verdicts are not imposed. Yet the volume is by no means problematically esoteric. As Jonathan Brockopp acknowledges, he selects problems that are widely debated in many circles, both religious and secular. Moreover, individual chapters show explicit awareness of how the problems are approached in non-Islamic contexts. In short, readers gain insights into Islam itself and the problems themselves, and into ways that particular religious and moral convictions may coalesce.

The volume exhibits three associated strengths. First, we find careful scholarship. In each chapter, analyses and conclusions depend on painstaking study of texts, study that assumes in turn demanding linguistic competencies.

Second, we find accessibility. Nonspecialists will not be at sea, and so the volume lends itself to classroom use. For example, it can aid those, like myself, who teach courses in colleges and universities under the umbrella of "religious ethics." (I regularly offer a course in Yale College entitled "Religious Ethics and Modern Moral Issues," that canvasses all three problems.) And I welcome the possibility that the volume makes more viable, namely, of adding Muslim perspectives to the analyses of Jewish, Christian, and secular perspectives on which I have heretofore concentrated. To widen conversations on such important questions is a gain, and the volume helps to place this goal within reach.

Third, we find efforts to understand the Islamic tradition that combine respect for and candor about its approaches to each of the problems. We should not take such efforts for granted, or withhold our gratitude.

For writings of this kind are frequently in shorter supply than the literature of partisan pronouncements and sweeping denunciations.

These strengths warrant, in my view, commending this volume in enthusiastic terms. Still, my enthusiasm does not stop here. For we also find that the chapters in each part range across classical sources and contemporary debates in a way that permits us to gain insights not only into salient features of Islamic approaches, but into other approaches by comparison as well.

Two examples must suffice. On abortion, we learn that a pivotal claim for Muslims is that God is the author of life and death, so that individual life is judged to be indisputably good and still one good among many, for example, the life of the larger community. Respect for human life is basic and generally determinative. But it is not supreme or always overriding, and in certain situations, other considerations may trump it. Muslims tend both to draw back from absolutes and to limit flexibility. Abortion is prohibited beyond 120 days after conception, except to preserve a mother's life. Before 120 days, abortion may be allowed on additional grounds, but nonetheless remains disapproved. There is theological insistence on the reality of human potential that inheres in the fetus before 120 days, so that respect is enjoined for potential as well as for actual human life. That grief following a miscarriage is entirely fitting supports this theological insistence. The consent of the husband, and not only that of the wife, is mandated for an abortion judged otherwise licit.

Missing is a stress on a woman's right over her own body that is allowed always to dominate other considerations. General worries go deep that permissibility on abortion can mutually reinforce other kinds of permissiveness (sexual relations outside marriage, prurience, and self-referential control that refuses to trust that God will provide when an unexpected or unwanted pregnancy occurs). Patient autonomy is extolled less than in many western societies; physicians are more likely to be asked to defend why they did what their patients (including pregnant women) wished, in contrast to cultural settings where they will be asked to defend why they did *not* do what their patients wished.

These represent only a sample of the judgments on abortion that the volume discusses. I cite them not because they are totally representative (differences among Muslims on this problem are plentiful), but to illustrate how they offer a distinctive mixture of judgments less conservative than official Roman Catholic teaching but more conservative than unqualified pro-choice stances. Those who are not Muslims are given a rich array of judgments to consider. They may say yes to the appeal to potentiality, for instance, but no to granting the husband veto power. Such selective agreement and disagreement, whether or not it is right, attests to the importance of wrestling with Islamic perspectives, and once more, the volume provides much-needed assistance in this process.

On war, the Islamic perspectives discussed here generally show a commitment to peace, but not to pacifism. It remains a moral duty to see that God's laws are enforced in this life. The combination of respect and candor to which I alluded is conspicuously in evidence in these chapters. So the authors do not shrink from referring to certain classical teachings that offend, for example, that unbelief is a grave sin, deserving death, and that norms governing wars against other Muslims may differ from those governing wars against unbelievers (and the latter are divided further between wars of defense and expansion). Yet the authors go on to describe modern developments that respond to western apprehensions of jihad and that address the regime of international law. Certain lacunae are identified, such as the need to confront more fully the implications of weapons of mass destruction and doctrines of deterrence. And notice is taken of contemporary struggles between proponents of neotraditional and of radical theories of jihad. Those in the former camp limit armed jihad to defense. Those in the latter camp view struggle and fighting in God's cause as a duty for individuals and not only communities; and no one who fights out of conviction should be treated as a common criminal, whatever judgments of "necessity" such a person may reach. Each camp draws different and sometimes rival conclusions about how Islam should comport itself in the future. The diverse fatwas on jihad issued during and since the Gulf War testify to the depths of these struggles. Jihad also contends against more general cultural attitudes and practices, bringing together in some cases premodern and postmodern arguments to oppose patterns of decadence that predominantly western sources are thought to inculcate.

Again, I cite only a sample of the judgments on war that the volume discusses. Attention to war yields more complicated and difficult comparative possibilities. The authors themselves make instructive points of contact with the Christian just war tradition, both with *jus ad bellum* (criteria for just resort *to* war) and *jus in bello* (criteria for just conduct *in* war), and document other recent comparative work along these lines that holds promise. The principle of noncombatant immunity from direct and intentional attack is a point, for instance, where Islamic and Christian construals may be usefully juxtaposed. Yet insofar as pacifism (or at least "practical pacifism") and the just war tradition are both commended in Christian communities, though the just war tradition is hardly on its way out, and insofar as the two camps in Islamic communities noted above vie for dominance, fruitful engagements may depend in part on how debates internal to each tradition further resolve themselves.

Despite my professed admiration for descriptive inquiries in ethics, these should not substitute for reaching normative judgments of our own at the end of the day, judgments about each of the three problems, and judgments about how adequately each is addressed by various Muslim thinkers. Yet these inquiries are indispensable if our judgments are to be, at a minimum, informed ones. And the authors inform with exemplary care. Chapters expose readers to key points of continuity and points of diversity and possible change. Continuity is evident where certain affirmations recur and authorities and sources stay intact. Possible change is evident where developments and revisions intrude and innovations, technological and otherwise, make their presence felt, and are variously resisted, embraced, or selectively incorporated. At a time when Muslims are an increased presence in North America and Europe, it becomes more practically urgent on all who dwell in these places to take cues from the absence that this volume displays of either defensiveness or rancor. We improve thereby our chances of acquiring a more reliably informed understanding of what is at stake. And the events of September 11, 2001, have demonstrated that what is actually at stake is momentous enough.

GENE OUTKA

Preface

This book was written to help fill a significant gap in the teaching of ethics in our colleges and universities. Such courses are now a common and popular part of a liberal arts education, but they tend to concentrate more on Christian and secular ethical positions than on the ethics of other religious traditions. However, the growing diversity of the United States, and other nations of the "western" world, demands that we also engage the ethical traditions of other major world religions.

Not only is Islam the second largest religion in the world, it is the third largest religion in Chicago. London, Paris, New York, and many other metropolitan areas also have substantial Muslim communities. While this book is not meant to serve as an introduction to the study of Islam, it can provide a basis for inquiry into Muslim ethical positions on some of the central questions of our time. Our aim is not to provide the "Muslim answer" but rather to show how Muslims frame the questions in terms of their particular religious viewpoint.

As a central unifying theme for our inquiry we have chosen ethical issues that focus on injunctions to save life and to avoid killing. We grant from the outset that these particular categories—abortion and euthanasia in particular—are of more concern for western ethicists than for traditionally engaged Muslim ethicists. But our purpose here is to construct a bridge between the Islamic discussion of ethics and issues of primary concern to secular ethicists and ethicists of Judaism and Christianity. Further, although the categories may be of western origin, the issues they point to are of universal concern. Taken together, the study of abortion, war, and euthanasia help to map out the boundaries of an ethics of killing and saving in both religious and secular schools of thought.

While the organization and initial approach of this book derive from similar texts on Christian ethics, the nine chapters are written by scholars of Islamic history and society, all of whom base their research on extensive use of primary materials. The introductory chapter first describes the most important of these sources and provides some context for their use and interpretation over the course of Islamic history. It then attempts a characterization of some of the guiding principles of Islamic ethical thought, analyzing the interplay of these principles with the three issues addressed in this book.

The remaining eight chapters are more narrowly focused, each addressing a specific aspect of abortion, war, or euthanasia. The first chapter in each section provides an overview of the key classical texts for the subject. This initial chapter not only lays the foundation for subsequent chapters on modern interpretations of these texts, it also reveals the historical contexts which shaped their reception. This foundation is essential for making sense out of Islamic ethical presumptions concerning, for instance, the very nature of human action in relationship to God.

The next chapters in each section address abortion, war, and euthanasia in the eyes of modern Muslim interpreters. For abortion and war, modern discussions are rather extensive; therefore one chapter first provides an overview of the subject, while another provides a more in-depth view of a specific issue. As we will see, however, euthanasia has not received the same interest accorded to it in the west. Therefore, only one chapter focuses on the modern issues surrounding determination of the actual moment of death. Finally, an afterword emphasizes the preliminary nature of our findings, critically assessing the project of comparative ethics and offering suggestions for future directions.

This project has been some four years in the making and is the result of a truly collaborative effort. All of the contributors to this volume have helped to shape the final version through their generous comments on each others' papers and through their participation in a series of conferences and workshops. I have learned a great deal from all of them, but I would particularly like to thank Sohail Hashmi for his constant encouragement and for his keen insight into ethical issues.

The first fruits of our work were presented to the 1998 meeting of the American Academy of Religion in Orlando at a joint session of the sections for the study of Islam and of Religious Ethics, and I would like to thank the co-chairs of the sponsoring sections for their support of this early stage of our work. Those papers were revised and appeared in the April 1999 issue of *The Muslim World* in a special issue devoted to Islamic ethics, and three of the chapters in this book (those by Abou El Fadl, Hashmi and Rispler-Chaim) originally appeared as articles in *The Muslim World*. I am grateful to the editors and board of *The Muslim World* for permission to reprint revised versions of those articles here. Two contributors to that issue, Daniel Brown and Therisa Rogers, were important influences in the early stages of this project, and I am grateful to both of them. Evidence of Daniel Brown's ideas are to be found throughout this volume, particularly in the introductory chapter.

A second workshop and panel were presented to the 1999 meeting of the Middle East Studies Association, and I am grateful to Kevin Reinhart for his help in guiding our workshop discussions. Mark Louder and the MESA secretariat generously provided us with a conference room for our workshop. In addition, I would like to thank the participants in the various sessions for their many useful comments.

The initial ideas for this book arose from my experiences in the classroom as student and teacher. I am particularly grateful to Gene Outka and Gerhard Bowering for encouraging my first forays into Muslim ethical thought. Students at Yale University and Bard College have sharpened my ideas with their incisive questions, and endless discussions with my philosopher-wife, Paula Droege, have helped to keep my arguments cogent. Colleagues and friends who have contributed indirectly to this book are countless, but I would like to name Bruce Chilton and Jacob Neusner for their active support of this project. I am also grateful to the faculty and administration of Bard College for generously granting me a research leave to complete the editing of this book. Joyce Kloc McClure, assistant professor of social ethics at Oberlin College, read through the entire manuscript and greatly improved the final version with her many useful suggestions, and Deming Brush was of great assistance in preparing the index. Finally, I thank Fred Denny for including this volume in his series, and Barry Blose and Barbara Brannon for shepherding me through the editorial process.

I dedicate this book to my son Noah, in hopes that he may grow up in a world that continues to respect the values of human life and dignity.

One

Taking Life and Saving Life

The Islamic Context

Jonathan E. Brockopp

The great ethicists of the western world, Augustine, Aquinas, Kant, and others, were all Christian and found themselves steeped in Christian convictions about good, truth, and beauty. Modern Christian ethicists, both Protestant and Catholic, often refer to these convictions and continue the tradition of Christian writing on matters of life and death. And in Europe and the Americas, the study of "religious ethics" is largely, though by no means exclusively, the study of this Christian tradition of ethical writing.[1]

But what happens to religious ethics as a field of inquiry when we depend on the Qur'an and the words of the prophet Muhammad (d. 632 C.E.) for our religious knowledge instead of the Bible? What happens to the philosophical definition of ethics, when in addition to principles and their necessary conclusions we add dependence on divinely revealed law? Can the category of religious ethics expand to include Islamic ethics, and if it can, what will the result look like?

These theoretical questions are ones that every student of ethics must keep in mind when reading this book, although this collection is far from a theoretical treatise. Rather, it is an attempt to understand Islamic ethics by looking at three specific issues: abortion, war, and euthanasia. Like Jews, Christians, and adherents of other major religious traditions, Muslims have explored these issues at length and responded to them in books, in articles, and in social policy. Reading and analyzing these responses alone, we can identify some of the distinctive features of Islamic ethical thought as it pertains to questions of life and death. When this book is read in combination with similar works from other religious traditions, moreover, it sheds light on issues that go beyond the borders of the Islamic religious tradition.

For example, in all religious traditions abortion, war, and euthanasia focus our attention on the value of human life. Abortion addresses questions of when human life is understood to begin as well as the ancillary injunctions against killing "potential life." In extreme situations, a doctor may even have to choose between the life of the fetus and the life of the mother. War addresses both the issues of licit killing of combatants, as well as the inviolability of noncombatants. Euthanasia urgently raises questions of response to human suffering, what a "good death" might mean, and the ethics of prolonging a life beyond God's appointed span. In sum, these issues explore questions of human responsibility at the beginning, middle, and end of life.

To group these three issues together heightens the comparative possibilities with other religious traditions. Still, it must be admitted that this combination is not found in traditional Islamic sources. Following the lead of these sources, modern scholars still prefer to deal with the ethics of warfare apart from the ethics of medicine.[2] To a large extent, this separate treatment is reasonable, since at first blush they seem to be entirely different ethical issues: war is a matter of public relations between states, while abortion and euthanasia center more on personal decisions within the family. Yet bringing these three issues together allows us to study normative judgments about taking life and the surrounding criteria that affect these judgments—for example, God's position as the ultimate arbiter of life and death; the human duty to protect life; and the realization that dire necessity and other extenuating circumstances may cause rules to be suspended.

These issues and the analysis of these judgments allow for comparison to secular and religious writings on the same subjects. But fruitful comparisons of ethical statements require equal familiarity with the religious traditions involved. In this chapter, I will first describe the primary textual sources for the study of Islamic ethics. Further, since this material only makes sense within a living context of interpretation and use, a second section will list the principal personnel involved in making ethical decisions. Then, in a final section, I will characterize in more general terms how Muslim scholars tend to approach the issues of killing and saving life.

Sources of Islamic Ethics

When Muslims look for guidance on questions of abortion, war, and euthanasia, they look to religious texts: the Qur'an, the collections of Prophetic stories, and the books of Islamic law that depend on these sources. Over the course of time, Muslims developed a highly advanced theoretical literature concerning the authoritative sources. This science, known as *uṣūl al-fiqh,* not only identifies sources for law, it lays down specific rules for using these sources and for cases when one source contradicts another. But while everyone agrees on the broad outlines, there is no single accepted formula for identifying and using the sources. Further, there is an uneasy relationship between the theoretical primacy of the sources and the application of this theory in the giving of ethical opinions.

No one disputes, however, that the Qur'an must serve as the basis of all inquiry. Revealed to the prophet Muhammad from 610 until his death in 632 C.E., it is understood as God's own speech. That is to say, Muslims believe that the Qur'an is not merely inspired by God, it is exactly what God meant to say to the early Muslim community and to the world in general. Furthermore, God spoke to Muhammad (usually through the angel Gabriel) in Arabic, and to this day Muslims resist translation of the Qur'an into any other language. The Qur'an is about as long as the Christian New Testament. It is divided into 114 chapters (called suras), which range in size from a few verses to a few hundred.

The Qur'an is a fixed, limited text. The process of its compilation and canonization was quite different from that of the Hebrew and Christian scriptures.[3] There is no apocrypha of texts that were not adopted into the canon, and no competing pseudepigrapha of texts written from the same period. Further, the Qur'an is not a book of law; it contains only a few hundred verses with clear directives to believers on ethics, ritual, and law. Rather, the Qur'an is more closely related to the prophetic writings of the Hebrew scriptures, and like those writings it appears to be dependent on a common body of religious knowledge. It refers to tales of Noah and the Flood, or the creation of Adam and Eve, in oblique language, drawing out implications from these stories rather than repeating the narrative. Likewise, its ethical statements are bound up in hortatory declamations, and not neatly placed in codes or lists.

Nevertheless, most religious authorities look first to the Qur'an for guidance, even when the subject is something that the scriptures do not address at all, like abortion or euthanasia. In these cases, the general command against killing is probed for its possible relevance to the case at hand. One of the most important verses, cited several times by the contributors to this volume, is "*wa-lā taqtulū al-nafs allātī ḥarrama Allāh illā bi-l-ḥaqq* (do not kill the person that God has made sacred, except by right)" (Qur'an 6:151; 17:33; 25:68). Yet even this clear verse raises a host of interpretive issues. For instance, in the case of abortion, is the fetus to be considered a "person" (*nafs*) before God sends down the soul? In the case of euthanasia, can one speak of a right (*ḥaqq*) to die as is commonly discussed in the west? To answer these sorts of questions, the commentary literature is an essential tool.

If religious texts are to inform us about the communities which hold them sacred, then they must be read within the context of those communities. Commentaries can limit possible interpretations; in the above case, commentaries would quickly clarify that no one has a "right" to die, rather God alone has power over life and death. Commentaries also expand the original source, often collecting interpretations of many previous generations together. The results can be massive. The Qur'an, for instance, is only one volume, but a typical commentary can run twenty volumes or more.

Specialized commentaries concern themselves with questions of grammar, sacred history, legal or mystical implications of the text. In the present volume, the authors depend on several different commentaries, all of which are listed in the bibliography. Among the most important classical commentaries are those by al-Tabari, al-Zamakhshari, al-Qurtubi, and al-Razi. Abu Ja'far al-Tabari (d. 923) was a historian and polymath; his text (*Jāmiʿ al-bayān*) is the earliest of the classical commentaries, combining many different types of exegesis. The Mu'tazilite theologian al-Zamakhshari (d. 1144) includes important grammatical and theological explanations in his *al-Kashshāf*. Fakhr al-Din al-Razi (d. 1209) was a famous philosopher and Qur'anic commentator who wrote *al-Tafsīr al-kabīr*. Finally, Abu 'Abd Allah Muhammad al-Qurtubi (d. 1273) was a noted commentator and jurist of the Maliki school; his commentary (*Jāmiʿ aḥkām al-Qur'ān*) often reflects these legal concerns. In the modern period, Qur'an commentary has continued in an unbroken tradition, and the following sources are cited in this book: Abu al-A'la Mawdudi (1903–1979), *Tafhīm al-Qur'ān*; *Tafsīr al-Manār*, written by Muhammad 'Abduh (1849–1905) and his student Rashid Rida' (1865–1935); and *Tafsīr al-Qur'ān*, by the current rector of al-Azhar University, Muhammad Sayyid Tantawi.

The importance of commentary in the Islamic tradition demonstrates that the Qur'an is not usually subjected to a literal reading. Rather, Muslims have depended on learned men and women to interpret the divine word and to add their own teachings to this tradition.[4] Therefore, these commentaries also serve as valuable sources for understanding the religious beliefs of Muslims through the centuries, since they provide a continuous expression of Islamic religious writing from scholars, mystics, and theologians across almost fourteen hundred years.

The second major religious source for Muslims is the prophet Muhammad himself, particularly his general way of doing things, or his Sunna. Unlike the Qur'an, which is the single source for God's word in Islam, the words and deeds of the Prophet are found in many different sources. These words and deeds were preserved and passed on from generation to generation in a precise form of oral transmission known as hadith, and early collections of these hadith were written down a few centuries after the Prophet's death.

The prophet Muhammad ibn 'Abdallah was born almost six centuries after Jesus' birth, around 570 C.E., and for the first forty years of his life he organized trading caravans. Around the year 610, he began meditating in a cave near his hometown of Mecca, when he was overwhelmed by a vision of the angel Gabriel commanding him, "Recite!" This event changed his life forever and he began, slowly, to preach to his relatives and neighbors. After years of effort, Muhammad and a small group of followers moved to the town of Medina. This *hijra,* the emigration of Muslims from Mecca to Medina in 622, marks the beginning of the Muslim calendar and was a turning point for the early community. In Medina, hundreds flocked to the new religion, and when the Prophet died ten years later, he left behind thousands of believers. The importance of this early group is testified to by the one billion Muslims in the world today. Now, as then, Muslims see the Prophet as an example of the ideal believer. Muslims often name their boys after the Prophet, wear clothes like he did, and try to live according to his precepts.

Stories about the Prophet were quite popular among early generations of Muslims, but no one attempted to collect and organize these hadith for legal purposes until over a hundred years after the Prophet's death. Two important early collections are those by al-Bukhari (d. 870) and Muslim ibn al-Hajjaj (d. 875). Hadith are also found in works of history and in commentaries on the Qur'an. It is worth emphasizing that Muslims do not believe that Muhammad was divine. A careful distinction was maintained between divine words that originated with God and therefore were put into the Qur'an, and Muhammad's general advice to his community. Both sets of words were spoken by the Prophet, but the first were written down and carefully preserved, while the second were handed down through the more informal vehicle of hadith.

As with the Qur'an, hadith are often consulted through commentaries. Particularly the earliest, and shortest, collections have important commentaries that expand and restrict the text just as Qur'an commentaries do. For instance, the Egyptian scholar, judge, and historian Ibn Hajar al-'Asqalani (d. 1449) wrote a popular commentary on al-Bukhari's collection, titled *Fatḥ al-bārī.* Muslim's collection also received significant commentaries, such as that by Muhyi al-Din al-Nawawi (*Sharḥ Ṣaḥīḥ Muslim*), the Syrian jurist who died in 1277. Since there is no single canonical collection of hadith, collections and commentaries are very numerous and continue to be produced to this day.

The growth of the Muslim community and the establishment of a world empire in the eighth and ninth centuries led to an explosion of information. With the loss of the earliest generations of Muhammad's companions and their followers, it was necessary to establish and train a group of scholars to understand and interpret the religious sources. After all, Islam had by then spread from Arabia across the Mediterranean to Spain and to the east as far as India. Life in the imperial city of Baghdad (founded in 761), or in the mountains of central Asia, was quite different than life two hundred years earlier in the deserts of Arabia, and many of the metaphors, usages, and even language of the Qur'an and hadith needed explanation.

Scholarship grew quickly, embracing the riches of the Byzantine, Persian, and Indian cultures. In the process, theological and legal schools grew, as did mystical orders. This variety challenged the power structures, and from 833 to 848 an inquisition was set up to impose a single set of theological doctrines. That inquisition failed, and as a result, no single school of law or theology has ever been able to dominate Islamic thought. The importance of this event cannot be overemphasized. Had the inquisition succeeded, authority for judgments on Islamic ethics may have been centralized, forming a hierarchy similar to that found in other religious traditions. Its failure led to a highly decentralized system, with many different influences.

Among these influences was a strictly philosophical trend that was only loosely tied to religious sources. Rather than turn to Qur'an and Sunna, the philosophers developed ethical arguments based on the requirements of reason and larger cosmological schemes. Some of them, like Abu Nasr al-Farabi (d. 950 in Damascus), were heavily dependent on Aristotle; consequently, their ethical writings are limited to matters of state and government.[5] Others, like Kay Ka'us ibn Iskandar (d. ca. 1098 in Tabaristan) wrote "mirrors for princes" in the Persian tradition, depending therefore on Persian ideals of state and kingship.[6] These texts were highly sophisticated products of the larger Islamic world, and as we will see, they affected the thought of religious authorities in both form and content.[7] More usually, however, these philosophical texts were written for princes and courtesans and are therefore not overly concerned with such individual matters as abortion, euthanasia, and killing in war.

This variety in ethical thought was balanced by a strong trend toward conservatism within the teaching institutions, many of which excluded "foreign sciences," such as Aristotelian virtue ethics, from their curriculum. The growing power of these institutions eventually led to the acceptance of a common theory of religious sources. This theory suggested that Islamic precepts were to be based on the following four sources, in descending order of importance: Qur'an, example of the Prophet (Sunna), consensus of the scholars, argument by analogy. In practice, however, these sources are seen as living harmoniously with one another, so a particular jurist is more likely to consult an important handbook of law rather than page through a collection of Prophetic hadith. Particularly in later centuries, these handbooks and commentaries dominated the teaching and transmission of law, so much so that until the modern period scholars would rarely seek to develop an independent analysis of a Qur'anic verse.

In the past two centuries there has been a rejection of the classical schools, which have been seen as both too moribund to adapt to the modern world and also too separated from the original sources of law. Modern authorities that depend on religious texts are therefore more likely to do their own Qur'anic exegesis or publish their own collection of Prophetic hadith; others resurrect philosophical arguments and reject some traditional interpretations as "irrational."[8] A second feature of modern ethical interpretation is the prevalent authority of science. In medical ethics, scientific facts, such as the form of the fetus in inter-utero photography or the absence of electrical activity in the brain, are often cited. These facts may be used to supplement or to verify religious truths, leading to some uneasy interactions, especially in traditional centers of learning, such as the Azhar University in Cairo.

For the general public, not trained in the ways of Qur'anic interpretation, opinions on matters of law and ethics are sought from religious authorities. Their opinions, called fatwas, are not binding and not legally enforced, but they provide invaluable evidence for gauging Muslim opinions on a given topic. Historically, fatwas of great jurists were collected and organized by legal topics, while fatwas today may be published in magazines and newspapers. Of the many important collections of fatwas, the ones most commonly used in this volume are the *Miʿyar* of al-Wansharisi (d. 1508) and numerous modern collections, such as *al-Fatāwā al-Hindiyya*, *al-Fatāwā al-kubrā al-fiqhiyya* and *al-Fatāwā al-Islāmiyya*.

At best, fatwas are only a rough guide to Muslim morality. Inherently personal and nonbinding, they do not determine law, although published fatwas of important persons, such as the rector of al-Azhar University, exert tremendous influence.[9] Still, fatwas provide some notion of the way in which ethical precepts are applied in everyday situations. This record of application is particularly useful in the medieval period, when we have few descriptions of daily life; in the modern period fatwas may be supplemented through anthropological observation and sociological studies.

Despite this wealth of historical sources and jurists' opinions, we must also keep in mind the limitations of these texts. Recent studies of Yemen and Morocco, for instance, suggest that even court records may be misleading, since women only go to court when other, more informal venues, are exhausted. Particularly for the medieval period, then, one may assume that most cases involving private matters, such as abortion and euthanasia, went unrecorded. This, in turn, helps to explain the rather theoretical nature of the discussion in the classical sources, far removed from practical application.

Whereas public issues such as war are discussed in great detail, abortion is mentioned primarily in terms of damages and recompense, while euthanasia is almost entirely absent.

Another limitation of these sources is that they are usually oriented around cases, real or imaginary; therefore, Islamic ethics are sometimes derided as "casuistry," a word which has come to suggest a form of reasoning without regard for principle. As will be discussed below, paradigmatic cases can serve much the same function as principles, but the ability to identify these paradigms, and the principles underlying discussions of detail, requires a very broad knowledge. Finally, these texts are generally written for those who are already familiar with the religious sources and their common interpretations. Like the Talmud, they are highly rhetorical works that can hardly be understood in isolation. Argument and disagreement are found even in the most authoritative collections of hadith, and the multiplicity of interpretive possibilities is further institutionalized by the establishment of four equally valid schools of jurisprudence within Sunni Islam alone. For these and other reasons, it is useful to keep track of which sources are being cited and how these sources are being used.

Ulema: The People of Knowledge

The elucidation and application of these sources naturally involves a wide variety of people, from scholars and teachers to the officials of the court. As in other religious traditions, the authority of a particularly charismatic person can be just as important as the authority of the textual sources they use. Certain individuals, such as the so-called founders of the four orthodox schools of law who lived in the eighth and ninth centuries, are understood to have had particular insight into the meaning of Qur'an and hadith of the Prophet. Their opinions and interpretations are given special weight, and books attributed to them are still consulted today.

These founders lived at a time when the scholastic system was just developing. Eventually an elaborate program of training would arise, culminating in the establishment of great colleges (*madrasas*) for the teaching of Islamic law in the major cities. Many of the important medieval sources for Islamic ethics were written by teachers in these colleges, and their students wrote some of the commentaries used in this text. As confusing as all these names and titles can be, the dozens of works quoted in this book represent only a tiny fraction of the thousands written on subjects of ethics and law. Scholarship in Islam is a *farḍ kifāya*, a duty upon the entire community, and it is the responsibility of those in power to see that centers of learning are properly maintained and endowed.

After undergoing long years of study, a graduate of one of these colleges might well seek a career in the court system. The Islamic legal court system, headed up by a judge, or Qadi, existed from a very early date. Although usually a political appointee, the Qadi had to be well versed in the process of making legal decisions on all sorts of matters. Furthermore, Qadis had significant societal responsibilities, such as guarding the possessions of minor orphans, distributing endowment income, and even declaring war. Court records from the medieval and modern period are valuable documents for tracing the application of law, and the written rulings of the Qadis sometimes contain detailed ethical justification for their verdicts.

Graduates of colleges might also be employed more informally as muftis. While Qadis render binding rulings that are legally enforced, muftis are scholars who provide answers (fatwas) to legal questions, usually in writing. This twofold system worked in a number of ways and still functions in many parts of the Islamic world.[10] For instance, plaintiffs might seek a fatwa to see if they have a viable case in advance of going to court. Alternatively, judges addressing a particularly difficult case might seek a fatwa from another judge to back up their opinion. Finally, a mufti can offer moral guidance on issues too personal or too insignificant for court, and some muftis host call-in radio shows to provide fatwas. On the web, "Ask the Imam" (http://www.islamicity.com/qa/) is a popular site for obtaining fatwas.

Not all influence comes through the education system, however. Abu l-A'la Mawdudi, for instance, is often cited as a source for modern discussions of the ethics of war and abortion. In fact, it is hard to imagine an overview of modern Muslim thought without a chapter devoted to Mawdudi's writings, yet he was a journalist and politician, not a trained scholar. Other famous figures throughout history have had similar influence, but the modern vogue of encouraging direct access to authoritative sources has led to an even greater proliferation of opinion. Therefore, modern works on Islamic medical ethics, for instance, are just as likely to be written by medical doctors as religious scholars.

Of course, none of this variety prevents individual Muslims from blithely speaking in the name of "Islam" or recommending the proper course of action for a "Muslim society." In part, this language is merely a matter of convenience, but it must also be seen as a serious claim. Such authors are engaging in normative ethics, and by speaking in the name of Islam they are making claims about their own scholarship and trying to move Muslim consensus in their direction. This book, by contrast, is concerned primarily with describing and analyzing ethical positions, and the authors (both Muslim and non-Muslim) seek to expose some of the variety to be found in specific patterns of Islamic ethical argument.

The Nature of Islamic Ethics

From the above discussion, it should be evident that there is no single set of Islamic ethical positions on war, abortion, and euthanasia. Moreover, ethical discussions in the Islamic world cover a broad territory that may challenge the boundaries of what is normally referred to as religious ethics. The reasons behind these facts reveal much about our presumptions of what fits into the category of religious ethics and could even change the way we think of this category.

For example, as Kevin Reinhart suggests in his afterword, the comparison with Islam (and Judaism) suggests that Christianity values individual over communal salvation. One might further speculate that the Christian concept of the soul, heavily influenced by Hellenistic thought, directly impinges on its view of religious ethics, which has been characterized by the positing of a rationalism universally accessible to individual human beings. In contrast, many Muslim thinkers see rational schemes as the tool of inquiry, not the proof; rational schemes guide one to the proof, found in revealed sources. If this assessment is correct, then it suggests that the concept of ethics as based on rational proof should be regarded as one form of religious ethics, and not as ethics *per se*. The hegemony of this rationalist view is already being challenged from within Christian ethical circles, as theologically intuitionist stances demand attention for instance, but the comparison suggests that we should be wary of presuming similarity between religions when there may be none.

If we look for an Arabic word to translate "ethics" we find either *akhlāq* or *adab*. Further, we would find a substantial literature under each of these categories, building on an illustrious tradition of character ethics and advice literature. These works are products of the rich Islamicate culture, but they do not always reflect Islamic values and ideals. Further, we would look in vain here for practical application of Islamic ideals to matters of daily life. We further complicate matters in the reverse when we translate the Arabic term *sharīʿa* as "Islamic law," a term suggestive of a fixed body of rules, the product, not the process of inquiry. In fact, sharia simply means "the way," and *fiqh* is not merely "jurisprudence" but "insight." For these reasons, Islamic "law" is better characterized as an ethical system than a legal one. It does not merely separate action into categories of required and forbidden, but also includes intermediate categories of recommended, reprehensible, and indifferent.[11] Further, there is no universally recognized code of Islamic law that applies this fivefold system of legal value to every act. And there is no earthly religious authority that could enforce such a code, even if it existed. Rather Islamic law is guided, much like western scholasticism, by disputation, argument, and finally consensus and tolerance. This tolerance of difference is exemplified by the existence of four equally valid schools of Islamic law within Sunni Islam, and the (sometimes begrudging) acceptance of Shi'i Islam as a fifth valid interpretation.

Yet sharia is far too large a category to be reduced to ethics. However wide-ranging the subject of ethics may be, it certainly does not address questions of the proper time of prayer or rules for undertaking the pilgrimage to Mecca, yet these issues are essential to Islamic law. Furthermore, Islamic legal handbooks tend to be rule-oriented, laying down required action without any need for explanation of the reason behind that action. This does not mean that principles do not operate within Islamic ethics; in fact, several key principles are identified and discussed by the contributors to this volume. However, Islamic law does not usually reason from principle to application. In fact, the very structure of legal reasoning (*ijtihād*), with primary recourse to a revelation and Prophetic example steeped in salvation history, tends toward the description of ethics in terms of normative cases, not principles. As a result, Islamic legal rules may be exceedingly rich in their relation to Islamic history and tradition, but also exceedingly difficult to translate and compare with other religious traditions.

This preference of cases to principles is one of the key traits of Islamic ethical argument,[12] a trait that may ultimately be rooted in the Muslim conception of the nature of God. In a recent article, Daniel Brown finds in Islamic thought both a tendency toward extreme theological voluntarism and also a counterbalancing tendency to presume that God's commands are purposeful.[13] These two tendencies are often in tension with one another, and each deserves further explication. By "theological voluntarism" Brown refers to the concept that God is the absolute and only source of volition. Simply put, nothing can occur, no bird can fly, and no human decision can be made, without direct dependence on God's will. In the classic "Creed of al-Ash'ari" medieval theologians stated

> that nothing on earth, whether a fortune or a misfortune, comes to be save through God's will; that things exist through God's fiat; that no one can perform an act prior to its performance, or be independent of God or elude His knowledge . . . ; that there is no creator save God; and that the deeds of the creatures are created by Him and predestined by Him, as it is written: "He created you and your deeds" [Q 37:94]; that the creatures can create nothing but are rather created themselves.[14]

This theological school is known as occasionalism or atomism, and it is no mere theoretical speculation; rather it is a serious attempt to employ human reason to describe how the world functions. Importantly, God's power in this system is absolute. Not only does he constantly create all objects everywhere in the universe at every given moment, he also determines their characteristics, such as their color or flavor, and their position. As stated in the creed above, it is only through God's granting of the characteristic of power that human beings are able to act at all, that power does not reside in them inherently.[15] Unlike God, humans are not only finite, their power and life is contingent on God, not in some abstract way, but directly at every moment of existence. Al-Ghazali went so far as to say that "everything other than God, when considered in itself, is absolute non-being."[16]

In such a system, God has the ability to alter anything in any moment; were God to so choose, the shape of the whole world could change in an inkling, without natural laws blocking the way.[17] Secondly, God is in a position of absolute immediacy. His will and his sustenance are required for all action, and even for the existence of inanimate objects.[18] This immediacy accounts for the total rejection of causality in some theological schools, since restricting God to the role of "prime mover" would remove God from his creation and suggest that intermediates can take on some of the attributes that rightfully only belong to him. Therefore, Muslim philosophers argued that "the fundamental and eternal source of these essences lies in the mind of God or in God's thinking them; it is God's thought which is the ultimate formal and final cause of all things."[19]

This depiction of God in control of every atom of creation might well seem foreign to many Muslims. Indeed, it is hard for anyone to live out a normal life, convinced that every single act is ultimately and directly dependent upon God. But while this system may only have been discussed among Muslim theologians, its main premises have important effects on Islamic ethical thought. As Brown writes: "God's command alone establishes an act as right or wrong quite independently of any human judgment about resulting benefit or harm. . . . [There is no] intrinsic moral value in specific acts. From a strict voluntarist viewpoint, should God prescribe an act which appears evil, it would be right for human beings to do it."[20] Brown also argues that this "theological voluntarism" helps explain the characteristic form of ethical response literature in Islam, a literature marked by the tendency to argue from cases instead of principles. He writes:

> A contemporary Muslim scholar, for example, makes the startling claim that "for Muslims abortion is not an ethical question." By which

> he means, Muslims don't have to think about abortion, they just go to the Qur'ān and the Sunna to find out whether it is right or wrong. Within a voluntarist framework such logic is quite sensible. If God is the only sure source of knowledge of good and evil, then there is little need for ethical reflection—rather, the only proper method in ethics will be to go directly to revelation. An insistence on beginning with the Qur'an and Sunna faithfully reflects a basic assumption of Muslim ethical theory—that God alone defines right and wrong, hence sure knowledge of good and evil can only be gained through revelation.[21]

Ideally then, each case becomes a new occasion for reflection on scripture, a method which is meant to eliminate the risks of human interpretation.

As Brown readily admits, this theology paints a rather austere picture, and it is possible to overstate the extent to which it influences Muslim ethical practice. Already in the formative period, scholars were making fun of the possible effects of a determinist God on ethical action. One story recorded by the theologian al-Ash'ari tells of a man, Shu'ayb, who owed some money to his friend, Maymun. However, when Maymun told him to pay up, Shu'ayb responded, "If God had willed it, I could not have done otherwise!"[22] Further, such a system seemed both to prevent believers from performing good acts on their own, and also to see God as the cause of evil acts as well as good. Arguably, it is just this sort of fatalism against which the Qur'an tried to argue.

Muslim theologians answered this austere system with a series of fine distinctions, arguing that sinful acts are "not in accordance with Allah's commandment, yet in accordance with His will, not in accordance with His desire, yet in accordance with His decisions, not in accordance with His good pleasure, yet in accordance with His creation."[23] Brown clarifies the conviction that lies behind these distinctions: that while God is able to act completely upon whim, in fact

> God's will is presumed to be purposeful, so that human reason, in *dependence* upon revelation, can discern rules and apply them. . . . [God] is *unlikely* to command an act one day and forbid the same act the next. It is not impossible that He may do so but it is not His general pattern. What this means is that there is a regularity in the will of God which allows for extrapolation from the known commands of God to new cases.[24]

What Brown refers to here is not merely a paradox within Islamic theology, but also a tension between a radical depiction of God's power and the pragmatic demands to reach consistent practical judgments. In other words, accepting a theory of God's complete power over every action does not prevent jurists from reasoning as though they had sufficient liberty to issue coherent verdicts.

The prime example of this reasoning is the methodological debate over how one gets legal and ethical norms out of scripture. This debate was resolved through common acceptance of a method in which jurists first consult Qur'an, then the record of the Prophet's words and actions (his Sunna). Other sources, such as the custom of important companions of the Prophet or the consensus of the scholars, could then also be consulted, but only in limited circumstances. By the eleventh century, the great scholar Abu Hamid al-Ghazali could summarize the process:

> The foundations of the religious law are four: 1) the book of God, 2) the Sunna of God's messenger, and 3) the consensus of the religious leaders and the traditions of the companions of the Prophet. As for this consensus, it is a foundation to the extent that it directs one to the Sunna, for it is a foundation of the third rank. The statements of the companions are similar, for they also direct one to the Sunna. After all, the companions witnessed the inspiration of and revelation to the Prophet and they comprehended the clear meanings of the revelation due to their knowledge of its relationship to particular circumstances, which were concealed from others. It is possible that the obvious expression of the revelation does not encompass that which was obvious at the time. 4) Along these lines, the opinion of the exemplary scholars may also be seen as a foundation of the religious law, along with their traditions, although this is with special conditions, particularly regarding the person who gives the opinion.[25]

While in al-Ghazali's system the action of any individual jurist seems quite restricted, the very existence of this system bears out Brown's contention of purposefulness. By building a rational framework that focuses on applying God's commands, the jurists seem to suggest that the mind of God is accessible through the application of reason. As we will see below, however, it does not follow that God must conform to logic or that he is limited according to human conceptions of logic.

Brown's analysis is particularly helpful in explaining some of the distinctive patterns of reasoning in Islamic ethical statements. Theological voluntarism leads to the formal recognition of the primacy of the Qur'an and also accounts for the tendency to reason from case instead of principle. The presumption of purposefulness leads both to a logical system of legal reasoning and also to the existence of certain consequentialist principles, such as utility, necessity, and equity. As will be seen in subsequent chapters, these last three principles play a significant role in modern ethical reasoning, and Brown calls them "the open frontier of Islamic ethics."[26]

But as useful as this analysis is, it misses some important sociological consequences of theological voluntarism. By locating ethical knowledge in the mind of God, Islam significantly limits the human role in legislating ethical norms. As a result, there is no single person or council that establishes ethical norms in Islam, and many significant ethical acts are left up to individual conscience, effectively establishing a limited right to privacy.[27] If we are to portray Islamic ethics accurately, then, we must also understand the significance of this limitation on human power in the structure of Islamic societies.

For the researcher, the complete lack of a legal code or centralized ethical authority means that dozens of different kinds of sources must be consulted, not just one. Muslims may gather ethical guidance from mystical texts, philosophical treatises in the Aristotelian tradition, or local custom.[28] But while each of these other sorts of ethical authority play important roles for individual Muslims, that role has always been a contested one. Mystics have been accused of bringing foreign elements into Islam, or of ascribing special knowledge and power to certain "friends of God." Aristotelian philosophers have been accused of placing human reason in the position of a rival to God's knowledge, and of limiting God's actions to the realm of the rational. Likewise the local customs and the knowledge of village wisepersons can be seen as a rival to God's authority.

The absence of formal vehicles for establishing ethical norms also means that some important contemporary issues, such as nuclear war and euthanasia, receive little sustained attention. In the case of nuclear war, Sohail Hashmi finds that many modern ethicists have little to say on the ethics of using weapons of mass destruction (pp. 141–42). Likewise, Muslim authorities are reticent to respond to technological advances in medicine that may have significant sociological and theological consequences for the dying individual.

Unlike the issue of war, euthanasia falls within the broad category of family matters, over which Islamic law exercises limited authority. In a recent interview with a Tunisian ethicist, I was told that both doctors and scholars of Islamic law would be unlikely to pronounce upon a case where euthanasia was desired. Rather, the decision would be left up to the family.[29] This respect for family prerogative also attests to the conviction that God alone knows what is right and wrong in such cases. The individual conscience is considered a better guide for action, since it is ultimately the individual who will have to answer to God on the day of judgment.[30]

In a tradition that loves variety, theological voluntarism is only the most dominant depiction of God's action in the world. There are other depictions of God as limited to the role of creator, as "bound to do the better," or as driven by compassion for his creation. These depictions are not always considered to be contradictory of one another, and some have great significance for ethical behavior. Still, the very fact that human ethical action depends so heavily on God's characteristics reveals much about the value of human life in Islam, which is, finally, contingent and not intrinsic. While human beings are the pinnacle of God's creation, there is nothing essential to the human creature that always demands an overriding consideration for human life. Rather, in cases of war, abortion, or euthanasia, human life is to be preserved because of God's essential attribute as the author of life and death.

This dependence on a characteristic of God for the value of life, and not some intrinsic characteristic of the human creature, has important consequences. In terms of killing in war, the duty to take life may be as strong as the obligation to save life (see Hashmi's essay, chapter 6), since war can be seen as an extension of God's will for all humankind to recognize his authority. Dependence on God also helps explain the extreme reticence of jurists to describe any life as "wrongful" (Rispler-Chaim, chapter 4), since God is the one who brings life into being. Such a dependence on divine commands may also help explain the significance given to the role of "necessity" (*ḍarūra*) in ethical decision-making. A broad category of necessity allows for a wider range of choices in any given situation, even those with clear divine commands. By describing difficult ethical situations (such as abortion to save the life of the mother) as cases of necessity and not principle, one preserves both the integrity of the transgressed command and also the unique characteristics of each ethical situation.[31]

On the other side, it is clear from the strong presumptions against suicide and abortion that Islam places a high value on human life. Further, since God is author of life and death, anything that approaches the taking of life must be undertaken with a sense of awesome responsibility. Therefore, it is the rules of conduct leading up to war (*jus ad bellum*) that are the most extensive and least contested, and the establishment of the moment of ensoulment (at 120 days) that is the center of discussions on abortion. These principles determine the rules of engagement and establish the intention (*niyya*) of the Muslim involved in ethical situations. This does not mean that the act itself is unimportant or undifferentiated, but rather that by paying attention to the frame of the ethical situation they establish the intention of the Muslim actors to follow God's will in advance of both the action and its consequences.

Finally, the Islamic ethics of life combines a compassionate awareness of the unique features inherent in every individual case with a stance of awe at God's creative power. The consistent refusal to describe cases of abortion or euthanasia as matters of personal choice reflects, ultimately, a sense that the value of human life is not encompassed by its significance for one individual, or even for the whole of humanity. Similarly, rules that restrict and guide licit killing in warfare cannot be fully explained by the logic of military efficacy. For some extremists, such as Osama bin Laden, this disconnect leads to a stance of arrogance, a presumed ability to know the mind of God and therefore to stand in judgment of the relative value of human lives. The majority of Muslims, however, find themselves in a stance of humility, one that might well be imitated by non-Muslims. As ethicists we should consider joining with those Muslims who see rational schemes and interpretive powers as limited and partial, and in doing so we might all gain a sense of awe at the mystery and fragility of life.

Notes

1. As one example, note that the leading scholarly journal in the field, *The Journal of Religious Ethics,* remains largely devoted to analysis of Christian ethics, though since 1973 it has published eleven articles on the subject of Islamic ethics. Hindu and Buddhist ethics also have achieved some recognition, with four and five articles, respectively.

2. For example, Vardit Rispler-Chaim and Abul Fadl Mohsin Ebrahim deal with medical ethics apart from war, while none of the numerous works on the ethics of war in Islam (e.g., John Kelsay's books) addresses issues in medical ethics; see the bibliography for these and other references. In contrast, note the recent work by John Reeder covering western ethical traditions: *Killing and Saving: Abortion, Hunger, and War* (University Park: Pennsylvania State University Press, 1996).

3. The process and timing of this compilation and canonization are disputed by western scholars, but many agree that while the Qur'an may have existed as a ritual text from the time of the Prophet, it did not begin serving as a book of law until almost a century later.

4. Although all the major commentaries are written by men, women are not forbidden from any level of scholarship in Islam, and important women have served as transmitters of Prophetic stories, authoritative mystics, and experts on law.

5. See, for example, *Al-Farabi on the Perfect State,* trans. Richard Walzer (Oxford: Clarendon Press, 1985). See also Walzer's article on philosophical ethics in the *Encyclopedia of Islam,* new ed. (Leiden, E. J. Brill, 1962–), s.v. "Akhlāk."

6. *A Mirror for Princes,* trans. Reuben Levy (London: Cresset Press, 1956).

7. It is instructive to note that two of the most important theologians in

Sunni Islam, al-Ash'ari (d. 935) and al-Ghazali (d. 1111) were formally trained philosophers. The suggestion that Islam is somehow opposed to rationalist or scientific thought is to be regarded as nineteenth-century orientalist rhetoric.

8. See here, for instance, the many works of Fazlur Rahman, one of the more important modernist interpreters of the traditional sources.

9. Shi'ism, particularly in its modern form, differs in this regard, and the fatwas of Ayatollah Khomeini were often seen as binding—such as his famous fatwa against the Indian author Salman Rushdie.

10. For an important anthropological study of muftis in Yemen, see Brinkley Messick, *The Calligraphic State* (Berkeley: University of California Press, 1993). For more on Muftis and fatwas throughout history, see Muhammad Khalid Masud, Brinkley Messick, David Powers, eds., *Islamic Legal Interpretation: Muftis and Their Fatwas* (Cambridge, Mass.: Harvard University Press, 1996).

11. For a good introduction to Islamic legal categories, see A. Kevin Reinhart, "Islamic Law as Islamic Ethics," *Journal of Religious Ethics* 11 (1983): 186–203; for an analysis of Islamic law in terms of Weber's notions of religious law, see Baber Johansen, *Contingency in a Sacred Law: Legal and Ethical Norms in the Muslim Fiqh* (Leiden: E. J. Brill, 1999), 3–25.

12. For a recent defense of this sort of casuistic reasoning, see Albert R. Jonsen and Stephen Toulmin, *The Abuse of Casuistry: A History of Moral Reasoning* (Berkeley: University of California Press, 1988). Note also Marion Katz's discussion on page 47 of this volume.

13. Daniel Brown, "Islamic Ethics in Comparative Perspective," in *The Muslim World* 89, no. 3 (1999): 181–92. Brown adds to these a third that I do not address here: "an ongoing tension over the respective importance of God's specific commands and His general will."

14. Majid Fakhry, *Islamic Occasionalism* (London: Allen and Unwin, 1958), 56–57.

15. Shlomo Pines, *Beiträge zur Islamischen Atomenlehre* (Berlin: A. Heine, 1936), 29–30.

16. Fakhry, *Occasionalism,* 72.

17. Note here the assertion in the Qur'an: "who would have any power over God if he were to wish to destroy the Messiah, Mary's son?" (Qur'an 5:17).

18. W. M. Watt: *Free Will and Pre-Destination in Early Islam* (London: Luzac, 1948), 88.

19. Simon van den Bergh, "Djawhar" in *Encyclopedia of Islam,* 2:493.

20. Brown, "Islamic Ethics," 182. The "Creed of al-Ash'ari" states this very point in somewhat denser language: "good and evil are the outcome of God's decree and fore-ordination . . . and that creatures are unable to benefit or injure themselves, save through God's pleasure" (Fakhry, *Occasionalism,* 57).

21. Brown, "Islamic Ethics," 185. The quotation is from Abul Fadl Mohsin Ebrahim, "Abortion," in *The Oxford Encyclopedia of the Modern Islamic World,* ed. John Esposito (New York: Oxford University Press, 1995), 1:17–19. Brown continues to explain that although some principles exist with regard to abortion and

are widely known (for example, that ensoulment occurs at 120 days), these principles are not used in moral evaluations.

22. As recorded in Watt, *Free Will,* 32.

23. A. J. Wensinck, *The Muslim Creed* (Cambridge: Cambridge University Press, 1932), 126.

24. Brown, "Islamic Ethics," 187; emphasis in original. Brown is dependent here on the reasoning of the Muslim modernist Fazlur Rahman, "Law and Ethics in Islam," in *Ethics in Islam,* ed. Richard Hovannisia (Malibu, Calif: Undena, 1985), 14.

25. Al-Ghazālī, *Ihyā' 'ulūm al-dīn* (Beirut: Dār al-Fikr, 1991), 1:27–28.

26. Brown, "Islamic Ethics," 192.

27. For an important new inquiry into this subject see Vardit Rispler-Chaim, "Islamic Medical Ethics and the Right to Privacy" (unpublished paper presented to the first International Conference on Medical Ethics and Medical Law in Islam, Haifa, Israel, March 2001). Selected papers from this innovative conference were published in the Israeli journal *Medicine and Law* 21, no. 2 (2002).

28. In the following chapter, for instance, Marion Katz considers the significance of many different sources, including Islamic mysticism, for ethical positions on abortion in the classical period (pp. 39–45).

29. Discussion between the author and H'mida Ennaifer, professor of Islamic thought at Zaitouna University, Tunis, April 5, 2000.

30. This reticence to respond may also be seen by some observers as a sin of omission. Indeed, Muslims could draw on their tradition to make significant statements supporting human rights, protection of the environment, and elimination of weapons of mass destruction, and the lack of pan-Muslim activism on such issues is disturbing.

31. For a recent discussion of the principle of necessity, see Birgit Krawietz, "*Ḍarūra* in Modern Islamic Law: The Case of Organ Transplantation" in Robert Gleave and Eugenia Kermeli, eds., *Islamic Law: Theory and Practice* (London: I. B. Taurus, 1997), 185–93.

Abortion

According to Muslim authorities, abortion interferes with God's role as author of life and death. It is God who forms the fetus in the womb and gives it a spirit 120 days after conception. Since the power to procreate does not lie with womankind, it follows that women do not have an unquestioned right to terminate pregnancy. This does not mean, however, that abortion is always wrong in Islam. Rather, Muslim authorities differentiate abortion in the early stages from abortion later on in pregnancy. Further, authorities recognize that issues of pregnancy and child-rearing involve a larger community of persons with discrete rights and responsibilities.

The first essay in this section examines the classical texts and finds that life is not defined as beginning at conception; therefore abortion, even late in the term, may be allowable in order to save the life of the woman. Along these lines Islamic texts also distinguish between abortion and infanticide, though the two are sometimes seen as closely related. In her essay, Marion Holmes Katz seeks to explain some of the principal motivating factors behind these initial positions. First, Katz differentiates between Islamic law as a moral guide and as a set of legal injunctions. This helps explain why some sources see abortion at any point as a reprehensible act, but find that it is only punishable after the pregnancy has advanced to a certain point. Second, Katz explains that abortion takes place within a complex set of relationships: between the fetus and the parents; between the parents and God; and between the fetus and God. This, in turn, leads to her discussion of the larger theological context for these legal injunctions. She concludes that the case orientation of the classical sources may in fact present a positive example for entrenched debates on this issue in other religious traditions.

The variety of possible cases is made explicit in the second essay by Donna Lee Bowen. Here, Bowen gives us a broad overview of the practice of abortion in much of the modern Islamic world, demonstrating the significant differences in practice among Muslim countries. As in Katz's essay, Bowen finds that community relationships are of great significance in determining the ethical value of any given case. Bowen also demonstrates the seriousness with which the classical texts are taken, as well as the new pressures of the modern world. On the one hand, there are countries such as Tunisia that allow abortion on demand in spite of the fact that most Tunisians belong to the restrictive Maliki school of Islamic law. On the other hand, some medical doctors argue that the classical dividing line of "ensoulment" at 120 days has no basis in modern medicine; therefore, abortion at any time should be prohibited. Bowen concludes her essay by looking at some of the key principles, such as respect for life and community values, that operate in ethical decisions about abortion.

In the third essay, Vardit Rispler-Chaim focuses on a very specific question that tests the boundaries of Islamic ethical thought on abortion. By examining recent legal decisions (fatwas) in cases of abortion, Rispler-Chaim looks to see whether a "right not to be born" is emerging among Muslim ethicists. Such a right is now being widely discussed in the west, particularly when genetic testing and counseling are available, and Rispler-Chaim looks both at cases concerning deformed fetuses and cases involving pregnancy after rape. By focusing on issues at the edge of the abortion debate, this last essay helps define the limits of an Islamic ethics of life. On the one hand, Muslim authorities are reticent to call any life "wrongful," but on the other hand, they are increasingly open to arguments about the quality of life.

As is to be expected with a complex religious tradition, Islam does not speak with one voice on the question of abortion. For instance, there is no agreement as to when life begins. The medieval marker of 120 days for ensoulment does not mean that abortion in the first trimester is licit; in fact, only some Muslims (those of the Hanafi school) allow unrestricted abortion before that date. Other schools of law forbid abortion at any point, seeing God's hand as actively forming the fetus at every stage of development. Yet even the most restrictive of schools does not view this prohibition as an absolute. Medical, social, and economic conditions all play a role, as each case is evaluated individually by the authorities.

For Islam, as in other religious traditions, the purpose of God's act of creating life is a key part of understanding positions on abortion. But while Catholics and other groups see fetal life as intrinsically sacred, an incommensurable gift from God, Muslims seem more willing to regard fetal life as only one good among many others, such as the life of the woman and of the larger community. For Muslims, therefore, God's creating of life in the womb is only part of his manifold activity; conception is not an isolated event, but part of a complex web of relationships that change and grow over time. The propensity of Muslim ethicists to argue on the basis of cases reflects this recognition that ethical decisions take place within a world of changing relationships. The absence of absolute and universal principles, however, does not seem to prevent the tradition from coming to consensus on some of the key issues regarding the beginning of life.

Two

The Problem of Abortion in Classical Sunni *fiqh*

Marion Holmes Katz

Throughout Islamic history, law (the sharia) and its learned practitioners (the *fuqahā'*) have claimed the primary role in defining Islamic behavioral norms. Therefore, in this chapter I am primarily concerned with the received opinions on abortion from the four schools of Sunni law. After an initial overview of the salient features of classical texts, and the wide-ranging debates within and among schools, I consider both the various criteria for establishing the humanity of the fetus, and also the relationship between formal requirements and empirical evidence. Yet as influential as these criteria were, they never have represented the sole system of moral guidance, for Muslims. Rather, legal texts are best understood within a larger religious world, one that includes mystical and philosophical discourses. In the third section of this chapter, I therefore examine the question of abortion in the work of one particularly influential proponent of a moderate Islamic mysticism (Sufism), Abu Hamid al-Ghazali.

The Status of the Fetus

In premodern Islamic legal texts,[1] the scenario of accidental loss of a fetus is far more routinely and extensively covered than that of deliberate abortion. Loss of a fetus, due to such culpable actions as blows to the stomach of a pregnant woman, is treated in the sections of traditional compendia devoted to the law of torts, alongside the rules relating to compensation for a wound or the loss of a limb. Remarks relating to deliberate termination of pregnancy, in contrast, tend to be incidental and unsystematic. The reasons for this bias may only be speculated. It may be that miscarriages inflicted by the wrongful act of another were relatively likely to be brought to the attention of premodern jurists, while intentional abortion (whose "victim," if any, was not in a position to take legal action) generally remained within the purview of individual women and the midwives or other folk practitioners who assisted them. Another cause of this reticence may be that neither the Qur'an nor the Sunna (exemplary practice) of the prophet Muhammad directly addresses the issue of intentional abortion.

This necessarily left juristic opinion on abortion more fluid than in those areas covered by explicit Qur'anic verses or direct Prophetic precedents.

In verses such as 6:137 and 151, 17:31 and 60:12, the Qur'an interdicts in the strongest of terms the killing of one's offspring. While the Qur'anic prohibition of "killing children" is stern and repetitive, however, classical exegetes did not generally understand it to refer to abortion. Instead, it was interpreted with reference to another more explicit Qur'anic allusion: the destruction of live offspring. Qur'an 81:8–9 speaks of the buried female infant who will arise on the day of judgment to ask for what offense she was killed. Muslim exegetes inferred on the basis of this passage, another reference to the burying of daughters in verse 16:59, and their understanding of pre-Islamic mores, that it was a common practice for pagan Arabs to bury their daughters alive for fear of poverty or disgrace, a practice known as *wa'd;* they interpreted the interdiction on killing children, accordingly, as referring to the already born.

It is true that the concept of infanticide could sometimes be extended to stages before birth, or indeed, before conception had even occurred. In one widely cited hadith, the Prophet describes contraception by withdrawal (*coitus interruptus,* or *al-ʿazl* in Arabic) as "hidden *wa'd*" and cites Qur'an 81:8–9.[2] In another well-authenticated text, on the contrary, the argument that *coitus interruptus* is "hidden" or "lesser" *wa'd* is attributed to the Jews; the Prophet retorts that "the Jews are lying."[3] In general, the perception that the relevant Qur'anic prohibitions might constitute a blanket interdiction of birth control was tempered by an awareness of a countervailing Qur'anic theme, that of the gradual development of fetal life (see below). This is demonstrated by an opinion attributed to the Prophet's nephew Ibn ʿAbbas. Confronted with the argument that *coitus interruptus* is the "lesser *wa'd,*" Ibn ʿAbbas is supposed to have replied by reciting Qur'an 23:12–14, which refers to the successive stages of formation within the womb, then asking, "How can [the fetus] be a victim of *wa'd* until it has passed through these [stages of] creation?"[4]

Due to the complexity of the exegetical situation, only the occasional classical interpreter directly and unambiguously applies the Qur'anic prohibitions on "killing children" to the case of abortion. One of these is the highly independent Hanbali jurist Ibn Taymiya (d. 1328 C.E.), who gives the following answer to a questioner presenting the case of a man who tried to induce an abortion in his pregnant slave girl:

> Praise be to God! Causing the abortion of a fetus (*isqāṭ al-ḥaml*) is forbidden (*ḥarām*) by the consensus of the Muslims. It is a category of *wa'd,* about which God said: "When the buried child will be

asked / For what crime she was killed"; he [also] said: "Do not kill your children for fear of want."[5]

Although the prophet Muhammad is not known to have dealt with any case of intentional abortion, he did reportedly make a ruling on a case of wrongfully caused miscarriage. This case resulted from a fight in which a woman struck her pregnant co-wife with a tent pole, killing both the woman and her fetus. The Prophet required that blood money (the *diya*) be paid for the deceased woman, and a payment (known as a *ghurra*) of a male or female slave for the fetus. Both fines seem to have been imposed on the kin group of the offender, since one of her male relatives is supposed to have objected to the latter penalty in incantatory rhymed prose: "How can one pay blood money for someone who neither ate nor drank, neither uttered a sound nor cried out after birth? The blood of such goes unavenged!" (*kayfa yuʿqalu man lā akala wa-lā shariba, wa-lā naṭaqa wa-lā istahalla, fa-mithlu dhālika yuṭallu*) The Prophet is supposed to have replied, in wording that varies among versions of the report, that this rhymed utterance (*sajʿ*) was nothing but the ranting of a pagan soothsayer (*kāhin*).[6]

While the legal sources discuss reports of this incident in terms of concrete legal precedent rather than of general values, it would seem that this exchange represents a qualitative shift in the evaluation of fetal life. The offending woman's relative is clearly basing his objection on the idea that socially protected life begins only at birth and is substantiated by signs of stable functioning that stretch well beyond the moment of emergence from the womb. Such criteria as eating and drinking suggest that a newborn infant's place in the community of the living may have been finally secured only after certain signs of viability had been displayed. Perhaps it was within this liminal stage that pre-Islamic Arabs considered infanticide an option.

This report forms the basis of the provisions of classical law relating to damages for miscarried fetuses. The specification of a male or female slave as the compensation to the kin of a miscarried fetus would seem to suggest a rough symbolic equivalence between the potential life that has been lost and the life of the enslaved human being who is to be delivered in restitution. However, classical jurists generally focus not on the status of the slave as a human being offered in compensation to the fetus's bereaved kin, but on his or her monetary value. The value of the *ghurra* is conventionally set at one twentieth of the full blood money,[7] thus placing the fetus in an intermediate position between the complete disregard associated with the pre-Islamic period and the full protection accorded to the already born. Interestingly, however, most jurists agree that the *ghurra* belongs to the fetus, and thus is inherited by its kin.[8]

In cases of accidental killing, Islamic law also requires that the offender expiate his or her crime by a *kaffāra*, either the emancipation of a believing slave or a fast of two consecutive months (Qur'an 4:92). Unlike blood money, which plays the social function of compensating the kin of the deceased, expiation is intended to address the relationship between the culprit and God. (Intentional murder, in contrast, is not considered to be expiable; see Qur'an 4:93.) Interestingly, cases of abortion and wrongfully induced miscarriage are generally treated as instances of quasi-accidental killing, since actions towards the fetus—which is not directly accessible, and whose very existence is considered conjectural until it emerges from the womb—are not understood to reach the level of certainty necessary for complete intentionality. Thus, unlike intentional murder of the already born, the killing of a fetus would be subject to a *kaffāra* if the fetus were understood to be a human life in the full sense of the term.

Two interesting early reports support the idea that *kaffāra* may have been considered incumbent by at least some early Muslims in cases of abortion. In one, the scholar Mujahid (d. 718–722 C.E.) reports that "a woman massaged (*masaḥat*) the belly of another woman, and she miscarried. The case was presented to 'Umar [ibn al-Khattab, a caliph who reigned from 634 to 644 C.E.], and he ordered her to perform expiation by freeing a slave—meaning the one who did the massaging."[9] While the report is not explicit on this point, it is plausible to infer that the reference here is to a method of abortion; massaging of the stomach (unlike a hostile blow) seems most likely to be both deliberate and consensual on the part of the pregnant woman. It is interesting that, if this is the case, it is the practitioner rather than the pregnant woman who is held liable for the offense. In the second report, the early Iraqi jurist Ibrahim al-Nakha'i (d. ca. 717 C.E.) is asked about the case of a woman who has taken a medicine (*sharibat dawāʾ*) and miscarried her fetus. He says that she must free a slave (as expiation) and pay a *ghurra* to the father.[10] Of the four classical schools of Sunni law, the Shafi'is and the Hanbalis hold that the *kaffāra* is obligatory for a miscarried or aborted fetus, while the Hanafis and the Malikis hold that it is an optional act of devotion (*taqarrub*) since the fetus is not unqualifiedly a human life.[11]

In general, classical jurists find the status of the fetus anomalous in two ways. One is that the fetus, while sharing some of the legal protections and powers associated with human life (such as the ability to inherit property, including the *ghurra*), in other ways is clearly not treated as a full-fledged human being. The sixteenth-century Hanafi jurist Qadi Zadeh expresses this ambiguity succinctly when he writes, introducing the discussion of rules relating to the fetus in his commentary on al-Marghinani's *Hidāya*,

"Having mentioned the law of torts as it relates to those who are human in all respects, he begins the exposition of the law as it relates to those who are human in one respect but not in another, i.e., to the fetus."[12] Another key area of ambiguity lies in the relationship between the fetus as an emergent individual and its inseparability from the body of its mother. Jurists note that the *ghurra* penalty incurred by the death of a fetus in some ways resembles blood money for the death of a human being, while in others it parallels the compensation paid for the loss of body parts such as fingers and teeth. At least two very early jurists are supposed to have held that the *ghurra* was to be paid exclusively to the pregnant woman herself, on the grounds that it was analogous to a limb of her body;[13] while this opinion was not successful in the classical schools, the status of the fetus with respect to the mother's body remained problematic. The highly independent Zahiri jurist Ibn Hazm (d. 1064 C.E.) resolves this ambiguity by a strict application of the principle (discussed below) that the fetus receives its soul 120 days after conception. After ensoulment, Ibn Hazm argues, the fetus is indubitably alive; before it, however (i.e., within the first four months of pregnancy), it is not a separate life at all. "It is a part of [his mother], a portion of her flesh and blood and a piece of her vitals; *she* is the victim [of a wrongfully induced miscarriage]!" In keeping with this argument, Ibn Hazm argues that within the 120-day period before ensoulment the *ghurra* goes exclusively to the woman herself.[14] More mainstream jurists did not resolve the ambiguity so neatly, but retained it as a fruitful tension in their general understanding of fetal life.

The rules relating to payment of monetary damages for an aborted fetus, based as they are on an explicit and universally accepted Prophetic precedent, represent a relatively clear and uncontested element of the classical law of torts. However, they do not explicitly address some of the most vital and vexing questions relating to intentional abortion. Jurists generally assume that the *ghurra* is to be paid, whether to the fetus's remaining heirs or to the father of the child, if the pregnant woman herself induces an abortion. This could be taken to imply that there is little qualitative difference between termination of a pregnancy by the considered act of the pregnant woman and its violent termination by someone unrelated to the child; certainly, the payment of damages by the woman suggests that a wrong has been committed. Nevertheless, the rules relating to the *ghurra* address the loss of the fetus only after the fact. Is it permissible for a woman to choose to terminate a pregnancy, accepting the payment of the *ghurra* as the financial consequence of her act? Can the *ghurra* be waived if the pregnancy is terminated with the consent of those to whom it is due? There is, in fact, a Hanafi opinion (based on the minority opinion that the *ghurra* belongs to the father of the child) stating that if a woman aborts with her husband's permission, no *ghurra* is due.[15] However, jurists' reflections on the permissibility or prohibition of intentional abortion were generally based not on inference from the rules on monetary damages, but on their general religious understanding of the nature of fetal life.

Classical Islamic jurists unanimously base their understanding of fetal development on Qur'anic passages suggesting a gradual progress towards the physical and spiritual attributes of humanity. The most foundational of these passages is Qur'an 23:12–14, whose description of the stages of development provide the basic terminology for classical legal discussions of the subject:

> We [i.e., God] first created the human being from an essence of clay, then placed it, a drop of semen (*nuṭfa*), in a secure enclosure. The drop of semen We made a clot of blood (*'alaqa*), and the clot a lump of flesh (*muḍgha*). This We fashioned into bones, then clothed the bones with flesh, thus bringing forth another creation. Blessed be God, the noblest of creators.

The Qur'anic description of human development in the womb is elaborated by hadith specifying the period of time elapsed in each successive change. The most important of these is a report from the Prophet's famous Companion Ibn Mas'ud:

> The Prophet of God told us—and he is the one who speaks the truth and evokes belief—"Each of you is gathered in his mother's womb for forty days; then [he is] a clot of blood (*'alaqa*) for the same period; then he is a clump of flesh (*muḍgha*) for the same period. Then God sends an angel who is commanded regarding four things: [his occupation,] his livelihood (*rizqihi*), his span of life, and his felicity or damnation [in the afterlife]. Then the spirit is breathed into it. . ."[16]

Another tradition cited by many jurists is the following, from the same well-known Companion:

> From 'Abd Allāh ibn Mas'ūd from the Prophet: He said, "When the drop of semen has spent forty-two days [in the womb], God sends an angel to it and [the angel] forms it and creates its hearing, sight, skin, flesh, and bones. . . ."[17]

Almost the only possible generalization about the opinions of the four schools of Sunni *fiqh* is that they all hold abortion to be forbidden after ensoulment (literally "the inbreathing of the spirit"), which is held (in accordance with the first hadith cited above) to occur after 120 days of gestation. The only exception to this rule is in case of peril to the life of the mother, which is held to take precedence over the potential life of the fetus. About the permissibility of abortion before the expiration of this period there is unanimity neither among the different schools of law nor within any one individual school.

Fairly typical in this regard is the range of opinion within the Shafi'i school. Some Shafi'is hold that it is permissible to abort a fetus at any time prior to ensoulment, i.e., before the expiration of 120 days. Others hold that it is permissible only until the fetus has begun to take on the first signs of human form, which, according to the second hadith cited above, occurs forty-two nights after conception. Still other Shafi'is hold that it is forbidden to take steps to expel the semen at any time after it has been implanted in the womb (*ba'd al-istiqrār fī'l-raḥm*).[18]

The other schools of Sunni *fiqh* display a diversity of opinion similar to that of the Shafi'i school. The most liberal of the three is the Hanafi school, in which the opinion that abortion is permissible at any point before ensoulment (i.e., the expiration of 120 days) found many adherents.[19] Within the range of more permissive opinion, there is also disagreement about the precise conditions under which abortion is allowed. Some Hanafis, for instance, hold that before ensoulment abortion is *mubāḥ*—i.e., a religiously neutral action, and thus one that can be performed at will. Other Hanafis hold that it is not neutral, but requires a compelling justification (*'udhr*).[20] In the Hanbali school, many jurists hold abortion to be permissible only in the *nuṭfa* stage (i.e., the first forty days of gestation), although others allow it until ensoulment.[21] The most restrictive is the Maliki school, where differences of opinion are largely limited to the position that abortion is forbidden at any point after implantation in the womb and the position that it is permissible until the end of the *nuṭfa* stage.

Like other areas of *fiqh* (jurisprudence), the debate over the permissibility of abortion (which is carried on largely in passing remarks accumulating with the accretion of marginal commentaries) is overwhelmingly formal in nature. That is, it is founded largely on a system of logical correspondences between specific texts rather than on a well-articulated set of fundamental generative principles. Thus, it is frequently difficult to discern the fundamental attitudes towards the nature of fetal life that underlie the various positions on the permissibility of abortion articulated in the *fiqh*. It is clear from the above discussion that the fetus is understood by most jurists to progress gradually towards fully realized and fully protected human life. However, it is less clear precisely what the criteria for full humanity (and thus full legal protection) might be. The most obvious cutoff point is, quite obviously, ensoulment. Most jurists agree that after this point abortion is quite simply unconscionable. However, there are other factors that contribute to the gradations of moral and legal censure attached to abortion in the *fiqh* literature.

Criteria for Humanity: Human Features and Relationships

The emergence of discernibly human features (*al-takhalluq*) is an important factor in the Hanafi discussion of abortion, where *takhalluq* is understood to coincide with ensoulment. The prominent Hanafi jurist Ibn 'Abidin (d. 1842 C.E.) presents an interesting discussion of this issue while commenting on the statement that a woman's *'idda* (waiting period after being widowed or divorced) expires with the miscarriage of a fetus that displays some aspect of the human form, such as a hand, foot, finger, nail, or hair; and that "its form does not become apparent until after 120 days" have passed. In comment, Ibn 'Abidin cites a source stating, "It is permissible for [the woman] to undergo a treatment to expel the blood [i.e., to terminate pregnancy] as long as the fetus is a clump of flesh or a clot of blood and none of its limbs have been formed." The length of this period is understood to be 120 days. This is permitted simply because "it [i.e., the fetus] is not [yet] a human being *(ādamī)*."[22]

The connection between the fetus's displaying some aspect of a recognizably human form and its right to protection under the *sharia* is a somewhat complex one. On the one hand, it may be understood as expressing an underlying attitude towards the nature of human life: a living thing is human if it displays human form. This would seem to be the idea behind Ibn 'Abidin's terse statement that before this point "it is not a human being." However, the importance of the criterion of formation (*takhalluq*) is also connected to the rules of evidence: no legal ruling can be applied to a being whose very existence is in doubt. This consideration seems to be alluded to by the Maliki Qur'anic exegete al-Qurtubi, providing a rationale for the opinion (held by a number of Hanbalis and Malikis) that it is permissible to abort the fetus in the *nuṭfa* stage (i.e., first forty days), but not afterwards. Al-Qurtubi writes:

> The *nuṭfa is not definitely known to be anything at all* (*laysat bi-shay' yaqīnan*), and no legal consequences ensue if the woman expels it (*lā yata'allaqu bihā ḥukm idhā alqathā 'l-mar'a*), because it has not [yet] coalesced in the womb; it is as if it were [still] in the loins of the man.[23]

Indeed, there is a clear correlation between the different schools' dominant opinions about the point at which a fetus gains the status of protected human life and the evidentiary requirements applied in such situations as the expiration of the *'idda* and the establishment of a slave woman's status as an *umm walad,* both of which require some form of proof that a pregnancy had indeed existed. Thus, for instance, the Malikis regard it as possible to confirm that a clot of blood was in fact a developing fetus; in the words of al-Dasuqi, it is necessary that it be "blood clotted (*mujtamiʿ*) in such a way that if hot water is poured on it, it does not dissolve, not clotted blood that dissolves if hot water is poured on it"—and some Maliki jurists apparently rejected even this requirement.[24] For Hanafis and Shafiʿis, in contrast, only the appearance of recognizable limbs and features (or, in some cases, the subtle signs of such as detected by reliable midwives) was taken as proof that the woman had really been with child in the first place.[25]

Indeed, it might be argued that in fact none of the schools of law allow abortion, in the sense that in general each school of law forbids any action to expel the fetus at any point after it is definitely known to exist, according to the individual school's evidentiary standards for identifying a fetus. However, I believe that this would not be a correct interpretation of the overall classical understanding of fetal development. Classical jurists were perfectly aware that women might know of their own pregnancy long before the legal requirements for proof of a fetus could be fulfilled, and they recognized that women, along with their husbands (and, in the case of slave women, their owners) made moral decisions to continue or terminate such pregnancies. The wording of their opinions, which often explicitly state that it is permissible to terminate a pregnancy at some point before their evidentiary standards could confirm its existence, indicates this fact. It would be nonsensical to speak of termination (*isqāṭ*) if they did not recognize that the woman knew of her pregnancy; the legal nonexistence of the fetus before the fulfillment of the various school's evidentiary standards is a procedural requirement relating to the law of torts, which does not negate the jurists' recognition that morally significant decisions were made at earlier stages of pregnancy.

In fact, the issue of *takhalluq* (formation) is more than merely evidentiary. Instead, it is correlated with the Qur'anic description of the development of the fetus and with the all-important inbreathing of the spirit.[26] This logic obviously raises possible problems for later thinkers; modern science has made it possible to discern the form of the fetus far earlier than midwives could in earlier ages. Indeed, competing medical discourses also caused dilemmas for jurists in centuries past. Ibn ʿAbidin, for instance, admits that the contention that the formation of the fetus begins only at the end of three months is medically problematic; he cites a source stating that "it has been observed that its form appears before this period of time [has expired]."[27] On the other hand, some premodern jurists question the relevance of scientific observations to legal discourse; the eleventh-century

Hanafi scholar al-Sarakhsi notes that "al-Shafi'i stated that an aborted [blood clot] should be tested with hot water; if it melts, it is not a baby. . . . This is a matter of medicine and has nothing to do with Islamic law, so we do not adhere to it."[28]

The discussion of *takhalluq* suggests that in one respect the fetus gains the full protection of the law when it attains certain decisive elements of what is understood by jurists to be a complete human being. The two most important criteria are the emergence of a recognizably human physical form and the inbreathing of the spirit. The developing embryo and fetus, moving along a continuum, gradually approximate to the jurists' abstract conception of human life; at different points along this continuum, taking their cue either from the growing definition of its physical form or the decisive event of ensoulment, jurists draw a line of demarcation after which expulsion of the fetus is a morally odious and perhaps legally culpable act. Here the development of the fetus takes place in a metaphorical vacuum; the only important relationship is between the fetus and a set of abstract criteria which it fulfills more closely with the passing of time. Although this is the schema most apparent on the surface of the juristic discussions of abortion, I do not believe that it is an adequate description of the Islamic ethics of abortion (even as reflected in the juristic literature). Instead, the development of the fetus takes place within a complex web of relationships, some of which reinforce the independent value of the fetus and others of which may occasionally outbalance the interests of this potential life.

Most obviously at stake in the issue of abortion is one's relationship to God as the author of life and the provider of sustenance for all living things. The Qur'anic verses on infanticide, while they do not directly inform most classical discussions of the issue of abortion, provide the theological background of all discussions of reproduction. In Qur'an 6:137, infanticide is associated with polytheism and spiritual ruin: "[Their idols] have induced many pagans to kill their children, seeking to ruin them and to confuse them in their faith." The continuation of this passage associates the killing of children with wantonness or intellectual incompetence (*safah*) and lack of knowledge (*'ilm*), a word which in the Qur'anic context denotes not merely worldly wisdom but morally orienting insight into the nature of things. In verse 151 of the same chapter of the Qur'an, the killing of children features in a terse list of God's most fundamental requirements:

> Say: "Come, I will tell you what your Lord has made binding on you: that you shall serve no other gods besides Him; that you shall show

> kindness to your parents; that you shall not kill your children because you cannot support them (We provide for you and for them); that you shall not commit lewd acts, whether openly or in secret; and that you shall not kill the soul that God has made sacrosanct (*al-nafs allatī ḥarrama Allāh*) except for just cause. Thus God exhorts you, that you may grow in wisdom."

For evident reasons, this list has been identified by some Muslim exegetes with the Ten Commandments revealed to Moses. Within the text of the Qur'an itself, the interdiction on killing children is given quasi-covenantal weight when it is made one of a fundamental list of requirements imposed on women converting to Islam at the hands of the Prophet:

> Prophet, if believing women come to you and pledge themselves to serve no other deity besides God, to commit neither theft, nor adultery, nor child-murder, to utter no monstrous falsehoods of their own invention, and to disobey you in nothing reasonable, accept their allegiance and implore God to forgive them. God is forgiving and merciful. (Qur'an 60:12)

Finally, the Qur'an twice (6:151 and 17:31) instructs believers not to kill their children out of fear of want: "We will support both you and them."

Thus, the commandment not to kill one's children has more than one kind of theological significance. On the one hand, infanticide is a pagan practice reflecting the fundamentally misguided nature of those who deny the existence of God; conversely, as one of a list of basic covenantal requirements, its prohibition seals the believers' pledge of recognition and obedience towards God. Perhaps more importantly, however, infanticide is displayed in the Qur'anic text as a particularly dramatic instance of failing faith in God's function as the ultimate provider. It thus ruptures the correct relationship between the human being and her or his creator.

Also at stake in the issue of abortion is the relationship between the fetus and God. The existence of such a relationship is not, of course, necessarily obvious; it is argued on several different grounds. One of these is the basic theological principle, founded on several passages of the Qur'an and related hadith, that all human beings are fundamentally *muslim*. That is, all human beings are born in a primordial state of recognition of, and submission to, their creator. Only the adverse influence of non-Muslim parents and the misguidance of one's own egotistical desires can pervert this primal monotheism, a fundamental nature known as the *fiṭra*. Furthermore, all humans are party to a covenantal relationship with God even before birth; the primal covenant is pre-temporal and was concluded with all humankind when God drew all future progeny from the loins of Adam and bade them recognize His lordship (Qur'an 7:172). Jurists did not always follow the logical implications of this understanding; they did, in some cases, make invidious distinctions between Muslim and non-Muslim fetuses or infants. However, some jurists used the concept of the *fiṭra* as the basis for understanding abortion as the killing of a "believing soul" (4:92) and thus Qur'anically prohibited.

The Zahiri jurist Ibn Hazm uses the concept of primal monotheism as the basis for his argument that someone who unintentionally causes the miscarriage of a fetus is subject to an act of expiation (*kaffāra*). Citing Qur'an 4:92, he first notes that God has imposed both the freeing of a believing slave and the payment of blood money (the *diya*) on anyone who unintentionally kills a believer. But can a fetus be characterized as "believing"? Ibn Hazm argues that it can. Referring to the text of the Qur'an and the word of the Prophet, he argues that the primordial nature of all human beings (the *fiṭra*) is inherently monotheistic—in Qur'anic terminology, all persons are created as *ḥanīfs*. However, Ibn Hazm concedes, the killing of a fetus is murder only if the fetus possesses a spirit, that is, after ensoulment, occurring four months after conception.

A relationship between the fetus and God can be inferred not only from Qur'anic texts and hadith dealing with the issue of primal monotheism, but from hadith that suggest that miscarried fetuses play a role in the afterlife. Thus, the North African jurist al-Wansharisi cites the following rationale in answer to an enquiry about the permissibility of abortion:

> The [unborn] child has three states [i.e., stages of development]: [1.] A state preceding existence, in which it can be prevented by *coitus interruptus;* this is permissible. [2.] A state after the womb takes hold of the semen; at this point, no one may interfere with it to prevent its birth, as lowly merchants do, giving their maids medicine when their menstrual blood ceases to flow in order to loosen it so that the semen flows out with it and birth is prevented. [3] The third state is after formation and before the spirit is infused in it; it is more strictly prohibited and forbidden than the first two, because of the tradition that is recited saying that "The miscarried fetus lingers at the door of heaven, saying: 'I will not enter heaven until my parents enter.'"[29]

A hadith transmitted by the eminent traditionist Ibn Maja similarly states that

> The miscarried fetus (*siqṭ*) becomes angered at its Lord if He consigns its parents to Hell. It is proclaimed, "O you fetus who are

> angered at your Lord! Bring your parents into Paradise!" It draws them by its umbilical cord until they enter Paradise.

In yet another text cited by the same author, the Prophet is reported to have said that "Indeed, a miscarried fetus (*siqṭ*) that I send before me is preferable to me than a warrior (*fāris*) I leave behind me."[30] In these traditions, the fetus appears as an intercessor with God in favor of its parents; it is not only a human being destined for eternity, but a privileged soul because it precedes its parents into the afterlife and can speak on their behalf. Thus there is a three-way relationship including the fetus, the parents, and their Lord.

The fetus is implicated not only in its own and its parents' relationships with God, however. It also participates in a relationship with its parents; furthermore, it is inextricably entwined in the parents' relationship of marriage or ownership with each other. With respect to the fetus's relationship with its parents, the key issue is its evolving relationship with the mother, her body, her rights over her own body, and her worth to her husband or (in the case of slave women) owner. This issue is dramatized when jurists discuss the *ghurra,* the indemnity paid as compensation for the miscarriage of a fetus caused by the legally culpable action of another. We have already noted the existence of early jurists who held that the compensation was owed to the mother. Even in the classical period, when the opinion that the fetus is juridically a part of the potential mother's anatomy became marginalized, some opinions suggest that the woman has a decisive interest in her own reproductive potential that must be protected by law. Thus, Islamic law generally holds that a man may practice *coitus interruptus* with the consent of his wife—the consent of slave concubines not being required. Some jurists even hold that the wife may negotiate monetary compensation for her agreement to such an arrangement. While an analogy between *coitus interruptus* and abortion is rejected by many jurists, the principles of consent and compensation imply juridical concern for the autonomy and interests of the woman.[31]

Interestingly, some legal sources seem to suggest that the primary interest in the survival of the fetus lies with the father. Thus, the Mughal period compendium know as the *Fatāwā al-hindiyya* states:

> If a woman strikes her own belly or takes medicine to abort the child intentionally, or if she gives a treatment to her vagina so that the child is stillborn, her kin group is liable for the *ghurra, if she did it without her husband's permission; if she did it with his permission, nothing is due.* So the *Kāfī*. . . . In the *Fatāwā* of al-Nasafi he is asked about a woman who has been divorced with compensation (*mukhtaliʿa*)

> while she was pregnant and plotted to eliminate her waiting period by aborting the child. He says: "If she aborted it by her act, she owes the *ghurra* and *it goes to the husband.*" So the *Muḥīṭ*.[32]

In fact, some authors seem to make the prohibition of early abortion dependent on the existence of a husband. Thus al-Qasimi:

> It is legally obligatory for a woman, whose menstrual periods have ceased, to refrain from taking medicines which pose a threat to the fetus, *if she has a husband*.[33]

Thus, the developing fetus is the node of a complex of relationships, starting with its own relationship to the mother's body (which begins as that of part to whole and ending as that of two individuals) and extending to a large set of other relationships with members of its family or the wider society. In fact, the legal status of the fetus could be defined by its ability to enter into relationships, defined by rights and obligations, with others. We have already encountered the sixteenth-century Hanafi jurist Qadi Zadeh's characterization of fetuses as being "human in some respects, but not in others."[34] He understands this intermediate status to be defined by the fetus's recognized but circumscribed ability to exercise rights and duties towards others:

> This is elucidated by what was mentioned by Shams al-A'imma al-Sarakhsi in his *Uṣūl:* that the fetus (*janīn*), as long as it is contained (*mujtann*) in the belly, does not have legal responsibility, because it is tantamount to a part of a human being, although it has a separate life and is in preparation to become a person (*nafs*) with legal responsibility. In consideration of this aspect, it is qualified to have rights with respect to others such as manumission, inheritance, lineage, or bequest; in consideration of the former aspect, it is not qualified to have duties towards others. As for after birth, it has legal responsibility; thus, if it were to roll over on somebody's property and destroy it, it would be liable for damages; and it is liable for a woman's bridal gift if its guardian contracts [a marriage].

Finally, one might address the question of the fetus's value to society as a whole. One might imagine that, as the necessary precursors to increase of the Islamic *umma* (community of faith), fetuses would be the object of special concern to jurists. Interestingly, this theme rarely appears in the classical juristic literature. A rare exception is the following fleeting comment, from al-Hattab's commentary *Mawāhib al-jalīl.* Citing an interpretation of the *Risāla*'s statement that it is forbidden for a man to take any medicines that limit his procreative capacity (*an yashriba min al-adwiya mā yuqallilu naṣalahu*), he comments: "This is considered undesirable (*kuriha*) only because it gives aid and comfort to the unbelievers," a Qur'anically forbidden action. He also invokes the love that is Qur'anically enjoined between husband and wife.[35] Although extremely terse and elliptical, like many such commentarial texts, this passage suggests two sets of human obligations that are implicated in the choice to prevent conception: those between the husband and his wife, who is assumed to have an interest in bearing children, and those between the husband and wife and the community of believers, whose ranks may be thinned by the failure to procreate.

It is interesting that, as mentioned above, there seem to be very few passages in classical texts suggesting a link between the practice of contraception or abortion and the magnitude of the Muslim community as a whole. This dearth of references contrasts with the prominence of the concern for numerical growth of the Islamic community in modern debates on these topics, where both contraception and abortion may be perceived as population control measures foisted on the Islamic world by westerners concerned to contain the number and power of Muslims.

Thus far, we have concentrated exclusively on legal discourse (*fiqh*). This is justifiable, given that at least on a theoretical level, *fiqh* was probably the paramount normative framework for most premodern Muslims, both learned and unlettered. However, *fiqh* was never the sole system of moral interpretation available to Muslims. *Akhlāq*, or the science of character rooted in some aspects of the Greek heritage, was a very specific and somewhat marginal discourse for medieval Muslims. Nevertheless, it did become fully synthesized into one major stream of Islamic discourse, that of the Sufis—Islamic mystics who sought direct, experiential communion with the Divine.

Sufi Ethics: Legal Rulings in Religious Context

At least since the thirteenth century, Sufism has been an influential supplementary (and sometimes competing) frame of ethical and spiritual reference for many—or even most—Muslims. The nature of the sources makes it more difficult to address specific, concrete ethical issues through a Sufi lens than through that of *fiqh*. While *fiqh* works tend to deal with such issues as reproductive behavior in fairly exhaustive detail, works dealing with Sufi *akhlāq* frequently treat the issue of moral self-improvement in broad and general terms. Thus, it is relatively difficult to find explicit discussions of an issue such as abortion. At this point, however, it may be useful to examine one very widely respected example of the synthesis of Islamic law and Sufi self-improvement. This may give a more comprehensive sense of the religious world within which Sunni Muslims have made decisions about ethical issues such as abortion.

An interesting example of the interaction between the two discourses (*fiqh* and Sufism) is provided by one of the most influential Islamic scholars of the Middle Ages, the author of one of the most widely read and deeply cherished syntheses of Islamic teachings in the history of the tradition. This is Abu Hamid al-Ghazali (d. 1111 C.E.), whose magnum opus *Iḥyāʾ ʿulūm al-dīn* ("The Revivification of the Religious Sciences") is until today both ubiquitous and revered in most parts of the Sunni Muslim world. Al-Ghazali's religious life, touchingly described in his autobiographical work *al-Munqidh min al-dalāl* ("The Deliverer from Error"), was marked by religious upheaval. After a crisis of faith in which he became unable to teach Islamic law, al-Ghazali left his prestigious academic post in the imperial capital of Baghdad to spend years in searching and meditation. His survey of the various paths to faith available in his time (law, theology, philosophy, Shiʿism, and Sufism) led him to a synthesis in which adherence to the normative discourses of law and theology was informed by an experiential conviction nurtured by Sufi practice. For the mature al-Ghazali, Islamic law and Sufi ethics were complementary. Crucially, he believed that *fiqh* applied exclusively to externals, while Sufism addressed the conditions of the heart.[36] Thus, for al-Ghazali *fiqh* is essentially a branch of politics, a discipline devoted to regulating the this-worldly affairs of human beings so that they can pursue their final rewards in peace. The heart of the spiritual struggle, meanwhile, goes on in a subjective realm inaccessible to the discourse of *fiqh*.

Al-Ghazali's understanding of Sufi ethics is rooted in an Aristotelian schema in which every being forms part of a hierarchy in which it shares some powers with the beings below it and enjoys other, additional powers which link it with those above. For instance, human beings share the power of voluntary movement with animals, who in turn share the powers of nutrition and growth with plants. Each category of being can reach its greatest perfection by fully developing those powers that distinguish it from the beings below it and associate it with those above. Human beings can achieve perfection—and thus happiness—by fully realizing those potentialities which they share with the angels, rather than those which they share with animals and plants.

By al-Ghazali's time, this schema had been fully Islamized through interpretive linkages with the Qur'anic text and the statements of the prophet Muhammad (the hadith). In the *Iḥyāʾ*, al-Ghazali identifies the *akhlāq* which humans must develop in order to fulfill their potentialities both with the exemplary moral characteristics (*khuluq ʿaẓīm*, Qur'an 68:4) of the Prophet and with the attributes of God.[37] By purging oneself of negative characteristics caused by one's egoistic desires, one can more and more closely approximate to the loving, compassionate, and just nature of the prophet Muhammad and, ultimately, of God himself. This process of self-refinement is routinely likened, in al-Ghazali's works and those of other Sufis and ethical writers, to the polishing of a metal mirror. Thus, the core of human ethical striving is inward-directed.[38]

However, precisely because al-Ghazali's Sufi ethics (*al-akhlāq al-ṣūfiya*) deal with the subjective states of human hearts, they do not deal primarily with ethical problems as understood in the modern west. Sufi ethics, for al-Ghazali, is not ultimately concerned with actions at all. "How many a lower soul (*nafs*)," he reflects in the *Iḥyā'*, "is receptive to acts, but not to moral characteristics!"[39] Thus, the same act can have very different ethical evaluations depending on the subjective spiritual state of the actor. A Sufi's refusal to accept charity, for instance, can be good or bad depending on the state of the *nafs*.[40]

How would a schema such as al-Ghazali's, in which *fiqh* regulated external human affairs and sufi ethics disciplined individual hearts, apply to an issue such as abortion? As it happens, we need not speculate; al-Ghazali provides one of the most detailed and thoughtful medieval discussions of the issue of abortion in his *Iḥyā'*. Based on this passage, al-Ghazali is sometimes cited by modern authors as an example of the absolute prohibition of abortion;[41] however, on closer examination his discussion is as ambiguous as it is rich.

The idea that al-Ghazali was a firm opponent of abortion seems to be based on two analogical arguments that he makes, one negative and the other positive. Firstly, al-Ghazali states that neither infanticide (*wa'd*, or the burying of unwanted offspring) nor abortion (*al-ijhāḍ*) is to be equated with *coitus interruptus*, because both involve the destruction of an already extant being (*mawjūd ḥāṣil*). Secondly, he compares conception (in his medical terminology, the mixture of the male and female "semen," *mā'*, or the male semen and the woman's menstrual blood) to the "offer" and "acceptance" that constitute a legal contract. Withdrawal differs from abortion in that the man's semen in itself cannot form a child, just as an offer in and of itself does not create a contract. "After the offer and the acceptance [have occurred]," however, "reneging constitutes cancellation, nullification, and rupture [of the contract]."[42]

Al-Ghazali's argument does differ from those of some other authors in that he emphasizes the moment of conception (i.e., the mixing of the sexual fluids of the man and the woman) as a decisive dividing point in the creation of the child. Before conception, al-Ghazali argues, any steps taken to prevent conception (ranging from the refusal to marry, through refraining from sexual intercourse with the spouse, to *coitus interruptus*) simply represent failures to realize a potential good. Thus, such actions are not forbidden; they are, rather, instances of falling short of the ideal (*tark al-afḍal*). Abortion and infanticide are qualitatively different from contraception in that they involve an offense (*jināya*) against an extant being; they represent the infliction of a positive wrong rather than the negation of a potential right.[43]

However, it is not necessarily the case that al-Ghazali's argument that both infanticide and abortion constitute a *jināya* implies an equal and absolute prohibition of both actions. Islamic law, which represents a fully synthesized combination of law (in the sense of judicially enforceable norms) and ethics (in the sense of moral standards providing voluntary orientation for the actions of individuals), has diverse and ambiguous ways of identifying and treating "bad" actions. In this case, al-Ghazali places abortion and infanticide on a continuum of moral odium:

> [The destruction of the fetus] also has different degrees. The first degree of existence is when the semen falls into the womb, mixes with the woman's semen and becomes ready to receive life; spoiling this is an offense (*jināya*). When it becomes a clump and a blood clot[44] (*muḍgha wa-ʿalaqa*), the offense is more serious (*kānat al-jināya afḥash*). When the spirit is breathed into [the fetus] and the form is completed (*istawat al-khilqa*), the offense becomes even more serious. The utmost degree of seriousness in the offense is after the child is born alive.[45]

Thus, it is not entirely clear how serious an offense early abortion would be in al-Ghazali's schema. It certainly falls short of murder, which presumably would be the final degree in his progression. Interestingly, al-Ghazali is also credited with the opinion that it is permissible to abort a drop of semen or a blood clot but forbidden to abort a clump of flesh.[46] Samira Bayyumi explains the rationale for this position as follows:

> This [opinion] is based on the Shafiʿi teaching that the drop of semen and the blood clot do not have the subtle form of the fetus (*ṣūrat al-janīn al-khafīya*) that the midwives, who are the experts [in this area], know; thus, they [i.e., the Shafiʿis] require the *ghurra* for a clump of flesh but not for a drop of semen or a blood clot.[47]

The apparent conflict between the sliding scale of moral turpitude described in *Iḥyāʾ ʿulūm al-dīn* and this second opinion attributed to al-Ghazali may be a function of the dual application of the *fiqh* to ethical evaluation of one's own actions before the fact and to the definition of civil and criminal offenses to be demonstrated and punished after the fact. Following al-Ghazali's schema as a moral guide for one's own actions, one would ideally choose not to abort a developing fetus at any point after conception, although the lesser seriousness of the transgression might justify doing so early in the pregnancy under some conditions. Using his schema as a guideline for identifying and penalizing transgressions after the fact, however, one would need to introduce another factor: the necessity for some kind of proof that a pregnancy had existed in the first place. From this point of view, only at the point when medical personnel (in this case, midwives) could discern the emerging form of the fetus could an offense be demonstrated to have occurred. At this point, however, there is a disjunction between the two forms of *shar'ī* discourse, the normative and the legal. It is resolved by making an analogy from the case of legal investigation (primarily, the demand for compensation for a fetus miscarried as a result of assault) to the case of personal moral action. Thus, the moral odium of abortion is incurred only if a pregnancy can be proven to have existed.

Al-Ghazali also provides an interesting examination of the possible motives for contraception, motives that might also be considered with respect to abortion. He enquires into this matter because, while he considers contraception to be permissible, he allows that the motivating intention (*al-niyya al-bā'itha*) may in itself be morally reprehensible. He lists five possible motives, only two of which he considers illegitimate. The first applies to slave women; the owner may want to avoid conception so that a slave woman could not gain a claim to emancipation by bearing his child. The second is the preservation of the beauty and health of the woman. The third is the fear of hardship resulting from excessive offspring. Al-Ghazali endorses all of these motives as permissible, although the third represents a failure to achieve the ideal state of *tawakkul*, or reliance on Divine Providence. The only motives he brands as sinful are the fear of conceiving daughters rather than sons, and a woman's excessive fear of the pollution resulting from childbirth, an obsession with ritual purity that al-Ghazali associates with the Kharijite heresy.

How, then, does al-Ghazali's discussion of birth control and abortion fit into his two intersecting moral discourses—the legal and the mystical? In general, al-Ghazali would seem to appear in this passage primarily as a jurist. The analogical reasoning of the opening of the passage is a basic technique of Islamic legal analysis known as *qiyās*. His placement of birth control on a continuum from marriage, through intercourse, to the final goal of reproduction reflects the legal concept of *al-maṣāliḥ al-mursala*, in which actions without a clear status in the text of Qur'an or *hadith* are evaluated with respect to a basic set of ultimate objectives. In his work *al-Mustasfa,* al-Ghazali identifies these objectives as the preservation of five things: religion, life, intellect, offspring (*nasl*), and property.[48] This is, indeed, a standard list of fundamental objectives of the sharia among those jurists who accept this form of legal reasoning. The fact that the preservation of bloodlines (*al-nasl*) appears as one of the basic values underlying God's laws for humankind in itself, of course, reflects the worldview of the Islamic jurists who formed this theory.

Al-Ghazali's emphasis on the importance of procreation is firmly rooted in his understanding of the nature of the human person and its realization in married life. Like other Islamic jurists (and unlike many Christian thinkers), al-Ghazali does not consider procreation to be the sole rationale for the sexual tie of marriage. The satisfaction of sexual urges which might otherwise lead to corruption and sin and the spiritually restorative enjoyment of intimacy and companionship are both independent, although subordinate, objectives of marriage. The legitimacy of marital intercourse is in no way contingent upon the possibility of conception. However, al-Ghazali places sexual satisfaction and personal companionship second and third in his list of the benefits of marriage (the fourth and fifth are the time saved by delegating household responsibilities to one's wife and the moral fortitude gained by patient endurance of her bad behavior). The first and most important benefit of marriage, in al-Ghazāli's view, is procreation. Al-Ghazali considers procreation to be a fundamental objective of human nature as created by God (the *fiṭra;* see Qur'an 30:30).[49]

Interestingly, al-Ghazali expresses a somewhat divergent set of values when writing in a more purely Sufi mode. In his handbook of Sufism appended to his *Iḥyā'* and titled *'Awārif al-ma'ārif,* al-Ghazali represents marriage (and, by extension, reproduction) as a lesser alternative to be resorted to only by those mystics who are constitutionally incapable of celibacy.[50] Thus, al-Ghazali is fairly consistent in his bifurcation between *fiqh* and Sufi ethics; while his treatment of Sufi lifestyles takes the spiritual perfection of the individual as its frame of reference, his wider discussion in the *Iḥyā'* (which is framed largely in terms of *fiqh*) takes account of social concerns, such as the importance of reproduction to the perpetuation of the Muslim community. Al-Ghazali's Sufi ethics is reflected in his discussion of birth control and abortion, however, to the extent that he also ponders the possible subjective motives for the individual's actions and exhorts him or her to a standard of perfection transcending the bare requirements of the law. The law allows one to fall short, but the quest for self-refinement urges one on.

Al-Ghazali's Sufi orientation is also apparent in his treatment of the possible intentions motivating the practice of birth control. Ordinarily, in

Islamic law intention (*niyya*) is a condition for the validity of certain legal actions rather than a generative principle producing new norms. Thus, for instance, acts of worship such as prayer are valid only if performed with the appropriate *niyya*. However, the process according to which the rules for correct prayer are defined is a purely exegetical one; jurists identify the external actions enjoined by the Qur'an and modeled by the prophet Muhammad, rather than starting out from the spiritual objectives or internal states involved in prayer. Intention is involved only at the stage of individual performance. The only major exception to this rule is the Maliki principle of *sadd al-dharā'i'*, which states that any action performed in pursuit of a goal that is *ḥarām* (forbidden by Islamic law) is similarly *ḥarām*, even if it is in itself completely unobjectionable. This principle is very important to the Maliki law of contracts, which (unlike, for instance, the Hanafi approach) forbids legal "tricks" *(ḥiyal)* that circumvent rules such as the prohibition on interest by transactions that are formally unobjectionable, although achieving the same effect as the forbidden action. Al-Ghazali, a Shafi'i, is not operating according to this Maliki principle. Instead, his deep interest in intention is dictated by his underlying Sufi approach to right action. What is intended by acts of obedience, in al-Ghazali's view, is not merely formal submission to the Creator; what ultimately counts is the way in which such actions mold the states and proclivities of the heart. Such effects on the heart can only be achieved with right intention, for it is intention that links the actions of the limbs with the states of the heart.[51]

What can contemporary western observers learn from the medieval Islamic discussions of abortion? One basic feature of these discussions is their high level of tolerance for ambiguity and complexity, which avoids absolutist simplifications of the intricate moral issues raised by fetal life. In part, this multivocality and flexibility arise from the basic structure of Sunni law. The mutual recognition of the different schools of law, which always involved at least a tacit acknowledgment that Muslims of good faith could come to differing conclusions on matters of detail, is one such element of flexibility. The legal technique of analogical reasoning, which allowed jurists to place the fetus within various frames of comparison (an independent life, a limb of the mother, and so on) also lent itself to complex ways of understanding. Another aspect of this nuanced approach is the jurists' vision of a developmental process which is gradual and progressive. Despite enormous variation among different Islamic jurists, all of the authors I have examined use a Qur'anically based schema of the gradual development of the fetus. Although some jurists do forbid abortion at any time after implantation in the womb, the logic of the graduated schema of development and the force of *ijmāʿ* combine to reinforce a logic of gradually increasing protection for the fetus. The idea that "life begins at conception" does not unqualifiedly describe any school of Islamic law.

Furthermore, while they do not develop this theme explicitly or systematically, the jurists place the developing fetus within a complex of relationships linking the fetus with its parents, the fetus with God, the parents with God, the parents with each other, and all of these individuals with the Muslim community as a whole. These relationships provide a broad and flexible set of considerations that come into play, and must presumably be weighed against each other, in any potential case of abortion.

In its picture of gradual development and its preoccupation with the multiple human relationships in which the fetus gradually takes its place, the medieval Islamic discussion of abortion represents one of a range of cultural and religious alternative views which challenge the understandings of personhood that inform the American debate over abortion. Beth Conklin and Lynn Morgan note:

> Seeking a way out of the conceptual quagmire in which one individual's interests are pitted against another's, theologians, humanists, bioethicists, and others often advocate less individualistic, more sociocentric approaches to personhood. The contrast between individualism and relationality that has framed many anthropological models of personhood has found its way into North American discussions of abortion and other life-and-death decisions.[52]

Conklin and Morgan argue that in North America, "personhood is assumed to be located in biology";[53] it is "biological markers" naturally and automatically emerging in the physical fetal body that render the fetus a human being. Classical Islamic law certainly shares this point of view when it uses characteristics such as fetal formation to determine the culpability of abortion. However, it ultimately tends to use such biological markers merely as indices of the one component of personhood that truly counts, the presence of a human soul which allows the fetus to play the relational roles of servant of God and (should it die) intercessor for its parents.

One advantage of a shift to a more relational understanding of personhood, Conklin and Morgan argue, is that it obviates the "either/or, all-or-nothing" nature of American debates. The relative flexibility and openness of classical Islamic legal discussions of abortion also emerges from another feature of the texts, their underlying commitment to casuistry—that is, the examination of specific cases rather than the generation of abstract rules. While the word "casuistry" has a disreputable ring in modern English, recently it has been the object of efforts at rehabilitation. In their book *The Abuse of Casuistry,* Albert Jonsen and Stephen Toulmin argue that casuistic argumentation can offer renewed possibilities for reasoned debate in just such areas as the abortion issue. They write:

> In one respect the current debate about the morality of abortion bears on its face the hallmark of much present American thought, not merely about ethics but about law and public policy. Activists on both sides of the abortion debate have looked for *universal* laws and principles. . . ; and their insistence on framing those principles in unqualified and universal terms . . . has done much to make the whole debate irresoluble.[54]

In contrast, Jonsen and Toulmin point to the greater nuance and openness of the casuistic arguments of the past, such as those of Thomas Aquinas. Like many premodern Islamic scholars, "Aquinas acknowledges that the balance of moral considerations necessarily tilts in different directions at different stages in a woman's pregnancy, with crucial changes beginning around the time of 'quickening.'" In both their attention to relationality and their openness to the complex ethical taxonomies allowed by the casuistic method, classical Islamic law offers a paradigm for the discussion of abortion which is stimulatingly and perhaps usefully different from those prevalent in North America today.

Notes

1. In this section, I have chosen not to limit myself to a specific chronological period. Rather, I have included the opinions of a range of jurists whose analysis of Islamic law follows the patterns of legal analysis set around the fifth Islamic century; thus, I have not excluded early modern thinkers when their discussions clearly fit into the patterns set by their medieval predecessors.

2. Muslim ibn Ḥajjāj, *Ṣaḥīḥ Muslim* (Beirut: Dār Ibn Ḥazm, 1416 A.H./1995 C.E.), 863; Abū 'Abd Allāh Muḥammad ibn Māja, *Sunan Ibn Māja,* ed. Muḥammad Fu'ād 'Abd al-Bāqī ([Cairo]: 'Īsā al-Bābī al-Ḥalabī wa-Shurakāhu, n.d.), 1:638.

3. Al-Tirmidhī, *Sunan al-Tirmidhī wa-huwa 'l-jāmi' al-ṣaḥīḥ,* ed. 'Abd al-Raḥmān Muḥammad 'Uthmān (Medina: Muḥammad 'Abd al-Muḥsin al-Kutubī, n.d.), 3:402.

4. See 'Abd al-Razzāq al-Ṣan'ānī, *al-Muṣannaf* (Beirut: al-Maktab al-Islāmī, 1983), #12570. Number 12571 relates a similar response from the early Meccan jurist 'Aṭā' ibn Abī Rabāḥ.

5. Aḥmad ibn Taymīya, *Majmū' fatāwā shaykh al-Islām Aḥmad ibn Taymīya* (Rabat: al-Maktab al-Ta'līmī al-Su'ūdī fī'l-Maghrib, n.d.), 34:160.

6. Various versions of this report, some with and some without the relative's complaint and the Prophet's rejoinder, are to be found (among many other sources) in al-Bukhārī, *Ṣaḥīḥ al-Bukhārī* (Beirut: Dār al-Fikr, 1411 A.H./1991

C.E.), # 6910; Muslim, *Ṣaḥīḥ,* 1057–1059; Abū Dāwūd al-Sijistānī, *Sunan Abī Dāwūd* (Beirut: Dār Ibn Ḥazm, 1419 A.H./1998 C.E.), 693–94; 'Abd al-Razzāq, *al-Muṣannaf,* #18338, 18339, 18346, 18349, 18351.

7. *Al-Mawsū'a al-fiqhīya* (Kuwait: Wizārat al-Awqāf wa'l-Shu'ūn al-Islāmīya, 1987–)., s.v. "ijhāḍ," para. 11.

8. Some jurists hold that, in the case that the abortion is deliberated induced by the pregnant woman, the *ghurra* goes to the father of the fetus; this opinion is attributed to the early Iraqi jurist Ibrahim al-Nakha'i and to the Hanafi scholar al-Nasafi (*al-Fatāwā al-hindīya* [1310 A.H., facsimile Beirut: Dār al-Ma'rifa, 1393 A.H./1973 C.E.], 6: 35–6).

9. 'Abd al-Razzāq al-San'ānī, *al-Muṣannaf,* #18362.

10. Ibn Ḥazm, *al-Muḥallā* (Beirut: Dār al-Kutub al-'Ilmiyya, [1992]), 11:240.

11. *Al-Mawsū'a al-fiqhīya,* s.v. "ijhāḍ," para. 12.

12. Qāḍī Zādeh, *Natā'ij al-Afkār fī Kashf al-Rumūz wa'l-Asrār* (Cairo: n.p., 1389/1970), 10:299.

13. See Abū'l-Walīd ibn Rushd, *Bidāyat al-mujtahid wa-nihāyat al-muqtaṣid* (Cairo: n.p., 1353 A.H./1935 C.E.), 2:408.

14. Ibn Ḥazm, *Muḥallā,* 11:242.

15. *Al-Fatāwā al-hindīya,* 6:35.

16. Al-Bukhārī, *Ṣaḥīḥ,* #3332 (also 3208, 6594, 7454); Muslim, *Ṣaḥīḥ,* 1616; Ibn Māja, *Sunan,* 1:29; al-Tirmidhī, *Sunan,* 3:302.

17. Muslim, *Ṣaḥīḥ,* 1617.

18. Umm Kulthūm Yaḥyā Muṣṭafā al-Khaṭīb, *Qaḍīyat taḥdīd al-nasl* (Jidda: al-Dār al-Su'ūdīya li'l-nashr wa'l-tawzī', 1982), 152.

19. Samīra Sayyid Sulaymān Bayyūmī, *al-Ijhāḍ wa-āthāruhu fī'l-sharī'a al-islāmīya* (Cairo: Dār al-Ṭabā'a al-Muḥammadīya bi'l-Azhar, 1989), 19; al-Khaṭīb, *Qaḍīyat,* 152–53.

20. See *al-Mawsū'a al-fiqhīya,* s.v. "ijhāḍ," para. 6 and the references there.

21. Bayyūmī, *al-Ijhāḍ,* 18 (references to *Ḥāshiyat al-Raḥūnī,* 3:264, *Ghāyat al-muntahā fī'l-jam' bayna'l-iqnā' wa'l-muntahā,* 1:87, and *Tafsīr al-Qurṭubī,* 12:8); al-Khaṭīb, 153.

22. Ibn 'Ābidīn, *Ḥāshiyat radd al-muḥtār,* 2d ed. ([Cairo]: n.p., 1386/1966), 1:302.

23. Al-Qurṭubī, *al-Jāmi' li-aḥkām al-Qur'ān* (Cairo: Dār al-Kātib al-'Arabī, 1387 A.H./1967 A.D.), 12: 8. Emphasis mine.

24. *Ḥāshiyat al-Dasūqī 'alā l-Sharḥ al-kabīr.* Dār Iḥyā' al-Kutub al-'Arabīya (no facts of publication given), 4:268.

25. Cf. al-Marghīnānī, *Kitāb al-Hidāya sharḥ Bidāyat al-mubtadi'* (n.p., 1326 A.H.), 4:154.

26. Sometimes the inbreathing of the spirit is identified with "quickening," in the sense of the beginning of discernible movement of the fetus within the womb. This in turn can be understood in an essentially evidentiary light, as the point at which the woman can decisively confirm that she is pregnant, and/or as the actual beginning of life itself. Thus al-Qurtubi writes, "There is no dispute among the

religious scholars that the spirit is breathed into [the fetus] after 120 days; that is, four months and the beginning of a fifth. . . . This is the rule to which we refer when necessary in legal rulings such as determining the paternity of a child when it is disputed and assigning support for pregnant divorcées. This is because [the existence of the pregnancy] becomes certain through the movement of the fetus in the womb. . . . The inbreathing [of the spirit] is the cause by which God creates spirit and life in [the fetus]" (al-Qurṭubī, *Jāmiʿ*, 8).

27. Ibn ʿĀbidīn, *Ḥāshiyat,* 1:302.

28. *Kitāb Mabṣūt al-Sarakhsī* ([Cairo]: n.p., 1324 A.H.), 3:213.

29. Al-Wansharīsī, *al-Miʿyār al-muʿrib wa'l-jāmiʿ al-mughrib* (Ribat: Wizārat al-Awqāf wa'l-Shu'ūn al-Islāmīya, 1981), 4: 236 (citing Ibn al-ʿArabī).

30. Ibn Māja, *Sunan,* 1:513.

31. Cf. Abū ʿAbd Allāh Muḥammad ibn Muḥammad ibn ʿAbd al-Raḥmān al-Tarābulusī al-Maghribī, known as al-Ḥaṭṭāb, *Mawāhib al-jalīl li-sharḥ mukhtaṣar Khalīl* (Tripoli, Libya: Maktabat al-Najāḥ, n.d.), 3:476.

32. *Al-Fatāwā al-ʿĀlamgīrīya al-maʿrūfa bi'l-Fatāwā al-Hindīya* (Cairo: Būlāq, 1310 A.H.), 6:35–36 (emphases mine).

33. Al-Khaṭīb, *Qaḍīyat,* 108 (emphasis mine).

34. Qāḍī Zādeh, *Natā'ij,* 10:299.

35. Al-Haṭṭāb, *Mawāhib,* 3:477.

36. Al-Ghazālī, *Iḥyā' ʿulūm al-dīn* (Beirut: Dār al-Fikr, 1414 A.H./1994 A.D.), 1:28–9.

37. C.f. *Iḥyā',* 5:173–77 ("*Fī akhlāq al-ṣūfīya wa-sharḥ al-khuluq*").

38. The synthesis or conflation of Greek-derived ethical concepts with the spiritual discipline of Sufism becomes explicit in al-Ghazali's *Deliverer from Error,* where he critiques the philosophers' science of ethics as follows:

> Their whole discussion of ethics consists in defining the characteristics and moral constitution of the soul and enumerating the various types of soul and the method of moderating and controlling them. This they borrow from the teaching of the mystics, those men of piety whose chief occupation is to meditate upon God, to oppose the passions, and to walk in the way leading to God by withdrawing from worldly pleasure. In their spiritual warfare they have learnt about the virtues and vices of the soul and the defects in its actions, and what they have learned they have clearly expressed. The philosophers have taken over this teaching and mingled it with their own disquisitions, furtively using this embellishment to sell their rubbishy wares more readily (W. Montgomery Watt, *The Faith and Practice of al-Ghazālī* [London: George Allen and Unwin, 1953], 38).

39. Al-Ghazālī, *Iḥyā',* 5:176.

40. Al-Ghazālī, *Iḥyā',* 5:129–31.

41. See Khaṭīb, *Qaḍīyat,* 152; Bayyūmī, *Ijhāḍ,* 18; Maḥmūd Shaltūt, *Fatāwā: dirāsa li-mushkilāt al-Muslim al-mu'āṣir fī ḥayātihi al-yawmīya wa'l-ʿāmma* (Cairo: Dār al-Qalam, n.d.), 290–91. Interestingly, in his detailed fatwa on the

subject of abortion Shaltut cites the entire passage, quoted below in this article, in which al-Ghazali indicates the embryo's gradual progression towards fully realized life and the corresponding gradations of prohibition associated with abortion at the different stages. However, Shaltut follows this quotation with a discussion in which he points to al-Ghazali's emphasis that "it is forbidden to abort the embryo after the sperm has joined the egg" (291). Shaltut's discussion thus combine's al-Ghazali's recognition of subtle gradations in the development of the fetus with an emphasis on the independent life of the zygote and even of the sperm itself, whose struggle to fertilize the egg Shaltut describes in heroic terms.

42. Al-Ghazālī, *Iḥyā'*, 2:58.

43. Ibid.

44. Many Islamic modernist authors offer different translations of the word *'alaqa* that correspond more closely to contemporary scientific understandings of the embryo. For instance, the basic meaning of the verbal stem '-l-q, "to cling, to be attached," can be associated with the embryo's implantation on the wall of the uterus. I have chosen to use the phrase "blood clot" here to reflect the understandings of the medieval authors whose work I am discussing. They seem unanimously to understand *'alaqa* in this sense (cf. the classic *Tafsīr al-Jalālayn*, which glosses the word *'alaqa* in verse 23:12 of the Qur'ān as "solidified blood" [*dam jāmid*]).

45. Al-Ghazālī, *Iḥyā'*, 2:65.

46. Bayyūmī, *Ijhāḍ*, 19.

47. Ibid., 23.

48. Al-Ghazālī, *al-Mustasfā min 'ilm al-uṣūl* (Beirut: Dār al-Arqam ibn Abī 'l-Arqam, n.d.), 1:636. Al-Ghazali notes that these objectives often stand in conflict with each other in concrete situations, thus giving rise to a need for comparative balancing of the different aims of the law (1:654–655).

49. Al-Ghazālī, *Iḥyā'*, 1:28.

50. Ibid., 5:137–142.

51. Ibid., 4:386–88.

52. Beth A. Conklin and Lynn M. Morgan, "Babies, Bodies, and the Production of Personhood in North America and a Native Amazonian Society," *Ethos* 24 (1996), 660.

53. Ibid., 665.

54. Albert R.Jonsen and Stephen Toulmin, *The Abuse of Casuistry: A History of Moral Reasoning* (Berkeley: University of California Press, 1988), 3–4.

Three

Contemporary Muslim Ethics of Abortion

Donna Lee Bowen

Early reports from the 1994 Cairo Population Conference announced an alliance between Muslims and Roman Catholics based on mutual opposition to abortion. As days passed, however, spokesmen for various Muslim countries dissented from the initially announced position. As the delegates made clear, while both Muslims and Roman Catholics felt that abortion is a grievous sin, their official positions diverged sharply. The Roman Catholic position forbids abortion absolutely,[1] but delegates held that Islamic jurisprudence allows abortion under defined conditions. They stressed that an across-the-board prohibition misrepresents even the conservative Muslim position, which is more a soft "no, but" than an adamant "never." This position extends to allowing abortion under certain conditions for a good reason.[2]

Abortion poses considerable ethical problems in that it is an action most agree is wrong. Yet the imperfect realities that many individuals face in a lifetime pose religious and ethical dilemmas. Although respect for life is a paramount virtue, how does one respond to the following situations? A pregnant mother faces certain death if she carries the child full term. A woman faces the sacrifice of her own health and ability to care for her family if she gives birth. Parents face the certainty that their child will be born severely disabled and will pose a heavy burden. A child will be born deformed and thereby live a diminished life. A student, accidently made pregnant by her boyfriend, faces family and social disgrace. If the question hinges on preserving life, which life—that of the mother or that of the fetus—is deemed paramount? Statements from the Vatican articulate clearly that unborn life cannot be taken directly, whatever the circumstances. Muslim theology answers differently. In laying out their response, Muslim scholars recognize that abortion contravenes God's general command to preserve the life of children, but they also recognize that circumstances may call for a modification of that prohibition. The situation is complicated, for Islamic jurisprudence regarding abortion separates into two major currents. While most schools of Islamic law prohibit or strongly disapprove of abortion in the first four months, at least without a strong reason, a smaller number of schools permit abortion before 120 days and prohibit it thereafter.

In Islam, abortion is not forbidden across the board but is decided on a case by case basis. Thus, a person who would determine whether the decision to abort is ethically permissible, such as a religious leader, a physician, or one of the parents, is placed in a paradoxical position—how to deal with the religious imperative of producing and maintaining a strong community of faithful Muslims while at the same time recognizing that in some cases individual needs overpower community welfare. This paper examines how Islam approaches this predicament: discouraging abortion while yet allowing for practical responses that safeguard an individual's well-being.

Discussion of this problem will only make sense if we examine the complicated legal texts on abortion in concert with the ethical values of the community, as represented in decisions made by individual Muslims, as well as public policies. In Islam as in other religions, ethical values and religious values overlap and have much in common. At times religious values underlie ethical values. In working through the thorny question of abortion, Islamic religious values and ethical values converge and serve as a guide for individual Muslims trying to determine life choices. In terms of political influence, these values also affect policy formation in many Muslim nations. In doing this, I argue, Muslims are guided by ethical considerations that both reinforce the scriptural commands and weigh in on real life problems. The ethical stances Islamic law offers are highly responsive to circumstances, however. As I discuss below, this room to respond may open doors some Muslims would prefer to keep closed. Some religious scholars consider permitting abortion until 120 days to be overly permissive, while others see it as a response to crucial individual needs.

The intricacies of this problem suggest that individual Muslims actively consider their options, referring to Islamic law, the advice of religious leaders, then finally their personal situations in deciding whether or not to abort, though this view is disparaged by some Muslim commentators. For example, Abul Fadl Mohsin Ebrahim states that "the question for Muslims is not whether it is right or wrong, from an ethical standpoint, to engage in abortion. Rather, Muslims ask whether the sharia (Islamic law) sanctions abortion, and proceed accordingly."[3] This statement begs the question, for the wide range of jurisprudents' statements on abortion offers opportunities for abortion if Muslims chose to follow the more permissive tradition. But the fact that so many choose to restrict abortion shows the weight Muslim ethical beliefs carry in determining how to proceed.

As Marion Katz explains in the previous chapter, the Qur'an says nothing about abortion itself, nor do the hadith and Sunna. Rather, the prohibition of abortion is based on analogy and interpretations of hadith applied to Qur'anic verses, specifically the injunction against killing. Muslims consider that God's command prohibiting unnecessary taking of life overshadows any other question: "Do not kill the soul that God has made sacred, except for just cause" (17:33, 25:68).[4] The debate on abortion centers on a narrowly defined theological question as to when the soul can perish by harm done to the fetus, or at what point the soul enters the developing fetus. A significant number of jurists make a case that the fetus is not "ensouled," or created, until 120 days after conception.

On the surface, since the Islamic position on abortion is found in scriptural and legal sources, some hold that recourse to scriptural authority eliminates the need for a reasoned ethical approach. The philosophers al-Farabi and Ibn Rushd held that religion, as a transcendental truth, by necessity encompassed reason, and that in most cases, reason and religious truth would support each other.[5] The necessity of having a good reason or justifiable grounds to purposefully terminate a pregnancy brings questions of reason into play to complement references to the Qur'an, hadith, and legal texts. No matter which position on the creation of the fetus one follows, no one can choose abortion on a whim. All schools require a good reason, one accepted by religious authorities, for terminating a pregnancy.

The situation has become more complicated in recent years as countries with Muslim majorities have legalized abortion. Three Muslim countries, Turkey, Tunisia, and Iran, permit social abortion (abortion for reasons other than the health of the mother) during the first trimester of pregnancy. In Iran, before the Islamic Revolution, abortion was available from 1973 to 1979; abortion was again allowed in 1994, after fifteen years of prohibition.[6] While no abortion figures are available for Iran, the latest statistics for Turkey and Tunisia differ significantly. In Tunisia, 1996 figures show 19,000 abortions, or abortions at 7.8% of total pregnancies. In Turkey in 1993 there were 351,300 abortions, or 20.5% of total pregnancies.[7] Demographers estimate that figures for Turkey in 1993, the first year that abortions were legalized, were higher than they have been in subsequent years; as of yet we have no data to bear out this theory. The fact that accessible statistics on abortions are scarce reinforces the extreme sensitivity of the issue of abortion in Muslim nations. Although therapeutic abortions (those performed for medical reasons) are allowed, and no doubt, social abortions are performed in a clandestine manner, no statistics on either category of abortions have been made public.

Even in countries where abortion is legal, up-to-date statistics are not routinely published. To set these figures in worldwide perspective, several examples are instructive. Israel in 1995 registered a total of 17,600 abortions, a figure representing 14.8% of all live births and 12.9% of known pregnancies.[8] Newly independent nations of the former U.S.S.R. with sizeable Muslim populations in Central Asia register significant numbers of abortions. Azerbaijan in 1996 recorded 28,400 abortions, or 18% of total pregnancies. That year Kazakhstan (with a population that is 60% Russian) registered 178,000 abortions, or 41.3% of total pregnancies; Uzbekistan (with a 30% Russian population) listed 63,200 abortions, or 9.5% of total pregnancies. The Russian Federation recorded 2,442,074 abortions, 64.2% of total pregnancies.[9] Bangladesh recorded an estimated 700,000 abortions in 1996 which is 3.1% of total pregnancies. France recorded 152,693 abortions in 1994, or 17.7% of total pregnancies. Japan in 1995 recorded 343,024 abortions, or 22.4% of total pregnancies. In 1998, the Republic of Ireland listed 5,892 abortions, or 9.92% of total pregnancies, an increase of 10.4% over 1997.[10] In 1997 the number of abortions in the United States fell to the lowest level in two decades: 20 of every 1,000 women had abortions, a rate of 305 abortions per 1000 live births for a total of 1,184,758 legal abortions.[11] The Alan Guttemacher Institute estimates that worldwide, for every 1,000 women of childbearing age, 35 are estimated to have an induced abortion each year. About 26 million women have legal abortions each year; 20 million have abortions where abortion is restricted or prohibited by law. Of the women having abortions each year, 78% live in developing countries, the other 22% in developed countries.[12]

The dilemma for Muslims centers on the extent to which they wish to permit the use of abortion. Tunisia, Turkey, and Iran have set policy that allows abortions to be performed widely. The majority of other Muslim countries prohibit social abortion but allow physicians to determine whether a therapeutic abortion is needed. On one hand, conservatives could question whether Islamic law is sufficiently open to allow legalized social abortion. On the other, liberals on the abortion issue could ask why other countries that now prohibit social abortion resist liberalizing abortion laws.

The contradictions found in the different Islamic legal schools' teachings on abortion can be resolved somewhat by emphasizing the stress Islam places on the value of life. This stems from Qur'anic teachings of an individual Muslim's place in the divine purpose of creation and extends to the potential held by an embryo in a mother's womb. The Qur'an states that God "breathed [his] own spirit" into Adam to distinguish him from the rest of the creations of God (15:29). The Qur'an teaches the significance of men and women's creation and emphasizes that life is of fundamental importance. Respect for life, then, is the rule, and exceptions to that rule must be noted and justified. To a great extent the differing legal positions all spring from different means of resolving the conflict between Islam's value of life and the needs of the woman seeking an abortion.

The Positions of Contemporary Scholars (Ulema)

Abortion takes much of its onus from Muslims' horror at the pre-Islamic custom of *wa'd* (female infanticide). The Qur'an's insistence on the value of life, even for as socially expendable a creation as an infant girl, is taken from verses on not killing children. Working from analogy from *wa'd*, some schools forbid abortion (expulsion of the product of conception from the womb) as the killing of a defenseless child in the womb.[13] A physician and *'ālim*, Dr. Muhammad S. Madkur, citing legal experts, defines abortion as the deliberate expulsion of the fetus prematurely and without the presence of any need for such an action.[14]

Muslim legal schools differ both on questions of when the soul enters the fetus and also on the permissibility of abortion. All schools agree that abortion is prohibited after the soul has entered the fetus. The critical distinction becomes whether the act of abortion extinguishes a fetus that has been ensouled or an entity without a soul. However, as I outline below, the schools differ on interpretations of when the soul enters the body so they cannot reach agreement on when abortion is permitted.[15] Even after ensoulment, abortion may become permissible if the mother or family has a good reason, but it still carries a heavy stigma. Most, but not all, Muslims believe that it is an action better avoided, even if they feel an abortion is medically necessary.

Determination of the time of ensoulment is based upon an interpretation of a Qur'anic scripture: "We first created the human being from an essence of clay: then placed it, a living germ, in a safe enclosure. The germ We made into a clot of blood, and the clot into a lump of flesh. This We fashioned into bones, then clothed the bones with flesh, thus bringing forth another creation" (23:12–14). In one hadith, each of the four stages enumerated is assigned a time period of forty days; four stages makes a total of 120 days.[16] Other hadiths differ and give forty days as the total of the four stages. Reasoning from different hadiths, some schools of jurists determined that until the stages were complete, the fetus had no soul, or God had not breathed his spirit into the fetus, and therefore it had not been created yet. The Muslim theologian Abu Hamid al-Ghazali, a Shafi'i who disagreed with the majority of jurists of his school in opposing abortion, discusses this point in *Kitāb al-durra al-fākhira fī kashf 'ulūm al-ākhira*.

> When the individual sperm falls, it is established in the womb until its form is completed. The soul in it is lifeless, but its essential Malakūtī [divine] nature keeps the body from decomposing. Then God, may He be exalted, breathes into it His spirit, rendering to it its secret essence that had been taken and hidden for a time in one of the treasure houses of the Throne. The infant gets agitated—and how many an infant does so in the belly of his mother. Perhaps his mother pays attention to him, or perhaps she does not. This is a first death and a second life.[17]

As discussed in detail in the previous chapter, the different schools of Islamic legal thought complicate any attempt to fit Muslims neatly into one mold according to their views on abortion. Beyond their agreement that abortion after 120 days is forbidden, they differ greatly on the permissibility of abortion before 120 days. They posit different time schemes for when the spirit or soul enters the fetus, and their beliefs concerning at which point abortion is no longer permitted follow from these limits: at the moment of conception, at forty days, at or before 120 days, and thereafter. The Hanafi school is the most liberal, and some Hanafi scholars believe that abortion before the 120-day period is permitted even if the family or person seeking the abortion has no valid reason. (The Hanafi school, like most other schools, would require the permission of the husband to a wife's abortion.) Other Hanafi scholars disagree, holding that an abortion before 120 days is disapproved of, but not forbidden. The Maliki school (joined as well by some Shafi'is, Ibadis, and Imami Shi'a) is the most strict, holding that the fetus is ensouled at the moment of conception, or within the first forty days. They differ on whether abortion before forty days is prohibited (the majority position) or disapproved of without a valid excuse. Thus, most Malikis do not permit abortion at any point. The Hanbali school holds a somewhat ambiguous position, but many of its jurists would not prohibit abortion before forty days. The Shafi'i school splits, some following the Hanafi school, some following the Malikis, and others holding that abortion after eighty or ninety days is prohibited. For all but the Malikis, Ibadis, and Imami Shi'a, a case can be made that abortion at some point (determined by the school) before 120 days is permitted as technically not constituting abortion: although the product of conception has been expelled, no soul is being killed as the fetus is not yet animated; that is, no soul has yet entered the fetus. After 120 days, all agree that abortion is prohibited.

Despite the difference on the question of the entrance of the soul into the embryo or fetus, all schools except some of the Hanafis also agree that abortion at will is not permitted. All emphasize that the abortion before

120 days can only be undertaken for what religious scholars consider a "good" or acceptable reason. This emphasis on needing an Islamically defensible reason should serve as a means of discouraging the initiation of an abortion for less than an acceptable cause. The best example of a good reason is when pregnancy compromises the mother's health and well-being. All schools accept the necessity of sacrificing the unborn child to preserve the mother's life and put the weight of the decision on the shoulders of the physician attending the mother. In this case, the Islamic legal rule that "necessity knows no law" as well as the legal premise that "the greater evil should be warded off by the lesser evil" takes precedence.[18]

It is noteworthy that al-Ghazali's words as quoted above and the emphasis of the legal scholars upon preventing abortion after animation of the fetus all dovetail with the experience of Muslim women. Conversations with women reveal that they believe that the fetus is not alive until it quickens in the womb. By two to four months, most women, feeling the fetus, believe that it lives, is a separate being from the mother, and that she is indeed with child. Abortion before the fetus is physically perceived to be alive seems to be an abstract action; after that point, it involves killing a real being.[19]

Al-Ghazali, although he noted that the divine spirit is breathed into the fetus following the creation of the embryo, himself opposed abortion before 120 days as disapproved, if not prohibited. He held that the prohibition of abortion intensified as the fetus developed stage by stage, culminating in prohibition after animation. Al-Ghazali also stipulated that adultery can be considered a valid reason to allow abortion. "If the zygote is the result of adultery, then the allowance of abortion may be envisaged. If it is left until it reaches the stage of animation, then prohibition is certain."[20] He set up a continuum beginning with the contraceptive technique of *coitus interruptus* (*'azl* in Arabic) and ending with infanticide (*wa'd*) and analyzed how these practices differ from abortion:

> This [*coitus interruptus, 'azl*] is not the same as abortion and infanticide, for the two latter are crimes against a living being that is already in existence. The first grade of existence occurs when semen is injected into the womb where it merges with the ovum and becomes disposed to receive life. To destroy this is to commit a crime. The crime grows more and more serious as this lump of living matter passes from one stage into another, until it reaches consummation and it detaches itself and comes out alive.[21]

By this reasoning, abortion in an early stage is a sin and contrary to Islamic teachings, but the sin grows more serious as time passes and the fetus develops further. The Mufti of New Delhi summed up this position in 1995 following the Cairo Population Conference by saying that abortion following 120 days was a "great sin, rather than the smaller sin it is considered before 120 days."[22] This reasoning is analogous to the reasoning Justice Harry Blackmun set forth in *Roe v. Wade,* the U.S. Supreme Court decision that sets up a three-tier approach to abortion. The court ruled that in the first trimester, the decision must be left to the pregnant woman and to the medical judgment of her physician. In the second trimester, individual states may regulate abortion procedures in order to safeguard the health of the mother. In the third trimester, at which point the Court determined that the fetus is viable, each individual state, by reason of its interest in preserving potential human life, may regulate and prohibit abortion unless continuing the pregnancy threatens the mother's life.[23]

The fact that the Hanafi, Shafiʿi, and Zaydi schools permit abortion within 120 days does not negate their disapproval of the practice. Although they do not forbid (*ḥarrama*) the practice, as there are cases when abortion is necessary, they consider it *makrūh* (disapproved or detested) and therefore only a strong reason can justify its use.

At the time of the U.N.–sponsored Cairo Population Conference in 1994, Egyptian ulema joined in public debate in the newspapers about the religious permissibility of abortion. Their statements illustrated the variety of current opinions on this matter. The late Jad al-Haqq ʿAli Jad al-Haqq, then Sheikh of al-Azhar, issued a statement on Islam's position on abortion. He emphasized that abortion following the breathing of the soul (*rūḥ*) into the fetus is forbidden except in the case of danger to the mother's health. He noted that as for abortion before that time, the ulema are divided into four groups: those who hold that it is permitted totally and no conditions are necessitated; those who believe that some conditions permit abortion before 120 days; those who disapprove of it (*karaha*); and those who prohibit it. Finally, the sheikh called on physicians to be cautious in performing abortions and warned them that physicians who perform unnecessary or unlawful abortions will not be punished on this earth, but by God.[24] In an article in the next day's *al-Ahrām,* al-Qasabi Mahmoud Zalat, the dean of the College of Religion (*uṣūl al-dīn*) at al-Azhar University in Tanta, stated that abortion is forbidden from conception (literally from impregnation), and that whoever denies the presence of life in a fetus only denies the presence of movement, not life or growth, for the fetus is alive, as studies have proved.[25]

The legal codes of Muslim countries that permit or prohibit abortion do not necessarily reflect the jurisprudence of the dominant Islamic legal school in their countries. Political policies in Tunisia and Turkey, which allow social abortion at will with no legal restrictions, may have been influenced by the historical role the Hanafi school played in each country, even though Tunisia has traditionally followed the Maliki school. At this point in time, the laws of other countries of the Middle East and the Muslim world are far more restrictive, allowing therapeutic abortions narrowly defined, but not social abortion. The states generally levy heavy legal penalties upon individuals, including physicians, found guilty of assisting in an abortion.[26] Observers could question why in countries such as Egypt, where theoretically the influence of the Shafiʿi school could sway opinion toward permitting abortion before the fourth month, abortion at any time is not legal unless necessitated by the health of the mother. The nation of Iran, for the most part Imami Shiʿa, whose jurisprudence prohibits abortion before 120 days, quietly revised its policy six years ago to allow private physicians to perform abortions even in public hospitals with the permission of two doctors who attest to the mother's need for an abortion, in terms of either her physical or psychological health.[27]

Contemporary ulema make a case that the reasoning which justified abortion before 120 days has been outstripped by medical advances. Hassan Hathout, a medical doctor, states that medical science now recognizes that the fetus begins moving long before its mother feels this motion.

> Its gradual development from a cell to a full-blown infant is a smooth and continuous development, without there being any scientific dividing lines or clear boundaries separating one stage from the other.
>
> As we see it, a legal opinion based on a scientific belief must be modified in accordance with the change in this scientific belief. If the foundation changes, the structure above it must change too. Our forebears rested their legal judgments on old medical opinions.[28]

Reciprocity of Legal Opinions

Islamic legal schools show unusual tolerance towards each other by recognizing the validity of each school's legal positions within the broad arc of sharia law. This mutual tolerance permits Muslims who differ on a given issue from the jurists in their *madhhab* (school of law) to follow the teachings of another *madhhab* and grants unusual leeway to Muslims who are sufficiently educated to be acquainted with this legal doctrine. Given this legal reciprocity, theoretically there is little technical difficulty for Maliki Muslims who wish to find juridical justification for their decision to abort a pregnancy, since large schools such as the Hanafi school allow it as long as the woman or family possesses a justifiable reason. In the past, this reciprocity would have provided little scope for practice.

However, as pressure to legalize abortion intensifies in some circles, the doctrine would make abortion religiously possible.

Statements by the different schools of legal thought shed light on the permissibility of medical practices developed in recent years. The medieval Maliki scholar, al-Qurtubi, while holding that abortion before animation as well as after is prohibited, nonetheless stipulated that it is permissible to remove the sperm from the womb before a clot is formed. He stated, "The sperm is not subject to any legal provision if it is discarded by the woman before it settles inside the womb. At this stage it is as though it were still part of the man in his loins." The Egyptian physician and *ʿālim* Muhammad S. Madkur, author of *The Embryo and the Relevant Provisions in Islamic Jurisprudence,* notes that this means that "it is permissible to dispose of the fertilized ovum while it is still in the uterine tube and before it definitely assumes the form of a sucking clot or gastrula cleaving to the wall of the womb."[29] This reasoning can apply to the permissibility of IUDs, which prevent a fertilized ovum from implantation in the uterine wall, and also to the use of morning-after medication, RU-486 (widely used in France although not in the U.S.), which causes the fertilized ovum to be expelled. Many scholars would consider this medication to be permissible since it is used before a pregnancy is determined, and thereby may or may not cause an embryo to abort. In any case, al-Qurtubi and Madkur's argument would hold that it is permissible in any case inasmuch as if the ovum is successfully fertilized, it would not yet have attached to the uterine wall.

The Ethics of Abortion

In analyzing the Muslim ethical stance on abortion, one cannot ignore the general ethical principles that guide Muslim action. Respect for life and concern for community welfare, as defined by the Muslim concept of the *umma,* guide Muslim action in a broad sense. In a more specific sense, however, these principles are qualified by exceptions whereby these general principles are superseded by practical circumstances. The degree to which a fetus is regarded as a person becomes a major factor when Muslims are faced with a real-life case of whether to abort. At this point, Muslim ethical reasoning becomes more casuistry than an application of universal principles. In the area of abortion, Muslims have traditionally reasoned from individual cases from the hadith and jurisprudence.

Respect for Life

Respect for human life and the importance of preserving life at all costs is as integral to the fabric of Muslim life as the air they breathe. Muslims acknowledge the hand of God in all their doings, but particularly in the creation of new life. Thus examination of exceptions to these rules is highly meaningful, for the tension between theory and practice exposes ethical underpinnings to the conflicting guidance which the legal schools give.

In Islamic discourse, respect for life takes two forms. Both trains of thought reflect essential principles of Islamic law: stress on the importance of the individual and care for the welfare of the community. Both of these principles sum up long-established aims of Islamic jurisprudence, to guard the well-being of the individual, but also to care for community cohesion through attention to its moral standing. To this end, Muslims treat respect for life as basic to the religion, but not as the supreme ethical principle to which all others give way. It proves in practice, at least as far as the example of abortion, to be generally determinative, but in certain circumstances to be relative to other considerations.

The Qur'an emphasizes that men and women are not only God's creations, but after being fashioned from clay, Adam was distinguished from other created beings by God's breathing "[his] own spirit" into him, and appointing for him "hearing and sight and hearts" (32:9, also 15:29, 38:72). This tension between the divine aspect of God's creation of humankind compared to the pettiness, narrow vision, and downright sinfulness human beings can evidence in their actions is a primary theme of the Qur'an. Its record of humankind's susceptible nature when faced with evil compels revelation on what should be obvious: "Do not kill the soul that God has made sacred except for just cause" (17:33). The Qur'an implores parents, "You shall not kill your children because you cannot support them" (6:151). The practice of killing female infants was forbidden with a strong reference to Judgment Day, "when the infant girl, buried alive, is asked for what crime she was slain" (81:8). All references establish the primacy of life and emphasize the duty to take particular care of those who are vulnerable.

Ahmad Sahnoun, a Moroccan scholar, stated in strong terms that abortion counters Islam's respect for life.

> Abortion . . . leads to . . . the depletion, and eventually the extermination of the human race, involving the attempt to alter God's law of creation and go counter to his will.
>
> Abortion is the expulsion of the foetus before it is due for natural birth. It is an abhorrent and a most damnable act, interdicted by Islam in the strongest terms, with wrathful censure of the culprit, and severe condemnation by true humanity and by all those of upright nature, all for the fact that abortion is no less heinous than the

> committing of a murder sternly prohibited by God, and amounts, in other respects, to insubordination to God's will and to a deliberate attempt to change the divine order.[30]

An additional argument for preservation of life goes beyond the major question discussed by jurists, saving an ensouled fetus, and extends to the worth of the potential life—the importance of guarding a fetus before it is ensouled. As was stated above, much of the debate among the jurists turns on the point at which the soul enters the fetus or it is "created." This need to prove that the fetus is a person is a vital ethical point, as respect for life would deem that the created fetus be treated with the same care as a live person. In western pro-choice writings on abortion, concern for a potential person is termed a "slippery slope" argument and is countered by the analogy that not all acorns turn into trees.[31] However, the argument takes on more resonance with each biological discovery of how early the fetus takes on human characteristics. Late-term abortions (forbidden in Islam for all reasons but the health of the mother) have become increasingly challenged as medical science enables premature births to be viable at earlier stages of development. Islamic theology complicates a facile dismissal of the fetus's rights in the early months, say before the 120-day limit, by its theological insistence on the reality of human potential.

While there is room for debate as to whether abortion is equal to killing a child (for no child has yet been born), all agree that abortion destroys potential life. The Aristotelian argument on human potential was well known among Muslim theologians, philosophers, and jurists. Much of this argument has been distorted both among Muslims and in western circles. Over time, the term for potentiality (*qadar* or *taqdīr*) has been interpreted as meaning divine predestination or predetermination of all events in this world, including human actions. This belief is the origin of the popular Islamic doctrine that denies human free will and postulates all being fated or written. Fazlur Rahman maintains that this idea of predestination is "a grossly simplistic misrepresentation" of the idea of *qadar* laid out in the Qur'an. Rahman states that *qadar* means "to measure out," and while God is the infinite "measurer," all that he creates is portioned out, has a finite sum of potentialities. In the case of men and women, the Qur'an insists that their potential is great, as long as they can avoid the deadening results of sin. Rahman notes that according to the Qur'an, when God creates a thing or a person, he creates with it its potential, its nature, and the laws of its behavior.[32] As a modernist, Rahman had a particular interest in emphasizing an area of freedom where human actions are their own, not predestined. If one construes an area of free will, human potential becomes more meaningful, as human potential, in religious terms of doing right or wrong, can only be constrained by a person's own actions. An unborn child holds the potential measured by God, and Muslim opposition to abortion notes the loss of that potential.

This doctrine of undeniable potential that becomes embedded in the embryo at the moment of conception gives additional resonance to questions of abortion. While jurists can debate whether destroying an embryo or a fetus is an act of killing a person, it is undeniable that by destroying an embryo or a fetus at whatever point in its nine-month gestation, one destroys a *potential* human being.[33] In the quotation from *Kitāb al-durra al-fākhira,* al-Ghazali makes the point that even when the soul is lifeless, the divine nature of the soul keeps the body from decomposing until God breathes his spirit into it. By his opposition to expelling this embryo and then fetus, al-Ghazali affirms the value of potential life. Mahmud Shaltut speaks to how al-Ghazali's understanding of this potential underlies his opposition to permitting abortion before quickening:

> Scholars are agreed that after quickening takes place abortion is prohibited to all Muslims, for it is a crime against a living being. Hence blood-money becomes due if the foetus is delivered alive, and the *ghurra* if delivered dead. The jurists were not, on the other hand, agreed as to whether to sanction or prohibit abortion if performed prior to animation. Some felt it was permissible on the grounds that there was no life at that stage and, therefore, no crime could be committed. Others held that it was unlawful, maintaining that it was already possessed of inviolable life, of growth and development. Among the latter was the great master, al-Ghazali.[34]

Shaltut then proceeds to quote the statement from al-Ghazali given above, on the grades of development from semen and ovum through birth. Following al-Ghazali's explanation of the increasing severity of the sin of destroying potential life, he suggests the development of potential life should be accorded respect and protection. It is this deep-seated belief in the potential human as well as the actual human being that I maintain underlies the ethical debate on abortion. Awe for the potential of life and hope for a child to result from that potential is deeply embedded in the social fabric of Muslim life. Grief at the loss of that potential follows a miscarriage, and apprehension at its loss often accompanies an abortion.

Abortion falls into a category of its own as it is not usually considered murder, yet some Muslims hold that it is analogous to killing a person in that both abortion after the animation of the fetus (determined according to the stance of each school) and killing necessitate compensation in the form of payment of blood money or *ghurra* to the bereft family.[35] Islamic law exacts a legal penalty upon any person, whether a parent or a third person, responsible for the death of a fetus. Any blow that causes a pregnant woman to miscarry—whether by intent or accident—requires the attacker to pay blood money or indemnity (*ghurra*) in the sum of 75 gold dirhams (another source says 40 or 100 dinars)[36] to the family to compensate for the death of the fetus, just as if the fetus were a live child. This legal demand for blood money signifies that in the eyes of society, the unborn fetus, as a Muslim person, was as much a part of its fabric as a child. Both parents are also liable to pay blood money for aborting the fetus if they, and not a third person, are responsible for the abortion. If the pregnant woman deliberately undertakes an abortion without her husband's permission then she must pay the *ghurra*, which should be the same whether the fetus was male or female.[37]

A major ethical issue in the general debate on abortion weighs the life of the mother by the potential life of the child. As loss of each sacrifices a life—one actual, one potential—this dilemma of which of the two lives should be maintained has been the subject of considerable analysis.[38] Despite their interest in avoiding abortion, Muslims universally agree that on all levels, whether the family, the community, or religious teaching, the primary concern must be for the life of the mother, and her welfare precedes any concern for the fetus. Ibrahim Haqqi, a Syrian physician, notes that the mother's health problems which would justify an abortion include heart disease, serious kidney trouble, hypereremises gravidarum, albuminaria, and nephritic toxemia, among others. He goes on to state that in Syrian law, "in accordance with Muslim law and logic," the attending physicians are required to file a report regarding the disease that justifies the operation.[39]

In my interviews of numerous religious scholars and Muslim religious authorities about family planning and abortion in Morocco, all agreed that the most prominent exception is to preserve the life and health of the mother. Muslim society, including religious leaders at all levels and physicians, defends therapeutic abortion when the health of the mother is endangered, for the mother is the origin of the fetus, or the original source of life, and as such must be safeguarded.[40] This priority establishes a hierarchy of life; as the late *ʿālim* Muhammad Mekki Naciri said, "The mother cannot be sacrificed for the child."[41]

Jurisprudence texts cite concern for a nursing child as a second justification for abortion. The medical wisdom of early and medieval Islam held that pregnancy absorbed such nutrients from the mother's body that if she became pregnant before the end of the requisite two-year period of nursing, the nursing child would be starved of necessary nourishment. This situation was common enough to be given a name, the "small assassination" (*ghayla*) of the nursing child. This term is still used in parts of the Muslim world, and women still avoid pregnancy while nursing utilizing the same logic. Jurists held, again, that the existing life has priority over the unborn, and justified abortion (within the 120-day limit) in this case. In reality, this argument is a historical precedent permitting economic need as grounds for abortion, for a well-off father would have had the means to hire a wet-nurse, and the mother could carry on the pregnancy without interference.[42] Hassan Hathout counters this traditional belief, not by disputing, as breastfeeding experts do, that breastfeeding while pregnant does not harm the fetus. Rather, Dr. Hathout states:

> The question of pregnancy during lactation is not, in the Sharia, a circumstance justifying abortion. For it is possible to avert this situation by preventing pregnancy. Then if the woman becomes pregnant during lactation and is unable to produce milk, and the husband cannot afford to engage a wet-nurse, then the choice is between sacrificing the foetus by terminating the pregnancy and the hazard of causing permanent debility to the baby. I think the right to life has priority over the right to bodily strength. In any case it is possible to give the woman pills or tablets which make up for any deficiency in her milk or to give her artificial milk on which the foetus can be nourished.[43]

In the following chapter in this volume, Vardit Rispler-Chaim even explores whether some ulema believe that seriously deformed fetuses may have a right not to be born. The late Sheikh al-Azhar, Jad al-Haqq, stated the opposite, that abortion should not take place after four months even if the fetus is found to have congenital defects. He argued that the fetus is nevertheless a human being, and barring danger to the mother's health, the fetus should not be killed for his illness. He added that modern science can often compensate for these defects as medicine continually progresses in these areas.[44]

At the Rabat Conference on Islam and Family Planning in 1974, the Indonesian scholar Achmad Gazali lists a number of conditions that would lead physicians to perform an abortion in Indonesia. He includes rape, incest, and the psychological state of the mother, stipulations the Middle Eastern ulema and physicians did not mention. He lists a number of conditions that in Indonesia would justify abortion:

> If pregnancy would make the woman liable to psychological illness harmful to her health;

If it is likely that the child will be born suffering from certain illnesses;
If pregnancy is the result of rape or incest, between brother and sister or father and daughter, and the termination of pregnancy in this case is due to psychological considerations.

There are also conditions relating to the mother's mental state, and psychiatrists considered these to justify abortion before the sixteenth week:

If it is likely that the pregnancy may be instrumental in causing hazard to the mother's psychological condition;
If the pregnancy harms the reputation of the woman when she is suffering from mental illness;
If pregnancy may induce the woman to do herself serious injury, or commit suicide.[45]

Community Welfare
The second area where ethics intersect with abortion is the concern Muslims demonstrate for community welfare. Jurists traditionally define the well-being (*iṣlāḥ*) of the larger community of Muslims as their paramount concern when issuing opinions on sharia questions. In speaking about opposition to abortion, ulema first mention the need to protect the community from its dangers. Their first concern, which is often implicit, is the need to recognize that respect for life is the basis of all community action. Without a reverence for life, the very existence of the community is endangered. Both ulema and local religious leaders cite the increased use of abortion as a prime factor in increasing social disintegration. Abortion, they claim, jeopardizes the self-evident truth that Islam is predicated upon—recognition of the divine spirit in humankind. Their second concern is a wider one: they worry about trends they see as harmful to the family, the basic unit of society. Ulema have devoted many sermons in mosques and articles in newspapers to the subject of family cohesion, the dangers of materialism, and in particular, the role of women in the family. During the 1994 Cairo Population Conference, Abd al-Aziz al-Tuejary, the head of the Muslim Organization for Science and Education (ISISCO), stressed in an interview in *al-Sharq al-Awsaṭ* that women are essential to the functioning and the maintenance of the Muslim family. He repeatedly emphasized that in Islam the main goal of a man and a woman should not be marriage alone, but the formation of a stable and pious family.[46] As the conference indicated, a central threat to twentieth- and twenty-first-century families is the attempt mounted by multi-lateral organizations and western governments, as well as technocrats within the Middle East, to limit family size or

prevent births. Many ulema adhere to a strong pro-natalist position, believing that large numbers of Muslims are critical if Muslims wish to confront the enemies at their borders. Other ulema are sensitive to the need to allow individuals to plan their families, and recognize that optional family planning, as opposed to mandatory birth control, is compatible with Islamic law. However, even for the latter group, abortion opens doors to forcible limitation of family size that ulema fear. The publicity given the case of China, in particular, causes ulema to react strongly to any mention of coerced birth control or public policies utilizing abortion for population control.

Probably the concern ulema voice most often is that of moral degeneration of the society. When Muslims discuss morals (*al-akhlāq*), sexual morality is first on their list of concerns. The term for corruption (*al-fasād*) generally refers not to financial dishonesty, but to sexual morality. Muslim religious leaders construe their role as guarding community morality, and this concern leads them to criticize contemporary sexual behavior. At the Rabat Population Conference in 1971, the Syrian scholar Abdul Rahman al-Khayyir presented the case often made in stronger language today following the advent of satellite television, sexually explicit films, and the Internet. The following quotation is part of the introduction to a long article in which he states his opposition to abortion at any point, without valid reason:

> It is all too evident that we are now being swept away by the hurly-burly and fury of material life through the rush of communications, and swamped by the destructive printed word, illustrated or otherwise, through the printing press. We look helplessly on as our rising generations are seizing on cheap and vulgar books and magazines that are invading our conservative Islamic countries. All these are causing fearful havoc in the social stream of our times, transforming our society from one of simple, guileless nature to one of hollow superficiality in today's material civilization, to which end the colonialists have mobilized huge resources under various deceptive guises.
>
> Intellectual stagnation, which has been the cause for concern to many of the educated classes as well as to the common people for several centuries past, has co-operated with weak and irresponsible regimes to firmly implant certain serious social evils, such as the spread of alcoholism, venality, fraudulence, rapid tribalism and factionalism, inter-strife for power, apathy, dissipation and indulgence of one's sensual desires. All these ills have paved the way for foreign penetration to do as it will with our people. As a result of this concentrated onslaught,

> our Islamic society is on the verge of disintegration, if it is not already disintegrating. . . .
>
> The family, which but a few years back was still preserving within the sanctum of the home certain genuine principles of Islamic education, now stands bewildered before this sweeping onslaught. It can no longer act in accordance with its beliefs and convictions, except in very limited and rare cases, for radio and television inside the home have shared with movies, theatres and wanton entertainment haunts outside the home in infixing more firmly the impression of this crushing overpowering invasion.
>
> Under the impact of all these forces collectively and severally, the relationship between husband and wife as well as between parents and children is growing day by day lax and lifeless, and the family bonds as a result are disrupted in many, if not in most cases.[47]

Abu al-A'la Mawdudi, the late conservative Pakistani *'ālim* and head of the Islamist League, *Jama'at-i Islami,* voiced an opinion on family planning that echoes general Muslim concerns:

> It [family planning] would, certainly, lead to illegitimate sex relations on a scale unprecedented in the history of our society. Our social conditions are already going from bad to worse. Our educational system is being systematically deprived of all emphasis for developing moral sense. Cheap amusements, sensuous songs and music, obscene pornographic literature, near-nude pictures have become a common feature of our social scene. Co-education, employment of women in offices, mixed social gatherings, immodest female dresses, beauty parades, are now a common feature of our social life. Legal hindrances have been placed in the way of marriage and on having more than one wife, but no bar against keeping mistresses and having illicit relationships, prior to the age of marriage. In such a society perhaps, the last obstacle that may keep a woman from surrendering to a man's advances is fear of an illegitimate conception. Remove this obstacle too . . . and you will see that the society will be plagued by the tide of moral licentiousness. All the forces that make society a cesspool of corruption are being encouraged and peddled. If we choose to walk along this road to destruction, how could destruction be avoided.[48]

Many other ulema echo Mawdudi's sentiments in condemning what they term the promiscuous drift of the society in the Islamic world. His charge that birth control opens doors to illicit sexual relationships is based on western figures on cohabitation and on abortions. The rise in abortion rates worldwide since the last edition of Mawdudi's book in 1968 has fueled the vehemence with which conservative ulema attack the incidence of abortion in the west and oppose its practice in their countries. Ulema assume that abortions in the west are performed routinely when pregnancies are unplanned or unwanted.[49] As Mawdudi states, Islam is adamant that sexual relations are to be confined to marriage, and women are to be chaste preceding marriage (no such charge is given to young men). The corollary follows that bearing and raising children is a fundamental precept of Islam. Both ulema and individual Muslims quote the Qur'an that "wealth and children are an ornament of the life of the world" (5:46).

Islam prohibits adultery and sexual relations outside of marriage. When asked the reasoning for this prohibition, ulema explain it less in terms of preserving ties of marital trust than preserving social order. Ever realists, Muslim ulema acknowledge (as the centuries of legal scholars have as well) the importance of sexual desire among both men and women. In order to preserve any attempt at social order, they reason, sexual activity must be regulated and restrained to marital relations. The alternative would be social chaos. Traditional restrictions on women's activities, emphasis on their virginity before marriage, and insistence on chastity after marriage tie into these beliefs. Without a belief in the fidelity of one's spouse, the parents of a child, or more properly the father, could not accurately identify offspring, and the family ties that order society would be severed or severely strained. Ulema see abortion, which allows sexual activity without the consequence of pregnancy, as an extreme danger to this social order. They attribute the same concerns to contraception, but abortion carries the additional load of striking a living soul dead. Thus abortion not only kills an existing soul or eliminates a potential one, but it destroys the social fences of chastity, sex within marriage, relations among men and women and respect for family values.

Muslims take the obligations and responsibilities of adulthood and parenthood very seriously. Muhammad Mekki Naciri, a professor of Islamic law and former minister of Islamic affairs in Morocco, was a major exponent of family planning at a time when it was unpopular in his country. He phrased his defense of family planning as a moral as well as a material and health-related issue:

> Family planning, as it is most usually accepted today, aims at giving parents a broader and deeper perception of their moral and material responsibilities, as father, mother or together. They will, therefore, be more concerned for the future of their children and contribute to a

> healthier future generation, physically and morally, that will know how to serve the country with more efficiency and devotion.[50]

For Naciri, as for most ulema and the majority of Muslims, these obligations structure life. They are critical to the smooth functioning of society as well as the religious obligations of following Qur'anic precepts.

Al-Qasabi Mahmoud Zalat, in the above-quoted interview in *al-Ahrām,* emphasized Islam's concern with the children's welfare at every stage of their lives, both before and after birth. He pointed out that various factors are critical in raising good children: a strong marriage, a good environment for their development, prioritizing religious values before wealth or beauty.[51]

Probably the most hotly debated justification for abortion centers on economic and financial concerns. The Qur'an prohibits killing children for financial reasons: "You shall not kill your children for fear of want. We will provide for them and for you. To kill them is a great sin" (17:31). Muslims maintain that material needs are secondary to faith in God's provision for his creations; no life should be shed for lack of financial sustenance. In response to Qur'anic exhortations, Islamic jurisprudence erected a safety net for poor and needy Muslims within the bounds of family organization specifically for women and children. As the prophet Muhammad was an orphan and his mother a widow, his concern for the vulnerable is manifest throughout the hadith and echoes Qur'anic precepts of social and economic justice. Women and children are to be cared for by their husbands and children, but beyond that by their natal family when in need. Today the safety nets have developed alarming gaps. These include increasing divorce and desertion of wives, the easing of ties among extended families, increased urban migration and the corresponding rise in nuclear families, high male unemployment and underemployment during the imposition of IMF-mandated economic liberalization plans which have the by-product of raising prices for basic commodities and throwing individuals out of work. For women finding themselves newly pregnant, responsible for support of their family, with their husbands either absent from the home or unemployed, the question of bearing another child may be daunting. The justification when social abortion was legalized in Tunisia centered not on women's rights, but on economic development, Tunisia's pressing need to lower its birth rate to better utilize resources to generate a higher standard of living for its citizens.

One *'ālim* in a popular quarter in Fez, Morocco put the problem to me by telling me a story of two families. One night a mother and father came to him. The mother had recently discovered that she was pregnant.

They were worried about finances, supporting the children they already had, and feeding them, dressing them for school, purchasing their books and papers, plus caring for another child. The *'ālim*'s advice was unlike that of any other religious figure I interviewed. He told them that abortion would be religiously permissible in their case. But he added afterwards, "Go home, look at your other children, particularly the youngest who was born at a time when you were strapped for funds, and ask where you would be without that child." That family decided to keep the unborn child, and according to the *'ālim* have been happy that they did. A second family whom he gave the same advice decided that they could not handle another child and went ahead with an abortion.

The recognition of the financial realities of bearing additional children is not new. As was detailed above, a good justification for abortion has always been the financial inability to afford a wet-nurse for a baby when the mother finds she is pregnant again. One justifiable reason for abortion in the medieval jurisprudence texts was to prevent the birth of a slave's child so as to avoid the subsequent obligation toward the slave mother (who could not thereafter be sold) and the child, who as the child of the master, would be freed.

Another hardship related to economic reasons that ulema recognize as justifying abortion is the likelihood of birth of a seriously ill or deformed child. Hassan Hathout, now of the Southern Californian Institute of Islamic Studies, believes from his experience as a doctor and his sentiments as a Muslim that there are only two sufficient grounds for abortion, the health of the mother and the strong probability of the baby being born deformed or afflicted with a serious disease.[53] Other ulema have phrased much the same thing differently, saying that abortion is allowed when the life of the child would be a hardship for himself or for his parents. They may be speaking of the additional effort to care for a disabled or ill child; however, an interpretation of those words could include economic reasons.

Muslim scholars have been outspoken in emphasizing that the Muslim community must take action to assure that demand for abortion decreases among Muslim women. Numerous scholars have pointed out that two important preventions can be undertaken. Benazir Bhutto, the former prime minister of Pakistan, articulated the first—to raise the status of women—on September 6, 1994, before the Cairo Population Conference. This would include increasing women's access to education, making prenatal health care available, guaranteeing access to contraception, and guaranteeing women's rights in national personal status law codes.[53] The second is to emphasize that Islam erects no barriers to use of temporary contraceptive methods, including birth control pills, IUD's, or prophylactic measures, as well as traditional measures such as *'azl* (*coitus interruptus*). A few Muslim scholars or religious leaders contradict this position. One, interviewed at the time of the Cairo Population Conference, claimed, "Population growth is normal. We need not confront it because it is controlled by God himself, in other words, it should be allowed to take place without interference for it is determined by God."[54] However, the majority of educated ulema across the Muslim world agree with the ulema assembled for the International Islamic Conference held in Rabat, Morocco, in December 1971, who, although disagreeing on many details, agreed that temporary contraceptive measures are permitted in Islam, and indeed should serve as a means of preventing abortion. Mahmud Nadjmabadi, an Iranian scholar, concluded:

> Islam forbids unjustified abortion.
> Concerning procreation of children and lack of adequate means of subsistence, the parents must use appropriate means for control and limitations of birth.
> In countries with no birth control, medical establishments, charitable persons and especially those with no children must offer a great deal of assistance to large families.
> If a woman procures an abortion for herself for one reason or another, she must be judged by the laws of her country.
> It is the obligation of social and medical service centers and social scientists to participate in drawing up plans leading to the logical control of births and to help large families.[55]

Who Should Determine If an Abortion Takes Place?

Part of the difficulty in writing about abortion is that three subjects are part of the argument: the theory of Islamic law, the legal realities in Middle Eastern countries, and social realities in these countries. Much of the discussion of this paper about the legal schools that permit abortion up to a certain point and those that prohibit it may give the impression that abortion is readily available for any Muslim who wrestles with their conscience and determines that their reason for abortion is religiously justifiable. In practice, this is far from the case. At the present time, abortion is only available easily in three Muslim countries, Turkey, Tunisia, and Iran. In Iran, the consent of two physicians is necessary, and it is not everywhere available in the public health hospitals. In other countries, selected private physicians who are willing to sign health certificates—or who pretend that the procedure was routine and the woman was not pregnant—offer abortions to women who have the means to pay for their services. Therapeutic abortions that technically should be available through national public health services are often not easily accessible. Decisions made by the state restrict legal and easy access to abortion. Nevertheless, rumors circulate about numerous abortions taking place among women of all ages, social classes, and marital status.

In most Middle Eastern countries where abortion is not legal but therapeutic abortions are possible with the consent of a physician, the husband's consent is also necessary. On the one hand this safeguards the rights of the father of the unborn child. On the other hand, the need for the husband's consent means that a wife who wishes an abortion does not have the right to seek one herself. She lacks what western ethicists term the right over her own body. It is precisely the lack of this right to bodily integrity that many writers on ethics question. Within Islam, unlike in some pro-life discussions in the west, women have the right to life if pregnancy endangers their health. However, the inability to determine and contract an abortion if one is needed without outside consent (medical, religious, state, spousal) severely constricts a woman's rights over her person. The factor that cannot be resolved is the right of the father to his parenting of the unborn child if he and the mother are in conflict over bearing the child. One of them must lose.

The question of who determines whether an abortion takes place is what locks the ethical aspects of abortion into reality for a woman, her husband, and the community. If the rights of the woman to determination over her own body and life are paramount, then she should make the decision. If the rights of the family—husband and wife as parents of the unborn—outstrip other rights, then the two of them should confer (and this brings up questions of the wife's rights vis-à-vis the husband, or vice versa, requiring an examination of women's rights within the family and marriage relationship). If the rights of the community, nation, or religion dominate, then community spokespersons, state authorities, or religious authorities should resolve the issue. In the majority of Muslim states, the state, acting for the community at large, has assumed leadership in this issue and has outlawed abortions unless the health of the mother is endangered. The state, recognizing that it lacks medical expertise, defers to the judgment of physicians, who can determine whether an abortion is necessary. This deference to medical authorities opens doors for women to obtain abortions. In most Muslim countries, the public health services are closed to women wanting abortions. Private physicians willing to perform abortions are the women's major recourse, and names of physicians willing to grant an abortion are passed among women. Physicians may be either genuinely willing to help a woman in need, going along with the woman's dissimulation, or seeing it merely as an opportunity to gain a fee for service.

Although no official figures exist, most observers believe that private abortions are performed and are on the increase in the Muslim world. Reasons cited for abortions include women's unwillingness to use contraceptives, often from fear of the effects of their use; contraceptive failure; and lack of access to contraceptives—increasingly common as unmarried high school and university students become sexually active but do not utilize contraception. I also have heard women speak of utilizing abortion—in some cases numerous repeated abortions—as a means of contraception. A woman seeking an abortion may simply not be able to bear the idea of another pregnancy or an additional child; she may be self-supporting and unable to afford another child; she may plan to separate from her husband and not wish another child to further bind them together.

A Response to Circumstances

The contrast between the Islamic and the Roman Catholic positions lies in two areas of difference: first, not all Muslims consider the soul to be placed in the embryo/fetus at conception, thus for some schools, abortion before 120 days does not truly constitute an abortion, for no soul lives in the fetus. Although differences are found within the Roman Catholic community, the official Roman Catholic position considers life to enter the fetus at the moment of conception, and aborting the pregnancy at any point thereafter is a mortal sin. Second, Muslims recognize a graduated hierarchy to the value of life. They consider the health of the mother to be more important than that of the fetus and will authorize abortion if the mother is in danger. The Roman Catholic Church recognizes no difference between the two and declines to prioritize the life of the mother above that of the fetus.[56] In terms of conforming to ethical principle, the official Roman Catholic position espouses a consistent ethics built on religious values. The Church refuses to compromise the importance of potential life, placing the life of the fetus at the heart of their stance. Muslims, while they emphasize the importance of life and potential life, are prepared to bow to other necessities when the needs of two lives, those of the mother and the fetus, are in conflict. Thus Muslims follow a more circumstantial, casuistic, end-based system of moral imperatives, showing willingness to deal with circumstances in a practical fashion when two undesirable conditions collide. This pragmatism does not recognize absolute moral principles, but may be better suited for dealing with the difficulties brought up by the health aspects of pregnancy. While an imperfect solution, abortion may at times be the only practical means of dealing with an intolerable situation—sacrificing a mother to possibly save the life of an unborn child.

The Muslim position, while sufficiently flexible to respond to the often tragic dilemmas individuals encounter in their lives, may pose ethical difficulties in the long run. Once one admits circumstantial arguments to determine ethics, the question becomes where the stopping point is. One argument discussed above is the allowance of abortion when a mother needs to nurse, and a pregnancy precludes nursing, while the family cannot afford a wet nurse. Although at one level this argument is health-based, it is at another level an argument of economic need. As we have seen in the United States, once health or economic need becomes viable cause for abortion, the thin end of the wedge has been jammed into the door. It is difficult to draw a line and judge which cases may or may not apply. In the west, arguments based on the health of the mother have been extended beyond physical well-being to include psychological well-being. Economic arguments can include judgment calls regarding the financial resources of a family. While not judging the merits of these claims to provide justifiable reasons, nonetheless, the room given by the minority position which allows abortion for a justifiable reason can be and has been stretched to fit the needs of those seeking abortions. The Muslim approach is highly realistic and responsive to human needs, and the flexibility Islam grants serves Muslims in dire circumstances well. However, in the end, an approach that responds to circumstances may prove to be overly accommodating and be used for more exceptions than many Muslim religious leaders would wish. The numbers of abortions granted in Tunisia, Turkey, and Iran, as well as in the newly independent Central Asian states, give an indication of the demand for abortion. If more states gave the option of easier access to abortion, the result might be a similar demand despite the warnings the ulema voice about the accompanying social dangers. As we have seen above, while the voices of the Islamic schools of law differ on abortion, there are scholars that permit abortion without condition before 120 days and those that permit abortion with a justifiable reason after 120 days. At least theoretically, as far as Islamic law is concerned, doors are open to permit greater latitude in granting abortions. As the major question of this article concerns the ethical principles which guide Muslim action on abortion, and is not a prescription for action, I conclude that Muslims face a paradoxical situation. Their legal system provides a means to increase the incidence of abortion. However, the ethical climate of Islam discourages abortion by its emphasis upon life and community morality.

A final point to consider is the extent to which Muslims consider abortion to be part of a package that includes sexual immorality, substance abuse, and materialism imported by the West. Muslims acknowledge that abortion has long roots in Muslim medical practice, but many argue that the west has played a dominant role in encouraging the trend toward abortion brought about in response to premarital sexual activity, a desire to augment family wealth by having smaller families, increased levels of prostitution, and in general an atmosphere of moral laxness. The number of western countries that have legalized abortion and the high number of abortions these countries record supply data points for such arguments. Professor Abdul Rahman al-Khayyir made this point explicitly in a statement quoted above, but like arguments are implicit in much of what the ulema say about abortion.

Muslim scholars have clearly indicated that abortion is a complicated problem, one undertaken for a host of different reasons, most of which have to do with specific needs which individuals encounter at different points in their lives. While there is a clear consensus that the majority of Muslim ulema discourage or prohibit abortion before 120 days and definitely after 120 days as the taking of a life or potential life, ulema note that there are cases where need is so overpowering that necessity compels its use. This theologically based struggle is complicated because it is multilayered: interspersing theological concern for the life of the unborn child with a family's anxiety for the health of the mother and the community's need to maintain moral standards. Although the starting point of the argument springs from theological statements which grant or withhold sanction for an abortion, tangential arguments quickly spread into questions of ethics, politics, economics, and medicine. Islam's position of discouraging, but still dealing practically with, the tragedy associated with any need for abortion brings about is rooted in the ethical considerations of Islamic theology and law, ones consonant with the aim of Islamic law to ensure the well being of the Muslim community. Many of the ulema as well as many lay Muslims would state that the community's well-being is increasingly challenged by everyday practice in communities throughout the Muslim world today. These practices—availability of abortion, economic pressure on families, increased sexual activity outside of marriage, greater emphasis upon individual rather than community rights and well-being—all allow greater reliance on abortion and induce many to see abortion as a solution to unwanted pregnancy. While most Muslims respect the gravity with which Islamic sources inveigh against abortion, the possibility of arguing the necessity of an abortion has historical precedents. The trend today is increased availability of abortion. Islam's ethical principles provide strong reasoning against abortion, but a strict examination of precedents may open more possibilities for abortion than many Muslims may wish.

Notes

1. Pope Paul VI, "Respect for Life in the Womb," address to the Medical Association of Western Flanders, April 23, 1977, reprinted in Stephen E. Lammers and Allen Verhey, ed., *On Moral Medicine: Theological Perspectives in Medical Ethics* (Grand Rapids, Mich.: William B. Eerdmans, 1987), 396–97. Lammers and Verhey take it from *The Pope Speaks* 22 (fall 1977): 281–82. *Catechism of the Catholic Church,* section on abortion, English translation (Rome: Libreria Editrice Vaticana, Urbi et Orbi Communications, 1994), 547–48.

2. Donna Lee Bowen, "Islam, Abortion, and the 1994 Cairo Population Conference," *International Journal of Middle Eastern Studies* 29, no. 2 (May 1997), 161–84. While the Qur'an itself is silent regarding abortion, it forbids in strong language the killing of children. Building by analogy, jurists interpreted these statements as a prohibition of killing a soul that has the potential of developing into a person.

3. Abul Fadl Mohsin Ebrahim, "Abortion," *Oxford Encyclopedia of the Modern Islamic World,* ed. John Esposito (New York: Oxford University Press, 1995), 1:17.

4. The term translated as "soul" in this verse is the Arabic *nafs*. Jane Smith and Yvonne Haddad, in *The Islamic Understanding of Death and Resurrection* (Albany: State University of New York Press, 1981) elaborate the distinction between two Arabic terms *nafs* and *rūḥ,* both of which can be glossed as "soul" in English: "*Nafs* . . . refers primarily to the individual self in a reflexive sense. It also designates the soul . . . *Rūḥ,* appearing only in the singular, never refers to the human soul. Its usages are many; of them the only one suggesting the relation of the divine spirit to the human person speak of the 'breathing in' of God's *rūḥ* (p. 18)." The authors note that the terms were interchanged in Islam's general terminology. Likewise, this distinction is not maintained by modern writers on Islam. In contemporary religious terminology, ulema may utilize *rūḥ* to speak of the human soul with the understanding that God's spirit has been breathed into it (God has created the soul). The term *nafs* may also refer to "human being" or "person."

5. Al-Farabi, "The Attainment of Happiness," and Ibn Rushd, "The Decisive Treatise," trans. Muhsin Mahdi, in *Medieval Political Philosophy,* ed. Ralph Lerner and Muhsin Mahdi (New York: The Free Press of Glencoe, MacMillan, 1963), 74–81, 165–77.

6. Homa Hoodfar, "Devices and Desires: Population Policy and Gender Roles in the Islamic Republic," *Middle East Report* 190 (Sept.–Oct. 1994): 11–14.

7. http://www.galwayforlife.ie/global_figures.html (accessed October 5, 1999).

8. Unpublished data from the Israel Central Bureau of Statistics, Demography Division, 1997.

9. http://www.galwayforlife.ie/global_figures.html.

10. http://www.galwayforlife.ie./global_figures.html.

11. "Number of Abortions Drops to Two-Decade Low," *Salt Lake (Utah) Tribune,* January 7, 2000.

12. http://www.agi-usa.org/pubs/fp_0599.html (accessed October 5, 1999).

13. There is discussion whether abortion constitutes killing. The Imami Shi' a and Ibadi schools consider expulsion of the product of conception from the womb at any point following conception to be killing. Other schools (Maliki, Zahiri, some Shafi'is), while not permitting the expulsion of the embryo or fetus, do not consider it killing. See Abdel Rahim Omran, *Family Planning in the Legacy of Islam* (London: Routledge, 1992), 191–92. In interviews I conducted with Maliki ulema in Morocco in 1993 as well as in earlier years, a number of scholars characterized abortion as "killing the soul" (*qatl al-rūḥ*).

14. Muhammad Salam Madkur, "Sterilization and Abortion from the Point of View of Islam," in Isam Nazer, ed., *Islam and Family Planning* (Beirut: International Planned Parenthood Federation, 1974), 2:271.

15. Further, the reasoning put forth by each school also lays groundwork for positions on other issues such as contraception, IUD's, the use of morning-after medication, the number of children one has, and even whether a man should take more than one wife.

16. See the previous chapter by Marion Katz (pp. 30–31) for a full discussion of this verse and the classical interpretations.

17. Jane Idleman Smith, trans., *The Precious Pearl: A Translation from the Arabic with Notes of the* Kitāb al-durra al-Fākhira fī kashf 'ulūm al-ākhira *of Abū Ḥāmid Muḥammad b. Muḥammad b. Muḥammad al-Ghazālī* (Missoula, Mont.: Scholars Press, 1979), 21.

18. Madkur, "Sterilization," 272. Ibrahim Haqqi states that "necessity is the situation in which man finds himself compelled not to observe the strict rules of Muslim law for the sake of saving his life or property or in order to avert a danger, real or imagined, too oppressive to be ignored. Thus necessity does not arise only when man is sure that his life is in danger, but also when man believes that his strict observance of the law might involve serious health hazard or physical disability. Haqqi states that necessity needs to be determined by a physician who is trustworthy regarding both his knowledge and religiousness. He has to make sure that no other solution or remedy is available and that there is no alternative" ("Islam and Abortion," in *Islam and Family Planning,* 2:392–93).

19. Bowen, "Islam, Abortion," 175–77.

20. Al-Ghazali, as quoted by Shabramalassi in *Hāshiyāt al-Shabramalassī 'alā nihāyat al-muḥtāj,* 6:179, quoted in Madkur, 277.

21. Hassan Hathout "Induced Abortion," in *Islam and Family Planning,* 2:316. Hathout is quoting Mahmud Shaltut, *Al-Fatāwā: Studies on the Nature of Today's Muslim in His Daily and Public Life* (Cairo: Publications of the General Culture Administration at al-Azhar, 1959). Shaltut, in turn, is quoting al-Ghazali in *al-Islām 'aqīda wa sharī'a,* 3d ed. (Cairo: Dār al-Qalam, n.d.), 211–13. Compare Marion Katz's discussion of this passage on p. 42.

22. Abdul Rehman, mufti of New Delhi, quoted in John-Thor Dahlburg, "Faiths Disagree on Morality of Abortion," *Los Angeles Times,* January 24, 1995, 5.

23. Robert Blank and Janna C. Merrick, *Human Reproduction, Emerging Technologies, and Conflicting Rights* (Washington, D.C.: Congressional Quarterly Press, 1995), 38.

24. "Sheikh al-Azhar: Abortion Is Only Permissible under Islamic Law to Protect the Life of the Mother," *Al-Ahrām* (Cairo), September 7, 1994, 4.

25. "Islam Prohibits Aborting the Fetus," *Al-Ahrām* (Cairo), September 8, 1994, 14.

26. It is hard to generalize, but in Morocco, while the laws are on the books, authorities often turn their heads when physicians perform abortions. An exception to this was when a mid-1990s scandal involving the misdeeds of a Moroccan school instructor focused attention upon physicians with whom he had contracted to perform abortions on pregnant school girls upon whom he had forced his attentions. Both the inspector and the physicians received heavy sentences.

27. Private communication from Homa Hoodfar to author, October 2, 1999.

28. Hassan Hathout, "Induced Abortion," 315.

29. Al-Qurṭubī in *Al-Jāmiʿ li-aḥkām al-Qurʾān,* 12:8, quoted in Madkur, 274.

30. Ahmad Sahnoun, "Islam's View of Abortion and Sterilization," in *Islam and Family Planning,* 2:373.

31. Judith Jarvis Thomson, "A Defense of Abortion," in George Sher, *Moral Philosophy: Selected Readings* (San Diego and New York: Harcourt Brace Jovanovich, 1987), 631–32.

32. Fazlur Rahman, *Major Themes of the Qurʾān* (Minneapolis and Chicago: Bibliotheca Islamica, 1980), 23.

33. While the distinction between embryo and fetus can be arbitrary, generally embryo refers to the earliest stages of development, where the cells are not clearly differentiated. Fetus refers to a stage of further development as the spinal cord and rudimentary heart begin to form.

34. Shaltut, as quoted in Hathout, "Induced Abortion," 315.

35. It is disputed whether abortion can be murder, as the fetus is not yet born. Regardless of that legal point and the legal ramifications of abortion (paying *ghurra*), contemporary ulema utilize the rhetoric of "killing" and "murder" in referring to abortion. Among others, Hassan Hathout refers to abortion as "a murderous assault upon life and therefore a criminal act" ("Induced Abortion," 315).

36. The dirham for this reckoning was that used in the early days of Islam and weighed 3½ gold grams (Hathout, "Induced Abortion," 318). Also see ʿAbdul Rahman al-Khayyir, "Attitude of Islam towards Abortion and Sterilization," pp. 357–58, in the same volume as Hathout's essay.

37. See Shaikh Abdul Rahman al-Khayyir, "The Attitude of Islam toward Abortion and Sterilization," in *Islam and Family Planning,* 2:357–58.

38. Thomson, "A Defense of Abortion," 631–45.

39. Ibrahim Haqqi, "Islam and Abortion," in *Islam and Family Planning,* 2:394.

40. Ebrahim, "Abortion," 18.

41. Muhammad Mekki Nasiri, "A View of Family Planning in Islamic Legislation," *Islam Review* 62, no. 3–4 (Mar.–Apr., 1969): 17.

42. Hathout, "Induced Abortion," 318.

43. Hathout, comments in "Discussion: Justifications for Abortion," in *Islam and Family Planning,* 2:438.

44. "Sheikh al-Azhar: Abortion," *Al-Ahrām* (Cairo), 4.

45. Achmad Gazali, "Islam's View of Abortion," in *Islam and Family Planning,* 2:396.

46. "Marriage Is for the Furthering and Continuation of Procreation and Motherhood Is the Duty of Women," *Al-Sharq al-Awsaṭ* (London), September 14, 1994, 14.

47. Al-Khayyir, "Attitudes of Islam," 2:347–48.

48. Abul 'Ala' Maududi, *Birth Control: Its Social, Political, Economic, Moral, and Religious Aspects,* 3d ed., trans. Khurshid Ahmad and Misbahul Islam Faruqi (Lahore: Islamic Publications, 1968), 179–80.

49. Ebrahim, "Abortion," 17.

50. Nasiri, "A View of Family Planning," 11.

51. "Islam Prohibits Aborting," *Al-Ahrām* (Cairo), 14.

52. Hathout, "Induced Abortion," 325.

53. Benazir Bhutto in *Al-Ahrām* (Cairo), September 6, 1994, 1.

54. *Al-Sharq al-Awsaṭ* (London), September 12, 1994, 12.

55. Mahmud Najmabadi, "A Historical Survey of Abortion in Iran," in *Islam and Family Planning,* 2:370.

56. For a discussion of approaches to forming a personal Roman Catholic ethics of abortion see Daniel Callahan, *Abortion: Law, Choice and Morality* (London: MacMillan, 1970) and John Noonan, *The Morality of Abortion: Legal and Historical Perspectives* (Cambridge, Mass.: Harvard University Press, 1970).

Four

The Right Not to Be Born

Abortion of the Disadvantaged Fetus in Contemporary Fatwas

Vardit Rispler-Chaim

> Bringing a new person into the world is good for that person if he or she comes to find life worth living. It is not good to bring into the world people who will be miserably unhappy or who will harm or deprive others.
>
> —Mary Gore Forrester, *Persons, Animals, and Fetuses*

This contemporary statement of a western ethicist assumes that life is worth living only if it maintains a certain level of happiness, and only when the living person does not harm the society or people surrounding him or her.[1] If in the case of a human fetus these conditions are not met, that fetus may have a "right not to be born," and it should be possible to abort the fetus. The above statement also assumes that parents and policy makers are equipped with certain tools and medical data, and that they have the autonomy to decide whether to bring a new person into the world or not. By no means is this the only western voice on the subject of abortion, as will be shown later in this chapter, but it is representative of secular liberal thought, which, though linked to American and western European ethics, has spread in recent years to other parts of the world. Wherever in the world this thought has not been embraced wholeheartedly it has still left its mark and provoked an ongoing debate, and Islamic societies are no exception.

Human rights argumentation seems to be essential in justifying the legitimacy of the above choices, since both the protection of the yet unborn fetus and the well-being of the people who would be its family are based on notions of the value of human life central to human rights discourses. Yet the "right not to be born" is missing from all human rights agendas. This may be because this right depends on the age at which various cultures and legal systems bestow "personhood" on the fetus; when there is no "personhood" no rights are due, and as several sources have attested, "in most of the western world today personhood begins at birth."[2] The whole dilemma of "the right not to be born" is rendered irrelevant in face of the perception that fetuses are not persons.[3] If before birth no rights are due, and after birth the subject is irrelevant, there is no need to carry on the debate. This idea is representative of what H. Tristram Engelhardt Jr. calls "the secular morality." There are of course other definitions of "persons," which define fetuses as persons even at stages during pregnancy, and they are not solely derivatives of religious theologies. Engelhardt explains under "potentiality and probability" that the likelihood of one fetus to indeed become a person has an impact on the assessment that it is a person and the rights it deserves as a result.[4] The idea that being a "person" is in certain of the fetus's developmental stages "potential and probable" is shared therefore by both religious theologians and secular moralists, and influences their attitudes regarding fetus abortion.

Furthermore, the ethical dilemma of whether certain fetuses after being born will enjoy life at all, and whether their lives will be a burden on the lives of others, becomes a legal issue when the decision is made not to let certain fetuses be born. The means and the premeditation required for terminating pregnancy might be considered criminal behavior. Moreover, from a monotheistic religious point of view, not to let a fetus be born may be seen as interfering with the divine will, as "playing God." In these traditions, it is God alone, the creator of life, who may grant life or withdraw it from any human.

Nevertheless, recent years have witnessed, mainly but not only in the United States and western Europe, increasing litigation on behalf of sick and impaired infants; the infants are represented in the courts by their guardians, often their parents, against the medical staff that allowed them to be born impaired, knowing or not knowing about the "worthless" lives awaiting them. These lawsuits usually aim at securing financial compensation to cover the costs of raising an impaired child, a much more expensive matter than raising a healthy infant. This means that the right not to be born is believed to exist and is being claimed retroactively; although such litigation cannot undo the birth, it aims at compensating for the anguish and expenses involved.

The idea that a baby is born with impairment when the birth or the impairment could have been prevented, comes in the west under the controversial rubric of "wrongful birth" claims. The parents sue the medical staff for not assisting in terminating the life of the injured fetus while in the womb, or not warning the parents before pregnancy that an injured fetus might be conceived. There are also "wrongful life" claims, in which the impaired infants sue their doctors for malpractice in letting them enter a life of misery.[5]

In the Islamic world, medical ethics are formulated by means of legal opinions pronounced by well-known religious jurists (muftis), often in a question-answer format (fatwas). Fatwas are published in daily newspapers, periodicals, booklets, and compiled volumes, and/or broadcast on radio and television in most Arab and Islamic countries.[6] Since fatwas are non-binding legal opinions, different and even contradictory fatwas can appear on the same issue at a given period, in various geographic locations or even in the same country; thus a versatile range of opinions exists, and this helps in defining the ethical dilemmas involved in any particular subject.

The fatwas studied here are mainly Egyptian and Saudi, since the major Islamic institutions that issue fatwas in these countries, the Azhar Fatwa Committee (*Lajnat al-Fatāwā*) in Egypt and the Supreme Scholars Forum (*Hay'at Kibār al-ʿUlamā'*) of Saudi Arabia, are both very active and prolific, and since their fatwas are sought and respected by Muslims far beyond the borders of Egypt and Saudi Arabia themselves. Therefore, Egyptian and Saudi fatwas have a greater impact on Middle Eastern Muslims than fatwas issued elsewhere.

To return to the "wrongful birth" issue, the term itself in any of its possible Arabic translations does not appear in the medical fatwas surveyed so far. However, muftis have been struggling with the moral dilemma implied in the term "wrongful birth" for several decades. They have asked themselves whether there is a birth or a pregnancy that should not have occurred, and if there is, whether a society founded on Islamic ethics can morally prevent these occurrences, and if it can, at what stage of pregnancy and by what means.[7]

These fatwas also show no evidence of "wrongful life" claims on behalf of a living injured child, although physicians' malpractice was a much discussed topic in medieval Islamic law and has featured in legal literature ever since.[8] Physicians' negligence is hard to prove under Islamic law, since the art of medicine is guided and aided by God's will, and the practice of medicine is valued as a *farḍ kifāya* (a duty imposed by God on the community);[9] nevertheless, compensation for the injured party is often guaranteed.

The claim that one's life is "wrongful" or worthless is similar to arguments used to claim that suicide should be licit, but such thoughts are theologically forbidden to Muslims.[10] Every life has a purpose, which sometimes is comprehended by God alone; suicide, an elective violent termination of life, is therefore viewed as a protest against God's will and wisdom. This theological rule may provide a partial explanation for the reluctance of Muslim muftis so far to employ the "wrongful life" approach as a legal instrument.

But contemporary fatwas do raise two questions in the domain of the "wrongful birth" concept: first, whether an impaired fetus should be aborted or left to be born; second, whether a fetus produced by rape should be aborted or left to be born. (The Islamic sources have not as yet been concerned with the financial remedies that "wrongful birth" claims in their western counterparts often involve.) I have combined these two cases under the title "the right not to be born" because they share a similar outcome: a difficult life, sometimes with no dignity. Further, in both scenarios the parents may have wished to terminate the pregnancy for the sake of their own well-being as well as that of their infant. An impaired fetus may be the product of a desired pregnancy, but the resulting person may endure an unacceptable standard of living, absence of pleasure, and lack of independence. The fetus produced by rape is the fruit of an unwanted pregnancy, the growth of foreign seed unlawful to the mother who carries it. After being born the child, and then the adult, might encounter social discrimination, degradation, stigma, and isolation. The infant born of rape may well be physically healthy but emotionally and socially injured.

The child born of rape, theoretically at least, could, when legally qualified, make a claim for the right not to have been born ("wrongful birth") that he or she was obviously denied. The impaired child would generally require another person to make the claim on his or her behalf. Although in the fatwas I have not come across actual claims on these grounds, the problems of the fetus of rape and the impaired fetus are often discussed. I will try to answer the question of whether Islamic medical ethics recognizes the right not to be born for either kind of fetus.

The Impaired Fetus

Prenatal screening and other scientific advances make it possible to identify genetic disorders in the fetus while it is still in the womb. Some of these disorders can be cured in the womb. For those that are incurable, the parents can choose either to let the fetus complete its term and be born, or to abort it. The general Islamic attitude toward the pursuit of knowledge and "scientific research" is very favorable,[11] so Muslims need not object to the prenatal tests themselves. Abdel Rahim Omran even states that "Muslim children have the right to be born with no actual or potential genetic disorders," emphasizing the awareness that genetic disorders can be identified during pregnancy, and sometimes even prevented.[12] The real problem arises when the tests suggest that an abortion is in order.

Abortion is a complex subject in Islamic law and constitutes an action that is legally judged "reprehensible." This means that it is permitted only when a "good" reason can be furnished, and only up to 120 days into the pregnancy, which is the stage before ensoulment. Only when the continuation of pregnancy endangers the mother's life is abortion permitted later than 120 days of pregnancy.[13] The muftis debate extensively about what is a "good" reason and what is not. Genetic fetal disorders are part of this debate. Should a impaired fetus be aborted?

Even in the west, where "personhood" (according to some) starts at birth,[14] and in England in particular, where abortion has been legal since 1967,[15] it is not obvious that any injured fetus should be aborted. This is linked to the moral question of whether all people should be whole and healthy, or to put it more bluntly, whether a child "has the right to be born whole or not at all."[16] The answer will partly derive from the status a given society allots to the handicapped and disadvantaged, and mainly from its legal philosophy and codes.

During the last twenty years different views on abortion of impaired fetuses have been expressed in fatwas and essays. In Kuwait, permission was given in 1982 to abort impaired fetuses up to three months into pregnancy.[17] Mufti al-Qaradawi,[18] for example, does not allow abortion of impaired fetuses later than forty days of pregnancy. In support of his position he cites doctors who say that "not all that physicians say about this [i.e., the question of deformities] is correct." This forty-day limit might be workable for couples who are aware of their own genetic disorders or unhealthy genes, and who early in the pregnancy undergo prenatal screening. For others, who do not suspect fetal genetic problems, standard tests are usually conducted later than forty days into the pregnancy, and if abortion is the parents' choice, al-Qaradawi's suggestion might prove too late.

Abul Fadl Mohsin Ebrahim, a South African scholar,[19] and 'Abd al-Qadim Zallum, a Muslim scholar residing in Israel,[20] hold the same idea and recommend not performing an abortion, since injured fetuses can sometimes be cured in the womb. Both ignore the fact that most genetic diseases are still incurable. Jad al-Haqq, the late rector of al-Azhar University in Cairo, advised against abortion of impaired fetuses, since "an illness that cannot be cured today might be cured in the future."[21] Another opinion is that since the impaired fetus does not endanger the mother's life it must not be aborted.[22] Abortion of sick fetuses, it is further claimed, is like euthanasia of old, disabled adults who are perceived as a burden on society; therefore, such an abortion must be rejected on humanitarian grounds.[23]

Others claim that there are certain deformities that one can live with, therefore no need exists to abort after 120 days of pregnancy. Jeffery Botkin holds a similar idea.[24] Only very severe injuries and genetic diseases justify abortion, according to Jad al-Haqq.[25] Just recently Sheikh Nasr Farid Wasil, the "mufti of the Egyptian lands" (*mufti al-diyār al-miṣriyya*), declared that an impaired fetus may always be aborted if seventeen weeks of pregnancy have not yet lapsed (i.e., no more than 120 days). More surprising is a statement attributed to him, and for which I found no other reference, that if medical tests unquestionably indicate a deformity in the fetus, an abortion is legitimate until 230 days of gestation.[26] He does not stipulate the severity of the disorder in the second case, only its validity, but this definitely brings new hope for parents of fetuses whose disorder is discovered after 120 days. For the sake of comparison, note that in the last twenty years 79 percent of the American public has come to support the legitimization of abortion "if there would be a serious defect in the baby."[27] No time limit is pronounced there for the age of the fetus at the time of abortion.

What constitutes a severe defect or illness that would qualify for the optional abortion seems to be a common dilemma shared by both Muslim muftis and western ethicists. David Seedhouse and Lisa Lovett offered the following definition for the severity of an injury: "When there is substantial risk that if the child were born it would suffer from such physical or mental abnormalities as to be seriously handicapped."[28] Jad al-Haqq suggested a similar definition.[29] However, all attempts to define "severity" are still vague and generalized. For the muftis, life is associated with "dignity," sentience, and independence, not with "happiness." It was Mahmud Shaltut, the Sheikh al-Azhar in the 1950s and early 1960s, who said, "Who knows whether the retarded child or Down's syndrome child is unhappy as he is? It is often the projection of the healthy on the life of the handicapped, but not necessarily the truth."[30]

The muftis are more eager to offer advice on how to prevent injured fetuses from being conceived than on how to prevent them from being born once conceived. This means that we find in the fatwas more discussions of family planning and the proper use of contraceptives than of abortion in the various scenarios of undesired pregnancies. Sheikh Abu 'Id, for example, allowed family planning that could include pregnancy prevention for parents known to carry genetic disorders transferable to their offspring. This prevention had no time limit set for its legitimacy for parents who are never cured of their genetic disorders.[31]

On February 11, 1979, Sheikh Jad al-Haqq[32] gave permission for the sterilization of the sick parent in order to save the offspring from hereditary genetic diseases; he condoned this method despite the theological objection that sterilization challenges the wisdom of God in creating reproductive organs in man and woman.[33] According to Prof. Mahmud Zayid of the

American University of Beirut, as early as 1936 Sheikh Ahmad Ibrahim permitted the sterilization of carriers of genetic diseases. This was a very daring step, considering the views on sterilization held by most muftis in the second half of the century. Several muftis acquiesce to a temporary sterilization only, if at all. Most of them are against any type of sterilization.[34]

The more conservative approach claims that when the Prophet recommended that persons "marry from afar" (non-consanguineous marriages) and marry young, he took into account that genetic disorders are more prevalent in consanguineous marriages and with an older age of the mother at pregnancy. Whoever follows this approach in practice will supposedly minimize the risk of genetic disorders in their offspring; they will not have to contemplate whether or not to abort a sick fetus.[35]

This being the attitude, very little can be done under Islamic law to reduce the number of impaired fetuses conceived. We therefore return to abortion as the only alternative to raising handicapped children, and abortion encounters its own obstacles, as mentioned. At present, therefore, and until Sheikh Wasil's opinion proliferates, very few impaired fetuses of Muslim parents, and only those who have been diagnosed as handicapped early enough, may win the right not to be born.

The Fetus of Rape

When the pregnancy is unplanned and therefore unwanted, as in the case of rape, the parents have only two options: to complete the term and give birth, then give up the unwanted child for adoption;[36] or to abort the fetus and thus prevent the disgrace that awaits both mother and child, so that the woman, whether single or married, may return to her natural course of life. The first option, adoption, is not realizable for Muslim women since the institution of adoption is absent in society and prohibited by Islamic law, for reasons that are beyond the scope of the present study.[37] At the same time, the child born of rape, like the one born of adultery (*walad zinā'*), is a more lowly member of society with regard to the rights he or she is guaranteed and the social status he or she can attain.[38]

With regard to the second option, in recent years the muftis were urged by Muslim women to legitimize abortion for fetuses resulting from rape. This came following the atrocious raping of Kuwaiti women by Iraqi soldiers during the Gulf War of 1991, and after Muslim women were raped in Bosnia in the late 1990s. Most of the muftis who addressed the issue were unanimous that the child of rape, like *walad zinā'*, is not to blame for the mother's sin, and he or she does not fulfill any of the terms which justify an abortion.[39] The child of rape is a legitimate *shar'ī* child, they claim, and to kill him or her through abortion would be to add sin to the sin already committed in conceiving him or her.[40] Even those who tend to permit abortion for raped women continue to wonder, "What sin did the fetus commit which justifies its killing?"[41] They permit abortion only before the fetus is four months old, and after that age, only if the fetus endangers the mother's health.[42]

Sheikh Atiyya Saqr[43] is so opposed to the abortion of fetuses of rape that he portrays the future of the raped woman as the natural course of events; if she is married, she will raise the child after the birth, and her husband may choose to foster the child or disown him or her *(an yastalhiqahu* or *an yatabarra'a minhu*); in the latter case, the child will bear his or her mother's name only. If the woman is not married, the child is hers (genealogically). Sheikh Saqr does not reflect upon the mother's emotional trauma, the possibility, if she is married, that her husband will desert her or divorce her, or, if she is single, her slight chances of marrying. It seems that for the fetus of rape there is almost no right not to be born, especially if 120 days of pregnancy have elapsed.

However, a significant exception can be found in a fatwa by 'Ikrima Sabri, the Chief Mufti of the Palestinian Authority. In 1999 he permitted Muslim women who were raped in Kosovo to take an abortifacient medicine in order to prevent pregnancy from taking place.[44] He justified the permission by arguing that Muslim women should not bear children to the Serbs, since later on these children might be enlisted by the Serbs to fight against Muslims. This is a patriotic, not only a humanitarian, rationale.

The right not to be born is linked to abortion in most of its aspects. Therefore, several moral issues related to abortion have to be raised here, for they may shed light on the reasons for the muftis' obvious reluctance to legitimize abortion of fetuses of rape and severe deformation, despite the sympathy to human suffering that the muftis exhibit at other times. The first question is who can legally speak for the fetus in the womb, represent what is believed to be its best interest, and then sign the permission to abort it: the parents? the doctors? This question is especially crucial when the fetus is more than 120 days old. At this point, the fetus passes from one stage, which al-Sha'rawi calls *insān bi-l-quwwa* (potential human being, with few rights), to another stage entitled *insān bi-l-fi'l* (actual, real human being), when any aggression against it is punishable by law.[45] The question belongs to the human rights issues of autonomy and representation.

Muslims share with westerners the view that the doctor's role ends with informing the parents about the poor state of the fetus's health. It is then the mother's responsibility or her choice on behalf of the fetus, if she decides to undergo an abortion.[46] Muslims jurists also attribute liability to the father, if he is a participant in the decision to abort.[47] The Muslim doctor, having performed an abortion, becomes guilty under certain legal systems, such as the Egyptian civil law, of a crime sometimes defined as a "misdemeanor" or a "felony."[48] Doctors who fear being accused of a crime (even though none but the husband and the wife may bring charges against an abortionist) refrain from performing elective abortions. The result, according to M. Ismail Ragab,[49] is that Egyptian women seek illegal abortions. This, in fact, has become the main cause of mothers' mortality in Egypt.

By contrast, in British law a physician is never charged with breaking the law if he or she performed the abortion when "there is a substantial risk that if the child were born it would suffer from such physical or mental abnormalities as to be seriously handicapped."[50] Thus, physicians are covered by the law when aborting severely impaired fetuses. Moreover, in common law, as evinced by British law, a child can sue his or her mother (yet never win the case) for not performing an abortion, thus bringing the child to "wrongful life."[51]

The Muslim physician, who is well protected by Islamic law against accusations of negligence as long as he or she has acted with good intent, is apparently not similarly covered in cases of abortion. Only abortions performed as lifesaving measures do not border on criminal behavior.[52] In a way, Muslim abortionists have to be prepared to defend themselves against charges that they did what the patient asked for, while western physicians may sometimes face charges for not doing what the patients requested and expected. This may occur if doctors abstain from giving patients additional medical treatments and procedures because they see them as futile.[53]

The second moral question concerning the abortion of the impaired and the fetus of rape is whether it can be justified on the grounds that, if it is not performed, the born infant might cause harm to others. According to one statement, "a malpractice suit cannot be successful unless someone has been harmed."[54] Wrongful birth and wrongful life claims are based on harm caused to the child or the parents or both. What type of harm can a fetus or an infant cause to others? The only harm recognized by Islamic law is the risk to the mother's life, in which case abortion is always justified, even obligatory. Does an impaired fetus or fetus of rape cause harm to anyone? Obviously not, from the muftis' point of view.

In the west, the harm caused by a fetus is measured by the financial burden laid on the parents, by disappointment, by emotional distress,[55] and also by the infringement of the right to privacy and the right to make choices, if the mother was never informed that the fetus was injured. The fact that wrongful life lawsuits against physicians, in England for example, are often successful, indicates that the injured fetus who becomes an impaired child is believed to cause "harm" to his or her family members, or to him or herself.[56]

Since most muftis are generally against abortion of either fetuses of rape or impaired fetuses, they actually refuse to identify any harm in their continued existence except in cases where the mother's life is at risk. The harm I think is thereby disregarded is the harm to the quality of life, of both the parents and the child.

Quality of life is a newly emerging argument in medical ethics, and, true enough, it is a relative and subjective term. People in different places and at different times, with diverse upbringing and expectations, will have different ideas of what quality of life means for them. Can we speak of a "standard" or "normative" quality of life, that may be ignored or respected? "Quality of life" was brought to public awareness mainly, but not solely, through discussions on euthanasia, on life prolongation of the terminally ill and the comatose, and on whether persons, or somebody representing them, can have the right to request that their life be ended through withholding further medical treatment on the grounds of absence of quality in their life.

Muslims have taken part in this debate for the past two decades. According to Qur'an 5:32, "Whosoever killeth a human being for other than manslaughter or corruption in the earth, it shall be as if he had killed all humankind and whosoever saveth the life of one, it shall be as if he had saved the life of all humankind."[57] Nowadays "killing life" and "saving life" are not treated by the muftis as clear-cut acts, as a glance at the verse may hint. Muslim ethicists and muftis are asking themselves, and are being asked by the public, whether disconnecting life-sustaining machines from a comatose or a terminally ill patient falls within the definition of prohibited "killing," and further, whether saving the life of severely impaired fetuses is ultimately virtuous. The dilemma becomes even more complex when individuals carry living wills or equivalent documents in which they have earlier expressed the wish not to have their lives prolonged if and when the medical condition deteriorates to a specified stage. What guidance should then be followed: the Qur'anic verse as it stands or the individual's right to autonomy and to privacy?

When an individual expresses a desire to have his or her life terminated, suicidal intentions enter the discussion, and the Islamic position on suicide is uncompromisingly prohibitive.[58] When others suggest that someone's life has lost its quality, and that a person should be left to die (or be aborted, if still in the womb), racist discriminative fears arise. Lonny Sharelson, for example, fears that those who suggest euthanasia for people who are a nuisance to themselves might soon suggest it for people who are nuisance to others.[59] However, several muftis, like most western ethicists, have already come to accept that brain death signifies death, and in such cases they allow lifesaving machines to be disconnected and the heart and blood circulation to stop. This acceptance is helpful, especially for harvesting organs for transplantation, but also for allowing a comatose patient whose brain is irreversibly damaged to die. In support of this attitude are the late Sheikh al-Azhar, Jad al-Haqq,[60] the present Sheikh al-Azhar, al-Tantawi[61] and others.[62] This view is still fiercely opposed by scholars who want the *shar'ī* criteria for identifying the moment of death to prevail and who view disconnecting lifesaving machines upon brain death, while the heart is still beating, as killing.[63] Transplants are performed precisely with the aim of improving the recipient's quality of life, and most muftis welcome the procedure, with certain stipulations.[64]

Recently, quality of life was also taken into account by the muftis in cases where plastic and cosmetic surgery was at issue. The general Islamic attitude is against changing anything in the creation of God, in this case the human body, thus against plastic and cosmetic surgery.[65] However, when the person in need of such surgery stated, or threatened, that if the operation were not approved his or her other option would be suicide, the muftis, apprehensive of such an outcome, and resorting to the argument that maintaining life is the highest priority, approved of the desired surgery, and furnished it with the proper legal grounds.[66] The quality of life of those in need of plastic surgery was thus indirectly assured.

If the muftis are ready to consider quality of life in some cases, why do we not see the same consideration with regard to the fetus of rape and the genetically injured? The muftis do have sympathy for suffering, so the condition of the impaired child and the raped mother and her fetus are discussed, but the problem lies in abortion: the violent termination of innocent life. I would attribute the problem with abortion to Islamic attitudes, on the one hand to the miracle of the creation of humankind and the semi-holy role destined for humankind on earth (Qur'an 2:30), and on the other, to the haunting historical *jāhilī* experience of *wa'd* (burying girls alive). The custom of *wa'd* was practiced primarily, though not solely, against girls, because they were viewed as useless, an economic burden and a social disgrace to their community.[67] It was a discriminatory practice, and it was inflicted upon female infants, a weak group in pre-Islamic society.

For the muftis, admission of abortion as a legitimate means of resolving the difficulty associated with handicap or social stigma does not differ much from the historical purpose of *wa'd*. The objection of several scholars to *'azl* (*coitus interruptus*) as a legitimate means of contraception, despite Prophetic license for the method, is often based on the notion that *'azl* is equal to *wa'd khafīy* (disguised infanticide).[68] Anything that hinders the natural entry of children into life is classed under *wa'd* and is therefore forbidden. Abortion of the impaired fetus and fetus of rape is unacceptable for this same reason.

It has been observed more than once that the muftis are afraid of a "mudslide" in religious ethics.[69] They fear that once they approve in principle of abortion in the case of the impaired and fetus of rape, they will later be obliged to approve of other grounds for abortion as time goes on. However, on the individual case level we may believe that as with exceptional circumstances of abortion in the past, the muftis would offer humanitarian solutions. They are still not ready to acknowledge the right not to be born in the way this right is acknowledged in the west. But muftis' concessions to individuals' appeals have already become ethical precedents, and only time will tell if the right not to be born will follow this pattern too.

Notes

1. Mary Gore Forrester, *Persons, Animals, and Fetuses* (Dordrecht: Kluwer Academic Publishers, 1996), 195.

2. Ibid., 159; Adrian Whitefield, "Common Law Duties to Unborn Children," *Medical Law Review* 1, no. 1 (Jan. 1993): 28–52.

3. David Heyd, "Prenatal Diagnosis: Whose Right?" *Journal of Medical Ethics* 21, no. 5 (Oct. 1995): 292–97.

4. H. Tristram Engelhardt, *The Foundations of Bioethics* (New York and Oxford: Oxford University Press, 1996), 135–51.

5. Jeffery R. Botkin and Maxwell J. Mehlman, "Wrongful Birth: Medical, Legal, and Philosophical Issues," *Journal of Law, Medicine and Ethics* 22, no. 1 (spring 1994): 21–28; Anthony Jackson, "Wrongful Life and Wrongful Birth: The English Conception," *Journal of Legal Medicine* 17, no. 3 (Sept. 1996): 349–81.

6. Vardit Rispler-Chaim, *Islamic Medical Ethics in the Twentieth Century* (Leiden: E. J. Brill, 1993), 3–5. Muhammad Khalid Masud, Brinkley Messick, and David S. Powers, eds., *Islamic Legal Interpretation: Muftis and Their Fatwas* (Cambridge, Mass.: Harvard University Press, 1996), 31.

7. M. Ismail Ragab, "Islam and the Unwanted Pregnancy," in Jane E. Hodgson, ed., *Abortion and Sterilization: Medical and Social Aspects* (London: Academic Press, 1981), 507–18.

8. Rispler-Chaim, *Islamic Medical Ethics,* 66–71.

9. Ibid., 75.

10. Ibid., 94–99. See also the discussion of suicide in chapter 8.

11. Hassan Hathout, "The Ethics of Genetic Engineering: An Islamic Viewpoint," *Journal of the Islamic Medical Association of North America* 22, no. 3 (July 1990): 99–101.

12. Abdel Rahim Omran, *Family Planning in the Legacy of Islam* (London: Routledge, 1992), 33.

13. Rispler-Chaim, *Islamic Medical Ethics,* 15; Ragab, "Islam and the Unwanted Pregnancy," 507–18.

14. Forrester, *Persons, Animals, and Fetuses,* 159.

15. Jackson, "Wrongful Life and Wrongful Birth," 349–81.

16. Ibid.

17. Isam Ghanem, *Islamic Medical Jurisprudence* (London: Probsthain, 1982), 60.

18. Yūsuf al-Qaraḍāwī, in *Sayyidatī* 15, no. 778 (February 3–9, 1996): 84.

19. Abul Fadl Mohsin Ebrahim, "Islamic Ethics and the Implication of Biomedical Technology: An Analysis of Some Issues Pertaining to Reproductive Control, Bioethical Parenting, and Abortion" (Ph.D. diss., Temple University, 1986), 187.

20. ʻAbd al-Qadīm Zallūm, *Ḥukm al-sharʻ fī al-ijhāḍ wa-fī istiʻmāl ajhizat al-inʻāsh al-ṭibbiyya al-ṣināʻiyya al-ḥadītha* (Bāqa al-Gharbiyya: Maktabat al-Sunna, 1997).

21. "Ḥukm al-ijhāḍ," *Al-Fatāwā al-Islāmiyya* 9 (December 4, 1980): 3093–109.

22. *Al-Nūr* (April 17, 1991): 3; Ibn Jabarīn, in *al-Luʼluʼ al-mathīn min fatāwā al-muʻawwaqīn* (Riyadh: Dār al-Ṣamayʻī, 1997), 125–26.

23. Abul Fadl Mohsin Ebrahim, *Abortion, Birth Control and Surrogate Parenting: An Islamic Perspective* ([Indianapolis]: American Trust Publications, 1989), 86.

24. Jeffery R. Botkin, "Fetal Privacy and Confidentiality," *Hastings Center Report* 25, no. 5 (Sept. 1995): 32–39.

25. *Māyū* (Cairo), January 15, 1996, 4.

26. Naṣr Farīd Wāṣil, in *al-Ittiḥād* (Haifa, Israel), December 7, 1998, 8.

27. Botkin, "Fetal Privacy," 32–39.

28. David Seedhouse and Lisetta Lovett, *Practical Medical Ethics* (Chichester and New York: John Wiley, 1992), 111.

29. *Al-Fatāwā al-Islāmiyya* 9 (December 4, 1980): 3093–109; *al-Ahrām* (Cairo), February 6, 1981, 9.

30. Maḥmūd Shaltūt, *al-Fatāwā.* (Cairo: Dār al-Qalam, 1966), 293–97; Forrester, *Persons, Animals and Fetuses,* 231.

31. *Al-Liwāʼ Al-Islāmī* (March 8, 1990): 6.

32. Jād Al-Ḥaqq, in *Al-Fatāwā Al-Islāmiyya* 9 (February 11, 1979): 3087–92.

33. Ragab, "Islam and the Unwanted Pregnancy"; Muḥammad Mutawallī al-Shaʻrāwī, *Al-Fatāwā* (Cairo: Maktabat al-Qur'ān, n.d.), 3:29.

34. Omram, *Family Planning,* 187–90; Tahir Mahmood, *Family Planning: The Muslim Viewpoint* (New Delhi: Vikas Publishing House, 1977), 95–99.

35. S. O. Alfi, "Marry from Afar to Prevent Weak Progeny," in *Papers Presented to the First International Conference on Islamic Medicine* (Kuwait: Ministry of Public Health, 1981), 288–89; Fikrī Ḥasan Ismāʻ īl, "Zawāj al-aqārib" in *Māyū* (Cairo), March 25, 1996, 9; ʻAbd Allāh al-Mushidd, "Zawāj al-aqārib," in *al-Ahrām* (Cairo), April 4, 1986, 15.

36. Forrester, *Persons, Animals, and Fetuses,* 188; Jackson, "Wrongful Life," 349–81.

37. Amira al-Azhary Sonbol, "Adoption in Islamic Society: A Historical Survey," in Elizabeth Warnock Fernea, ed. *Children in the Muslim Middle East* (Austin: University of Texas Press, 1995), 45–67.

38. Etan Kohlberg, "The Position of the *Walad Zinā* in Imāmī Shī' ism," *Bulletin of the School of Asian and African Studies* 48, no. 2 (1985): 237–66; Uri Rubin, "Al-Walad li-l-firāsh: On the Islamic Campaign against zinā'," *Studia Islamica* 78 (1994): 5–26.

39. 'Alī al-Sālūs, in *al-Ḥaqīqa* (June 29, 1991): 7.

40. Muḥammad 'Abd Allāh al-Khaṭīb, in *al-Nūr* (May 10, 1989): 8.

41. Abul Fadl Mohsin Ebrahim, *Abortion,* 83.

42. *Al-Liwā' al-Islāmī* (April 6, 1989): 55; Abū 'Īd, in *al-Jum'a* (Sept.–Oct. 1989): 20; Aṭiyya Ṣaqr, "lā li-l-ljhāḍ," *Mimbar al-Islām* (Nov. 1994): 123.

43. *Mimbar al-Islām* (July 1995): 119.

44. 'Ikrīma Ṣabrī, *Fatwā shar'iyya ḥawla jarīmat al-ightisāb fī Kūsūvū* (Jerusalem: Publications of Majlis al-Fatwā al-A'lā, 25 April 1999).

45. *Al-Liwā' al-Islāmī* (April 6, 1989): 55.

46. Jackson, "Wrongful Life," 349–81.

47. Rispler-Chaim, *Islamic Medical Ethics,* 17.

48. Ibid.

49. Ragab, "Islam and the Unwanted Pregnancy," 507–18.

50. Seedhouse and Lovett, *Practical Medical Ethics,* 111–16.

51. Jackson, "Wrongful Life," 349–81; Alec Samuels, "Born Too Soon and Born Imperfect: The Legal Aspects," *Medical Science and Law* 38, no. 1 (1998): 57–61.

52. Rispler-Chaim, *Islamic Medical Ethics,* 12.

53. Lawrence J. Schneiderman and Nancy S. Jecker, *Wrong Medicine* (Baltimore and London: Johns Hopkins University Press, 1995), 83–96.

54. Botkin and Mehlman, "Wrongful Birth," 21–28.

55. Jackson, "Wrongful Life," 349–81.

56. In the United States only one case of wrongful life lawsuits has been successful as of 2000. This is the Curlender case of 1986, in which the parents sued the laboratory for failing to warn them that their fetus carried Tay Sachs disease. Had they received the information in time they would probably have chosen to abort the fetus. See Gregory E. Pence, *Classic Cases in Medical Ethics* (New York: McGraw Hill, 2000), 219. I thank Joyce Kloc McClure for this reference.

57. Mohammed Marmaduke Pickthall, *The Meaning of the Glorious Koran* (London: New American Library, n.d.).

58. Jalaluddin Umri, "Suicide or Termination of Life," *Islamic Comparative Law Quarterly* 7 (1987): 136–44; *Al-Liwā' al-Islāmī* (February 8, 1990): 7; Atiyya Saqr, in *Mimbar al-Islām* (Sept. 1994): 109.

59. Lonny Sharelson, *A Chosen Death* (New York: Simon and Schuster, 1995), 105–57.

60. *Al-Aḥrār* (Cairo), June 8, 1992, 5.

61. *Al-Naba' al-Waṭanī* (Cairo), May 11, 1997, 1.

62. Nadā Muḥammad Na'īm al-Daqr, *Mawt al-dimāgh bayna al-ṭibb wa-l-Islām* (Damascus: Dār al-Fikr, 1997), 167–75. See also the extensive discussion by Birgit Krawietz in chapter 9.

63. Fu'ād 'Alī Mukhayyam (a professor at al-Azhar), "laysa li-l-fard an yataṣarraf fī jismihi wa'in kāna ḥayyan aw mayyitan," in *al-Nūr* 655 (August 20, 1997): 12; al-Daqr, *Mawt al-dimāgh,* 155–66.

64. Rispler-Chaim, *Islamic Medical Ethics,* 42–43.

65. Ibid., 49.

66. Muḥammad al-Ṣāliḥ al-'Āthimīn, in *Fatāwā al-mar'a al-muslima* (Riyadh: Maktaba Ṭabariyya, 1995), 1:478–79; Ṣāliḥ b. Fawzān b. 'Abd Allāh al-Fawzān, "hal yajūz taqwīm al-asnān," in *Fatāwā al-mar'a al-muslima,* 1:476–477; 'Abd al-Salām al-Sukkarī, "*Jirāhāt al-tajmīl al-jā'iza wa-ghayr al-jā'iza,*" in *al-'Ā lam al-Islāmī* (January 22–28, 1996: 2; 'Aṭiyya Ṣaqr in *Māyū* (Cairo), July 29, 1996, 4.

67. Avner Giladi, "Infanticide in Medieval Muslim Society," in *Children of Islam: Concepts of Childhood in Medieval Muslim Society* (London: Macmillan, 1992), claims that the existence of material in the hadith against *wa'd* suggests that the custom may still have been practiced in the first centuries of Islam (102–15).

68. Ibid.; Rispler-Chaim, *Islamic Medical Ethics,* 10.

69. Rispler-Chaim, *Islamic Medical Ethics,* 146.

War

The Islamic tradition sees religiously sanctioned war as one of the means by which God effects change in this world. Therefore, it is no surprise that the subject of war occupies a large place in both historical texts and legal ones. Certain key wars were formative for the Muslim community. Among these are the wars fought by the Prophet, such as the battle of Badr (624 C.E.) and the conquest of Mecca (630), and also the great conquests of the Byzantine and Persian empires in the seventh century. But in the early years, Muslims also fought one another in a series of struggles, such as the war of apostasy (633) just after the Prophet's death, the battle of the camel (656) led by the Prophet's wife 'A'isha, and the battle of Siffin (660) led by the Prophet's son-in-law 'Ali. The centrality of war caused scholars to divide the world into three sections: the abode of Islam, the abode of treaty, and the abode of war.

Our concern here is not with the broad historical circumstances of war, but rather with the more specific question of killing in warfare. War is one of those occasions during which the prohibition of taking life sometimes disappears. Indeed, the means of winning a war is often by killing. This fact suggests that war aims at some good which conflicts with the good of human life, rendering it a means to an end. For this reason, religious traditions that place a high value on human life have an uneasy relationship with this most bloody of human endeavors, while other traditions condemn war outright. The authors in this section demonstrate that Islam also places clear limits on killing in war and provides for the protection of noncombatants.

The fact that war can constitute a moral good in Islam does not mean that killing in war is an undifferentiated act, or that enemies are somehow seen as subhuman. All life is valued in Islam; rules of war even protect vegetative life such as crops and trees. Further, the Qur'an explicitly recognizes a common humanity, all of whom are "children of Adam," so the simple state of unbelief does not cause one's life to be forfeit. The recognition of common humanity also means that voluntary conversion by the enemy, or submission to the rule of Islamic law without conversion, both make war no longer necessary. Territorial aggression between groups of Muslims is normally prohibited in Islam, but it may be accepted in cases of doctrinal differences.

The first essay in this section looks precisely at this distinction between war against Muslims and war against non-Muslims. After first distinguishing among the different sorts of moral statements found in the classical sources, Khaled Abou El Fadl looks at the way that the act of killing is portrayed in these two sorts of war. He finds that the classical jurists generally focus more on *jus in bello* (rules on the conduct of war) than on *jus ad bellum* (rules determining whether a specific war is licit). That is to say, the jurists seem less concerned that war exists than that it be fought correctly. In addressing the question as to why non-Muslims may be killed, Abou El Fadl finds that a minority of jurists regard unbelief to be a grave sin, deserving death. The majority of Muslim jurists, however, say it is only right to kill unbelievers if they pose a threat to Islam. Such reasoning leads to protection of noncombatants, such as women and children. But as in other areas of Islamic law, these rules are sometimes tied to specific cases and sometimes reflect a larger Islamic ethos. Abou El Fadl finds that the jurists in any given situation are negotiating between pragmatic rules and an underlying morality.

While many of these themes continue to be of importance to Muslims today, the second essay finds a significant break between classical texts and modern ones. In his review of three influential modern writers (Mawdudi, Hamidullah, and al-Zuhayli), Sohail Hashmi finds differences both in the way they formulate the questions and also in their use of authoritative sources. Hashmi then turns to five specific areas within the rules of conducting war (*jus in bello*) that address the question of killing and saving life. In these texts, there is a great concern that human life not be taken unnecessarily; therefore the rules of giving quarter to the enemy are quite generous, following Prophetic precedent. But there is also recognition that war may result in the accidental death of noncombatants, and along these lines, it seems that even nuclear weapons may be acquired and deployed if necessary to defend the Muslim community. Finally, Hashmi deals with the key concept of "necessity" in war, an issue relevant to all discussions in this book.

In the third essay, Richard Martin analyzes Muslim rhetoric of war in a postmodern world. While Hashmi notes that modern writers often take western (not Muslim) authorities as their interlocutors, Martin addresses radical Muslim voices that call for jihad and for the killing of enemies in ways that the classical sources would not sanction. In both these cases, it seems that ethical statements on war are not so much prescriptive of what a person should do as descriptive of how Muslims perceive their position over and against western powers. Martin continues by addressing two controversial cases: the use of jihad rhetoric in the slaying of Egyptian president Anwar Sadat in 1981, and the more recent declarations of jihad against western powers by Osama bin Laden. As Americans now know all too well, Muslim extremists use the rhetoric of jihad to justify terrorism and individual acts of violence against the enemy. By analyzing these voices on the edge of ethical discourse, Martin reveals the boundaries of Muslim morality, since even these angry, radical men root their arguments in the classical sources. But as examples of "global rhetoric" aimed to address larger issues of injustice, they reject what Martin terms "the quietism of traditional Sunni theories of jihad."

The focus on the rhetoric of jihad in this section may seem some distance from an Islamic ethics of killing and saving life in warfare, but the attacks on the World Trade Center and the Pentagon have demonstrated that these issues are intimately related. Pages of a devotional manual found in the luggage of Muhammad Atta, one of the hijackers, reveal a profound religious conviction as he cites both Qur'an and the example of the Prophet to justify his actions. Such rhetoric functions on at least two levels. From the perspective of non-Muslims, terrorist jihad begins to define Islam, so much so that film and television producers find it easy to depict Muslims as terrorists with no regard for life. These powerful representations, if left uncorrected, only succeed in blocking our examination of war in ethical terms. From the Muslim perspective, however, the rhetoric of extremists gains much of its shock value from the respect given to human life in Islam. Further, to justify terrorist acts such as assassination of a standing president or the killing of thousands of civilians, extremists must engage in such rhetorical gymnastics that they end up rejecting classical and mainstream jurists alike, isolating themselves from the rest of the tradition.

It is another example of the flexibility of the Islamic legal system that there can be no single, authoritative response to such voices. While Martin refers to a "war of the fatwas," in which opinions and counter-opinions do battle in the daily newspapers, there is no ultimate authority to which the parties can appeal. That such freedom of expression is a moral good can hardly be argued, and in the previous section, Marion Katz noted this flexibility with approval in private matters such as abortion. But the lack of authoritative response, just as the general focus on cases over principle, may undercut Muslims' ability to make substantial contributions to limiting the scourge of war and even terrorism. In the very public issue of war, it sometimes seems that the only principle that seems to hold is that great destroyer of principle: "Necessity makes licit the illicit." As emphasized several times by the authors in this section, however, there are both functional limits of warfare and also a clear commitment to hold human life as sacred. As Hashmi points out, Islamic ethicists will need to find ways to identify and enforce these limits in the future.

Curiously, it may be Abu l-A'la Mawdudi, the father of the radical Islamic party in Pakistan, who points the way. In his discussion of Qur'an 6:151 ("Do not kill the person that God has made sacred, except for just cause") Mawdudi lists five just causes, including that of religiously sanctioned war. But he continues to explain that the command not to kill can only be overridden in order to uphold the truth and justice that make life meaningful. In the modern world, where we have the ability to destroy civilizations and the environment on an unprecedented scale, it could be argued that Muslims must establish limits to uphold the integrity of creation that makes life possible. In so arguing, Muslims would have a powerful means to defend the sacredness of life even in the face of war.

Five

Between Functionalism and Morality

The Juristic Debates on the Conduct of War

Khaled Abou El Fadl

The Challenge of War and the Balancing of Moral Imperatives

War poses a formidable challenge to juristic discourses. To a large extent, juristic discourses must assume a certain degree of stability and order. It is the existence of a presumed stability and order that make the articulating of rules of conduct and the prescribing of parameters for the resolution of conflict intelligible. The assumption of a degree of order and stability facilitates a reasonable expectation of compliance with the prescriptions of a legal system. Furthermore, legal systems, which assume the supremacy of law, will also assume that pragmatic political considerations or discretion must be subject to some limits. War poses particular challenges because it is thoroughly political and thoroughly chaotic.[1] If juristic discourses rely on an unrealistic view of war, they risk marginality and irrelevance. In other words, if jurists are oblivious to the particular challenges and demands of war, their discourses appear idealistic and unimportant. At the same time, if jurists do not attempt to set any parameters upon the prosecution of war, they tacitly admit the irrelevance of law in this particular field. If jurists concede to the prosecution of war an unfettered autonomy from any rules, in a sense, the law becomes very pragmatic but also irrelevant. If law becomes a thoroughly legitimating discourse, without any proscriptive aspirations, it risks becoming a merely descriptive discourse, and it risks becoming marginal.

Muslim juristic discourses strike a balance between conservative legitimation and aspirational prescription. A balance, of course, does not mean that both functions are given equal weight or identical proportions. A balance simply means that legitimation and aspiration are both weighted and considered. This is sometimes a conscious act, but it is often an unconscious response to perceived moral imperatives, social or political demands, cultural assumptions, or even simple fidelity to the inherited doctrines or precedents of a juristic culture. Furthermore, a jurist's reading of actual practice or social or political demands could be imperfect and incomplete. Hence a jurist may believe that he or she is articulating an actual social or political practice, but what is ultimately articulated is, in reality, aspirational in nature. For instance, a Muslim jurist may write that a permanent state of peace may not exist between Muslims and non-Muslims, and that non-Muslims should be fought at least once a year. The jurist might believe that this describes an actual practice or that this responds to a pragmatic concern. Yet the jurist's imperfect understanding of reality or a change in circumstances might reveal that, more than anything else, this statement is aspirational or prescriptive in nature. For instance, the Shafi'i jurist Abu Ishaq al-Shirazi (d. 1083) states that Muslims should wage war against non-Muslims at least once a year. He justifies this prescriptive ruling by stating: "[This is so] because failing to wage war [against non-Muslims] for more than a year will cause the enemy to transgress against Muslims" (because the enemy might assume that Muslims have become weak).[2] What assumptions inform al-Shirazi's rule? Although the rule appears prescriptive in nature, it is based on a reading of a context. It is possible that al-Shirazi's statement is a straightforward documentation of a political and social reality of his time. But if al-Shirazi has misread his context or is challenging this context, or if the context once existed but has now changed, his statement becomes aspirational in nature. From a different perspective, to what extent is al-Shirazi stating a functional rule? Furthermore, to what extent is al-Shirazi's rule wedded to the practical utility it is supposed to obtain? If al-Shirazi is stating a functional rule, then the point of the rule is to accomplish a specific result, and if it fails to do so, then there is no justification for the existence of this rule. If non-Muslims will not transgress against Muslims, or if attacking non-Muslims once a year will not produce the desired effect of inspiring fear in non-Muslims, then the rule fails. On the other hand, if al-Shirazi's statement is a moral prescription, then regardless of the consequences or results, the rule remains valid, and non-Muslims, as a matter of principle, should be attacked at least once a year.

Functionality, as I am using the word here, is not necessarily synonymous with practicality or pragmatism. Pragmatism is not necessarily aspirational because pragmatism tends to look to what is feasible or realizable. Functionality could be aspirational; it looks to the possible benefit or utility to be obtained. A juristic discourse could be functional (that is, oriented towards the potential function) but not pragmatic because the benefit one hopes to obtain is not possible. Meanwhile, a moral rule, as I am using the term here, sustains a principle but does not look to the possible empirical or mundane benefits or utility of the rule. A moral rule could be pragmatic—it can be implemented and realized—but it is not functional because its primary role is to sustain a principle and not to produce utility.[3]

Between the reading of reality and the prescribing of rules to effect this reality, juristic discourses balance pragmatism, functionality, and morality. This is particularly true in the case of Islamic juristic discourses. Working within a religious legal system, Muslim jurists were not at liberty to ignore moral imperatives. But, as noted above, the balancing of these factors in the context of addressing the rules of war is particularly challenging for any legal system. Even a religious legal system, if it aspires to remain relevant, cannot completely ignore any of the three factors identified above. We will focus our attention in this essay on the balance between functionality and morality in the premodern juristic discourses on the rules that apply to killing at war. The purpose of this essay is to demonstrate that in discussing the conduct of warfare, classical Muslim jurists negotiated between functionality, and perhaps pragmatism, and near absolute moral imperatives. This is, however, not an exhaustive study of this negotiative process. This essay demonstrates the existence of the negotiative process, but it does not present a thorough review of its mechanics. By demonstrating its existence, I hope to refute many of the highly essentialistic and terribly ill-informed contemporary studies on the classical Muslim juristic heritage.[4]

Muslim juristic discourses dealing with the conduct of war do not demonstrate a clear tendency toward either moral or functional methodology. Rather, there is a tension between the articulation of rules that tend to look to ultimate benefits and interests, and the articulation of rules that uphold the supremacy of certain principles regardless of the material benefits or harms that might accrue. This tension is handled through a negotiative process. A balance is often struck between the two tendencies. But this balance is not stable or constant. A rule that might have been the product of a specific context and intended to respond to this context, by serving an identifiable interest, could ascend to the status of an absolute moral imperative. The opposite is also true. A rule could be articulated because of a perceived moral imperative, but, eventually, it becomes modified and compromised into a rule that is supposed to serve a specific interest.[5]

As discussed below, many contemporary commentators have tended to view Islamic juristic discourses on war as either predominantly moral or predominantly functional, and have tended to ignore the negotiative nature of these discourses.[6] This has often led to a sadly unbalanced understanding of the nature of the juristic discourses in Islam and to a fairly dogmatic view of the approach to war in juristic Islam. In order for us to properly assess the juristic negotiative process in the discourses on war, it will be necessary to compare the juristic discourses on both internal wars in which Muslims fought Muslims, and external wars in which Muslims fought non-Muslims. Often, moral trends within juristic discourses are expressed in terms of moral culpability. In other words, it is the assessment of the moral guilt of the actor, and not necessarily the expected benefit, which could justify the applicability of a certain rule.[7] By comparing the rules that apply to fighting Muslims with those that apply to fighting non-Muslims, we can evaluate the extent to which the rules of killing at war were founded on notions of moral culpability and guilt, or on functionalist considerations related to the benefits to be obtained from the rule. The advantage of such a comparative approach is that it looks to the general approach that Muslim jurists took in discourses on killing at war rather than simply focusing on external wars against non-Muslims. Put differently, it is useful to examine whether certain rules were adopted because of the religious status of the combatants or whether these rules are seen as functional necessities quite apart from the issue of status. In this context, one can better understand the balance struck between functionality and morality by premodern Muslim jurists.

A Clarification Regarding the Juristic Moral Constraints

Before turning to the subject of rules of warfare, I want to admit that I am not prepared to argue that the Muslim juristic view of morality is either deontological or teleological.[8] In part, this is because theories of ethics and their relation to Islamic jurisprudence is an under-explored subject in modern scholarship.[9] More importantly, however, for the purposes of this essay, it is not necessary to explore the exact nature of the juristic moral commitments, since I will focus on what Muslim jurists treat as moral imperatives regardless of their utility *to Muslims.* If Muslim jurists exhibited a commitment to normative principles regardless of the resulting consequence to Muslims, this might connote a deontological view of morality, but it does not necessarily mean that either I, or the jurists I study, regard consequentialist visions of morality to be inadequate.[10] For one, I am not sure that a deontological view of morality is necessarily incapable of dealing with hard cases where it would be necessary to violate moral constraints because of the dire consequences that would result otherwise.[11] Furthermore, I am not sure that a teleological view of morality is possible without a prior deontological commitment.[12] But more fundamentally, it strikes me as largely unhelpful to describe the workings of legal institutions as either deontological or teleological.[13] Legal institutions negotiate between the functional, pragmatic, and moral without being entirely one or the other. Often, moral values are asserted as *prima facie* obligations or rights that may be overridden by countervailing considerations. For instance, legal institutions may impose a duty to speak the truth before a court of law. It is difficult to conceive of a situation in which lying to a judge would be considered, from the perspective of the legal institution, as a rightful act. Yet, it makes little sense to describe this stance as deontological. The duty to speak the truth before a court of law is not necessarily based on an absolute view of morality, but could be based on a belief in the practical necessity of such a rule.[14] Furthermore, a defense of necessity in the case of criminal offenses does not necessarily mean the endorsement of a consequentialist view of morality. For instance, if a person is threatened with death unless he curses God, he may do so. But that does not mean that cursing God becomes either good or rightful but merely excusable under dire circumstances. In addition, some Muslim jurists argued that murder may be justified to save a large number of lives, but rape is never justified.[15] However, this does not necessarily mean that for these jurists, the moral value of life is teleologically conceived and the moral value of honor is deontologically conceived. In both situations, murder and rape, the offender incurs a sin and will be punished in the hereafter, but as far as the earthly law is concerned, one act ought to be punished (rape) and the other (murder) should not.[16]

Here, I am interested in examining the assertion of normative values as *prima facie* moral constraints in Muslim juristic practice. Such constraints could be absolute or could yield to countervailing considerations; they could be predicated on a notion of what is right or a notion of what is good or both. What strikes me as moral about a particular constraint is that it is not predicated on a sense of opportunism or that it is not focused on a singular interest in promoting Muslim welfare regardless of the consequences to others.[17] One final example might help in clarifying this significant point. Muslim jurists argued that if a Muslim enters the territory of war under a safe conduct agreement (*amān*), he is bound to fulfill all contractual obligations towards his non-Muslim counterparts. If a Muslim violates any such obligations, for example fails to pay back a debt to a non-Muslim, and escapes to Muslim territory, the Muslim government must compel the Muslim offender to fulfill his financial commitments. In fact, the government must collect the money from the offender and either hand it over to a representative from the non-Muslim territory or send it by means of an emissary to the non-Muslim polity. This rule is advocated regardless of its potential impact on Muslims—it is a moral constraint regardless of whether it hurts or benefits Muslims. Nevertheless, if a war breaks out between the Muslim and non-Muslim polities and the Muslim polity has reason to believe that the money will be used to further the war effort against Muslims, it may defer payment of the financial obligations of its subjects until the war ends, which could be an indefinite period of time. Importantly, whether Muslims lose or win the war does not affect the obligation of payment; only the persistence of the state of war is relevant. Furthermore, in all circumstances, the Muslim offender carries the sin of treachery until the money is paid to the non-Muslims. If the state of war continues for a long span of time and there is no reasonable expectation that it would end in the near future, the Muslim offender should donate the money to charity to clear his conscience before God.[18] I would identify this rule of compensation as a moral constraint upon the Muslim polity, but it is neither utilitarian nor consequentialist.[19] Yet the rule is not absolute either. I think that all one can say is that Muslim jurists have articulated a weighty *prima facie* moral constraint that is subject to modification in extreme circumstances,[20] and the way that premodern Muslim jurists negotiated between moral constraints and functional considerations is my major concern.

Moral Culpability and Fighting Muslims

Classical Muslim jurists distinguish between what they call *ḥarb al-bughāh* (war against Muslims) and *ḥarb al-kuffār* (war against unbelievers). The rules that apply to fighting Muslims are different from the limitations set upon the conduct of warfare against non-Muslims. If Muslims fight other Muslims, there are binding regulations that do not necessarily apply to Muslims fighting non-Muslims or apostates. If Muslims fight one another, the fugitive and wounded may not be dispatched. Muslim prisoners may not be executed or enslaved. Children and women may not be intentionally killed or imprisoned. Imprisoned male Muslims must be released once the fighting, or the danger of continued fighting, ends. Furthermore, the property of Muslims may not be taken as spoils, and any property taken must be returned after the cessation of fighting. Even more, means of mass destruction such as mangonels, flame-throwers, or flooding may not be used unless absolutely necessary. Additionally, Muslims may not be punished or held liable for acts committed during the fighting.[21] Importantly, however, these rules do not apply to just any fighting that may occur between Muslims and other Muslims. Rather, these rules apply to fighting that may take place between Muslims and a specific category of Muslims called the *bughāh*.

The special status of bughāh arises because, in principle, Muslims are prohibited from fighting each other; if they do, they are considered to have committed a grave sin. But the rules mentioned above specifically apply to

Muslims who fight other Muslims while relying on a plausible interpretation (*ta'wīl muḥtamal*) or cause (*dhikr maẓlama*). Muslims who rely on a plausible religious interpretation or a plausible just cause are designated as bughāh and are treated with a certain degree of benevolence. Therefore, Muslims who fight because of tribal reasons (*'aṣabiyya*) or out of mere greed are not considered bughāh and are not entitled to the treatment outlined above. According to classical jurists, those who do not rely on a plausible interpretation or cause are either bandits or apostates, and they are to be killed or executed, and in certain circumstances, amputated or crucified.[22]

It is not clear what the proper parameters are for identifying a plausible interpretation or cause. Muslim jurists do not elaborate upon this point. In describing a plausible interpretation, classical jurists rely on historical precedents rather than on theoretically systematic expositions. Hence, they argue that Mu'awiya, Talha, Zubayr, and 'A'isha relied on a plausible interpretation when they rebelled against and fought 'Ali. Furthermore, classical jurists describe various early rebels against the Umayyads and 'Abbasids as bughāh. Despite the ambiguity, a plausible interpretation appears to mean the citing of a religious disagreement that, in the view of the jurists, is not heretical, or a grievance from a perceived injustice.[23] In principle, Muslim jurists were not willing to equate Muslims who fight or rebel because of "higher motives" or unselfish reasons, with those who resort to violence out of the desire for prurient gain or out of blind allegiance to a tribe or family. Therefore, the bughāh, according to the majority of the schools, are not sinners or criminals. Furthermore, according to Muslim jurists, the term bughāh does not connote censure or blame (*laysa bi-ism dhamm*).[24] Hanafi jurists, however, have argued that the bughāh are sinners but not criminals. The bughāh are sinners because resorting to violence against fellow Muslims is never justified; but they are not criminals because criminals are motivated by prurient interests. Consequently, the bughāh, as a matter of law, cannot be treated as apostates or common criminals.

Although the bughāh are not treated as common criminals, Muslim jurists insist that if the bughāh commit a violent rebellion against a ruler, they are considered, as a matter of law, to be in error. Their *ta'wīl* is presumed to be erroneous, and the ruler and the loyalists are presumed to be rightful. Nevertheless, the mere existence of a plausible interpretation or cause, even if erroneous, separates the bughāh from others. Therefore, the Hanbali jurist Ibn Qudama (d. 1223–4) states: "The *bughāh* are not dissolute (*laysū bi fāsiqīn*), but they are wrong in their interpretations, and the ruler and the loyalists (*al-imām wa-ahl al-'adl*) are right in resisting them. All of them [the loyalists and the bughāh] are like jurists who disagree on specific points of law."[25] Comparing the bughāh to jurists who disagree on specific points implies that the bughāh should be *mujtahids* of sorts. Importantly, however, Muslim jurists specifically assert that the bughāh do not need to be jurists or of an equal degree of learning or knowledge in order to qualify for preferential treatment.[26]

For the most part, in dealing with the issue of fighting Muslims, the classical jurists do not focus on issues related to *jus ad bellum* or the justifiability of war. Rather, most of the discourses are focused on *jus in bello* or the treatment that should be afforded to the bughāh in the course of fighting. Muslim jurists do not discourse at length on when it is justifiable for a Muslim to fight another, or when a Muslim may properly rebel against a ruler. Of course, I am not arguing that Muslim jurists were uninterested in the justifiability of the use of force. Muslim jurists have, in fact, pronounced lengthy exhortations about the impermissibility of the use of force against fellow Muslims, and they have cautioned against the evils of rash and violent rebellions against unjust rulers.[27] Furthermore, particularly in the context of rebellion or enjoining the good and forbidding the evil, Muslim jurists have advocated a type of balancing test according to which the possible evils are weighed against the potential good.[28] This is similar to the notion of proportionality in the western *jus ad bellum* tradition, by which the act of resorting to force might be justified if the total good outweighs the total anticipated evil.[29] Nevertheless, the main focus of Muslim jurists has been on the practical rules of treatment, and not on the grounds of justifiability.

There is a certain degree of pragmatism in the approach taken by Muslim jurists. It is as if Muslim jurists presumed the occurrence of fighting, and simply dealt with the subsequent consequences. In other words, the main focus seems not to be so much on theories of justifiability, but on the technical rules of conduct that should apply once the fighting, regardless of its merits, takes place. Nonetheless, this pragmatic approach is also moral because it tends to focus on issues related to moral culpability. The bughāh are not morally culpable because they rely on a presumptively erroneous interpretation or cause. Because they are not morally culpable, they are entitled to be treated in a fashion that is not afforded to mere apostates or common criminals. Significantly, this moral consideration is not absolute. It is mixed with a limited degree of legal pragmatism. For instance, Muslim jurists argue that in order for the bughāh to qualify for preferential treatment they must have a degree of strength, or *shawka*. Strength, in this context, means that the bughāh must be of a certain number so that they are not easily overcome or defeated. Muslim jurists do not specify how many individuals are needed for *shawka* to exist, but they simply state that one or two people are not sufficient. The jurists justify this numerical requirement by arguing that since the bughāh are not held liable for life and property destroyed during the course of fighting, if the status of bughāh is given to individuals, regardless of the degree of support that they might enjoy, suffering will increase. As the jurists put it, without the requirement of *shawka,* anarchy and lawlessness will spread (*ḥattā lā tafsad al-siyāsāt*).[30] They contend that without the requirement of *shawka,* every corrupt person will invent or fabricate a *ta'wīl,* and claim to be a *bāghī* (singular of bughāh).[31] Hence, if a person resorts to force while relying on a plausible *ta'wīl,* but does not have a *shawka,* he will be treated as a common criminal and will be held liable for any life or property destroyed. Importantly, however, this pragmatic consideration is not without constraints. Even if individuals lack a *shawka,* they are to be held liable for their specific acts; but they may not be summarily executed and their property may not be confiscated without just cause. Therefore, neither moral culpability nor pragmatic considerations seem to be absolute. Rather, both moral and pragmatic considerations seem to constrain each other through a process of balancing. At the same time, however, this balancing act is placed within a context of certain moral absolutes so that, for example, under no circumstances may an individual be enslaved, tortured, mutilated, or denied a proper burial, even if he lacks a *ta'wīl* or *shawka.* One can clearly discern a certain degree of concern over the role that the rules will play and the consequences that will result from the application of the rules. But at least as far as the fighting of Muslims is concerned, there is a strong moral tendency. Regardless of the anticipated function of the rules, Muslim jurists have strongly affirmed the principle that a Muslim fighting out of conviction cannot be treated as a common criminal.

It is not entirely clear exactly what methodology is followed by the jurists in reaching the balance between moral and pragmatic considerations, nor is it clear what makes certain rules unwavering and absolute. For example, many jurists, particularly those from the Hanafi school, argue that a fugitive or wounded individual from a group that enjoys a *ta'wīl* and *shawka* may not be pursued or dispatched. However, if the group has reinforcements (*fi'a*), the fugitive and wounded may be dispatched. The reasoning behind this argument is largely pragmatic; as long as the bughāh have reinforcements, the danger posed from their rebellion has not subsided, and, in the interests of *siyāsa* (politics), a certain amount of latitude should be granted to the *imām* (ruler). Nevertheless, Muslim jurists also insist that under no circumstances may bughāh who enjoy a *shawka* and *ta'wīl* be held liable for life or property destroyed during the course of the fighting. The interests of *siyāsa* will not be accommodated in this context.

Furthermore, the classical jurists insist that if the bughāh take hostages and execute them, under no circumstances may the loyalists respond in kind. The taking or execution of hostages is invariably wrong.[32]

The strength of doctrinal sources, or what might be called the weight of sources, does not necessarily indicate which rule would be compromised in the interests of *siyāsa,* and which rule would stand as a foundational and absolute principle. In other words, the sources from which the rules of conduct were derived do not, by themselves, determine the weight that is given to a particular rule. For example, it is argued that the laws applicable to the bughāh (*aḥkām al-bughāh*) are derived from the precedent of 'Ali's conduct in fighting his opponents in the Battle of the Camel and Siffin. Purportedly, 'Ali refused to pursue the fugitive, dispatch the wounded, or execute prisoners. Yet as noted above, many jurists were not willing to assert this rule in an absolute or unequivocal fashion. At the same time, Muslim jurists insist that the rule against the mutilation or torture of the bughāh is absolute and unequivocal. As authority, they often assert that when Ibn Muljam assassinated 'Ali, 'Ali's dying wish was that Ibn Muljam not be mistreated or mutilated, and that 'Ali's commands were duly adhered to by the members of the Prophet's family. Interestingly, however, there are various historical reports that claim that 'Ali did not make such a testament, and that Ibn Muljam was tortured or mutilated after 'Ali's death.[33] Muslim jurists rarely cite or acknowledge the existence of these reports. This points to a selective and creative process by which the jurists construct and negotiate certain values.

In all probability, what emerges as a moral absolute in Muslim juridical culture is the product of an incremental and cumulative sociological and theological interactive and dialectical process. One suspects that if specific doctrines were examined in a progressive historical and sociological context, one would be able to better explain the process by which Muslim jurists negotiated religious and political imperatives.[34] For the purposes of this essay, however, it is important to emphasize that Muslim jurists hinge the treatment of Muslim combatants on a perceived moral culpability, but most of their efforts have focused on the morality of conduct and not the morality of purpose. This is consistent with the emphasis in Islamic theology on orthopraxy and not necessarily on orthodoxy. It would be inaccurate, however, to claim that Muslim jurists passively accept the inevitability of violence and then proceed to regulate its effects according to purely functional considerations. Rather, Muslim jurists seem to approach the issue of violence against Muslims pursuant to a gradation of rules; if the basic rule prohibiting violence against Muslims is not honored then a set of primary and secondary rules come into effect to regulate the conflict.

moral principle is stated in functional terms because the exception for bees and pigeons is based on the potential benefit to Muslims. Arguably, however, one can expand the justification for the protection of bees and pigeons to cover any animal capable of migrating. Therefore, the principle could be read to mean that any animal that is capable of moving or traveling cannot be killed. In that case, superficially, the logic appears functional, but in reality, an unequivocal prohibition against the killing of animals is reasserted.

One can observe the same type of dynamic and negotiative process in Muslim discourses on the duration of peace treaties. Muslim jurists have often argued that as a matter of principle, peace treaties with non-Muslims should not be indefinite in duration. Since Muslims are supposed to be in a perpetual state of spreading the word of God, it is preferable that a peace treaty not exceed four months. The maximum possible duration for a peace treaty, however, is ten years.[71] Nonetheless, the practice of Muslim states has not necessarily been consistent with this principle. Some peace treaties have had a perpetual status.[72] Furthermore, the principle of a cap on the duration of peace treaties must have posed considerable challenges to the Islamic polity. Importantly, however, we find that many late jurists have omitted the discourse specifying a ten-year limit on peace treaties.[73] Ibn Taymiyya goes further, arguing that those who attempt to set limits on the duration of peace treaties have violated the Qur'an and Sunna of the Prophet. Both the Qur'an and Sunna, Ibn Taymiyya argues, have not required any time limit, and, in fact, the Prophet entered into several perpetual peace treaties with non-Muslims.[74] Effectively, Ibn Taymiyya not only ends up negating an old normative principle, but also constructs a new normative principle that accepts a permanent state of peace.

There are remarkable similarities in the discursive practice of the classical jurists on fighting Muslims and non-Muslims. This intersection in itself indicates the emergence of certain moral absolutist trends in the juristic culture. Muslim jurists look to issues of moral culpability or guilt in articulating the appropriate rules of conduct that should be afforded to Muslim or non-Muslim combatants. But the assessment of guilt works in favor of Muslim combatants who rely on an interpretation or cause. Muslims who espouse unacceptable causes (such as tribalism), or non-Muslims who refuse to adopt Islam are considered morally culpable, and this, in turn, affects their treatment. Nevertheless, despite the consideration given to issues of guilt, Muslim jurists have not focused on a *jus ad bellum* style of inquiry. They seem to have adopted a functional approach, attempting to influence the conduct of war rather than the commencement of war. In this

Muslim jurists negotiate, through a complex dynamic, between primary rules, which do not seem to yield to the demands of *siyāsa,* and secondary rules, which are balanced against the demands and interests of *siyāsa*. The primary rules are moral in nature; they are fundamental and basic and tend to override any other practical consideration. They affirm a principle that is seen as necessary and foundational. The secondary rules are functional. They take into account pragmatic considerations. Secondary rules are articulated because of, and not despite, their consequences. The secondary rules could exist in tension with the primary rules, but, at least in theory, they do not override them. In other words, the secondary rules are not supposed to negate the basic principles. But as we will see later, the secondary rules might lead to the modification and reconstruction of the primary rules.

Culpability, Moral Constraints and Fighting Non-Muslims

Muslim jurists approach the issue of fighting non-Muslims within the same basic paradigm and framework of inquiry. As with rules on fighting the bughāh, Muslim jurists do not focus on considerations related to *jus ad bellum* or the justness of waging war against non-Muslims.[35] Rather, the overwhelming majority of their attention is focused on *jus in bello* or rules related to the conduct of war. There is no doubt that Muslim jurists do equate between just war and jihad, or religious war.[36] However, their discussions on the appropriateness or lawfulness of fighting non-Muslims are remarkably short and formalistic. For instance, Ibn Rushd (d. 1198) asserts that all polytheists could be fought, but he excepts the Turks and Ethiopians.[37] It is not permissible to attack either of these groups. Other than citing a hadith attributed to the Prophet in support of his assertion, he does not elaborate on the logic behind this exception. In essence, Ibn Rushd, like other Muslim jurists, assumes that the material interests of Islam should be served, and that Muslims should not be placed into a subservient or compromising position. But Muslim jurists concede a considerable amount of discretion to the ruler over issues involving interactions with foreign powers. Therefore, their discourses reveal a great amount of deference to the ruler as to when a ruler may or may not enter into a peace treaty or wage war against non-Muslims.[38] This could be a result of a tacit recognition of the political realities of the age—ultimately a ruler will do what a ruler deems fit. More importantly, however, Muslim jurists seem to purposely and methodically grant those in power substantial leeway in protecting Muslim territory and promoting Islam. Similar to the approach concerning the issue of fighting Muslims, classical Muslim jurists do not concede to rulers the same type of unfettered discretion when it comes to articulating the proper limits for conducting war against non-Muslims.

Despite the fact that Muslim jurists focus on the conduct of war rather than on the legality of war, they impute a degree of moral culpability to non-Muslims being fought. Muslim jurists insist that unbelievers must be offered a chance to adopt Islam before they are fought. If the unbelievers refuse to adopt Islam, they are to be offered an opportunity to recognize Islamic sovereignty and supremacy by paying a tribute (*jizya*) to Muslims.[39] It is not clear whether the payment of a tribute protects unbelievers from molestation due to a functional necessity or because, by recognizing Muslim supremacy, they have somehow mitigated their moral culpability. Nonetheless, it is rather clear that if the unbelievers refuse to adopt Islam or pay the tribute, they are considered to have committed a kind of moral infraction that compromises their entitlement to be free from harm. If the unbelievers are offered a fair opportunity to adopt Islam, and they refuse to do so, they have not committed an error in judgment similar to an erroneous *ijtihād;* rather, they have wrongfully and inexcusably rejected the truth, and waived away some of their rights. Certain categories of thought, such as tribalism, apostasy, and disbelief, are not excused, and the culpability of those who adopt these categories of thought compromises their right to safety. But, as we have seen, disagreements that are considered similar to *ijtihād,* or honest and excusable disagreements, are a privilege granted to Muslims, and perhaps *ahl al-dhimma,* but not the unbelievers.[40] Importantly, however, the moral infraction committed by the rejection of Islam does not, in itself, justify the killing of all unbelievers. Nor does the rejection of Islam deprive unbelievers of all rights.

Nevertheless, many Muslim jurists argue that if non-Muslims refuse to accept Islam or pay the jizya, the male unbelievers may be killed. This, of course, implies that the guilt of refusing to adopt Islam deprives a non-Muslim of the right to life, and therefore, such a person deserves whatever harm may come to him. In fact, according to some Muslim jurists, the moral guilt incurred when one fails to adopt Islam justifies their execution. However, this is not the majority view in Islam. For instance, al-Sarakhsi (d. 1090–1) argues that the failure to adopt Islam is a serious crime (*al-kufr min aʿẓam al-jināyāt*), but this is not why non-Muslims are killed. Disbelief, al-Sarakhsi argues, is a matter that is between a person and his or her God (*al-kufr bayn al-ʿabd wa-rabbihi*). Non-Muslims, however, he argues, are killed in order to avert the danger that they pose to Muslims (*li-dafʿi sharrihim*).[41] Ibn Rushd explains that there is disagreement among Muslim jurists on this issue because Muslim jurists disagree on the legal cause (*ʿilla*) for killing unbelievers. Ibn Rushd states:

> The source of their disagreement on the matter is that they [the jurists] disagree on the legal cause (*ʿilla*) for killing the unbelievers. The jurists, who claimed that the legal cause for killing the unbelievers is their disbelief, do not exempt [from killing] any of the unbelievers. Those who claim that the legal cause is the capacity [of the unbelievers] to fight . . . exempt from killing those who are unable to fight or who are usually not inclined to fight such as peasants and serfs.[42]

Ibn Taymiyya (d. 1327–8) presents a somewhat different emphasis on the same theme. He asserts:

> Since the basis for permissible fighting is *jihād* which strives to uphold religion, and make the word of God supreme, whoever obstructs [these purposes] must be fought. Those who normally do not fight or obstruct such as women, children, the hermit, the elderly, the blind, the crippled and anyone of a similar status, according to the majority of jurists, may not be killed unless they fight [Muslims] by word or act. Nonetheless, some have argued that the status of unbelief, in itself, merits execution, but they exempted women and children because they may be useful for Muslims. The first opinion, however, is more correct because we fight those who fight us when we seek to spread the word of God.[43]

As is clear from these passages, there were competing trends within Islam that battled for acceptance. The first trend believed that the failure to adopt Islam is a sufficient cause for execution. Women, children and others are not killed only because they are of potential use for Muslims. The second trend considered unbelief to be a grave crime, but it is not sufficient cause for execution. After the fourth/tenth century, it is clear that the second trend becomes the prevailing and predominant view. Among the important competing trends, not represented in the above quotations, is a school of thought that argued that under no circumstances could a prisoner be executed. In fact, the proponents of this view argued that there is a consensus among the companions of the Prophet on this point, and that the only options open to the ruler are pardon or ransom. This rule applied whether the prisoners were men, women, or any other category.[44] One can only speculate as to why this particular trend did not become predominant in Islam. In all likelihood, however, this view from a functional perspective was problematic because it was largely inconsistent with the war practices of the age.[45] As noted earlier, the majority of Muslim jurists has tended to gravitate towards a functional approach when it came to issues relating to the conduct of war.

The majority of Muslim jurists emphasize that the ruler may pardon, enslave, ransom, or execute male prisoners of war in accordance with the interests of Muslims. Therefore, the ruler must choose the option that best serves the welfare of Islam and Muslims.[46] The majority of the jurists also emphasize that even with regards to property there must be a defensible reason or cause for any destruction that takes place. Hence, if one destroys even a bird without cause, such a person is liable before God.[47] The ruler is granted discretion over the execution of male prisoners of a fighting age because of the risk that such males pose to Muslims. Arguably, people who are capable of fighting pose a continuing threat to Muslims, and the ruler is entrusted to evaluate that risk and act on it.[48] Importantly, this largely functional logic is somewhat mitigated by certain priorities. Therefore, for instance, if the execution of the able-bodied men will lead to the execution of Muslim prisoners held by the enemy, then execution is, at a minimum, reprehensible. If the enemy offers to exchange prisoners with Muslims, the ruler is duty-bound to accept the exchange, and not to do anything that would endanger the well-being of Muslims held by the enemy. In these circumstances, the discretion of the ruler is limited by the priority of liberating Muslim prisoners from captivity. However, if an unbelieving prisoner of war converts to Islam, then under no circumstances may such a person be exchanged or returned to the enemy.[49] The interests of one Muslim may not be sacrificed for the sake of another.

Many classical discourses do not focus on abstract notions of fairness or justice in dealing with non-Muslims. The classical discourses do, however, balance the rights of Muslims against the discretionary leverage given to the ruler in promoting the interests of Muslims. Often the question is one of how much discretion the ruler should be given rather than what the demands of justice and fairness are in dealing with non-Muslims. Therefore, often the balance to be struck is between the rights of Muslims and the interests of Muslims rather than the rights of non-Muslims and the interests of Muslims. The existence of this tendency in the classical discourses has prompted some contemporary commentators to conclude that the Muslim juristic discourses are overwhelmingly functional in nature. These commentators argue that the rules placing limits on the way non-Muslims may be treated are not induced by notions of justice, but by a desire to preserve the potential value that may accrue to Muslims. By not killing women, children, or peasants or needlessly destroying crops and vegetation, Muslim jurists were protecting the rights of Muslims to profit from these resources. In the words of James Johnson, "The reason given in the text is not that these [people] have rights of their own to be spared harm, rights derived either from nature or from considerations of fairness or justice, but rather, that they are potentially of value to the Muslims."[50] This, however, grossly overstates the case.

It is true that classical juridical sources, particularly from the Hanafi school, emphasize the proprietary rights that Muslims have in the spoils of war, including women and children. For instance, some Hanafi jurists have argued that once the ruler makes the decision to enslave war captives, the proprietary rights of Muslims become vested. Therefore, if a non-Muslim prisoner of war converts to Islam after the proprietary right has vested, he will still be enslaved despite his conversion to Islam.[51] But this does not mean that the classical discourses are devoid of moral insights or even that the overwhelming attention of the jurists was focused on issues of value. Rather, as in the case of the bughāh, Muslim jurists have negotiated and balanced issues of value and interest within certain moral parameters. As Johnson himself recognizes, certain rules adopted by the classical jurists seem to be "pure" acts "of moderation outside considerations of benefit."[52] As noted above, Muslim jurists assert that women, children, the elderly, the blind or crippled, the insane, hermits, and, according to some jurists, peasants, craftsmen, and serfs may not be executed unless they take an active part in the fighting. Contrary to what John Kelsay and Johnson argue, this is not due to the fact that such categories of individuals are presumed to be of diminished capacity, and thus, less guilty in failing to adopt Islam.[53] Rather, Muslim jurists argue that such individuals usually do not fight and, hence, there is no justification for killing them.[54] In fact, Muslim jurists claim that the Prophet expressly stated that women should not be killed because, normally, they do not fight. In other words, the operative cause (*ʿilla*) for not killing women is that they are presumed not to be a danger.[55] Some sources add that peasants, craftsmen, and hermits typically are preoccupied with work or worship, and thus pose no danger. Therefore these individuals should be left unmolested.[56] The presumption seems to be in favor of the inviolability of such individuals unless there is an actual threat. Importantly, in terms of a value analysis, the insane, crippled or hermit are presumed to be of no value for the purposes of enslavement. Nevertheless, that does not affect their protected status. Furthermore, Muslim jurists often express wariness about the ideological risk posed by hermits and clergymen.[57] Nevertheless, Muslim jurists argue that hermits may not be killed or enslaved, and, in the opinion of certain schools, enough property and money should be left for their sustenance.[58]

Furthermore, Muslim jurists assert that those who may not be executed must be set free if the Muslim army is unable to transport them back to the territory of Islam. In other words, having captured, for example, women, children, and elderly individuals, if it is not possible to take them to Muslim territory where they may be enslaved, ransomed or set free, the Muslim army is obligated to release them.[59] Vindictive or precautionary execution is not permitted. Here, direct material value or benefit is missing; yet that does not relieve Muslims of their moral obligations. In fact, a purely interest-based analysis would suggest that women and children, in this context, should be killed. If released, they may still provide substantial aid to non-Muslims. Nevertheless, Muslim jurists do not believe that such an indirect risk, or the absence of material benefit to Muslims, justifies the elimination of these individuals. Additionally, one of the rather interesting laws in Muslim discourses is that the same individuals who may not be killed do not have to pay the jizya. This, of course, is applicable only if the non-Muslims in question had accepted paying a tribute rather than war. However, the correlation between the protected categories and the obligation of jizya is fascinating. Al-Marghinani (d. 1196–7) explains this rule by stating: "This is because the jizya is demanded as a substitute to killing. Therefore, it [the jizya] is not obligatory upon those who may not be killed."[60] This seems to indicate that the prohibition against the killing of certain categories of individuals is a broad and principled imperative.[61]

Muslim jurists frequently assert other broad moral injunctions in the context of conducting warfare against non-Muslims. Torture, mutilation, and treachery are strictly prohibited. Pursuant to the prohibition against treachery, if male or female fighters are promised safety in return for a surrender, these terms must be complied with, and the prisoners may not be executed.[62] This creates a moral obligation higher than the value inherent in the discretion granted to the ruler over the treatment of prisoners. This also implicitly recognizes the legality of negotiating a treaty guaranteeing the safety of prisoners of war. The prohibition against torture or mutilation is somewhat vague, except that Muslim jurists argue that the beating or starving of prisoners is impermissible.[63] It is not clear if the prohibition against torture or mutilation may be weighed against other interests. However, as we saw earlier, Muslim jurists prohibit the use of torture or mutilation against Muslims as well as non-Muslims. For reasons that are not yet clear, Muslim jurists seem to have developed an ideological and principled aversion to the use of torture or mutilation.[64] For example, Muslim jurists prohibit severing heads, and displaying or transporting them back to Muslim territory.[65] Furthermore, as noted above, there are certain values that seem to have competed for acceptance in the juridical culture of Islam.[66] Often these values are articulated in the context of certain discourses, but it is not clear to what extent these moral ideas had gained acceptance in the juristic culture. For instance, some jurists argue that weapons of mass destruction such as fire, flooding, or mangonels may not be used unless for dire necessity or in self-defense. Other jurists express a distinct distaste for the use of fire, in particular. According to this view, fire is particularly brutal, and therefore, unacceptable.[67] Regardless of whether a particular point of view had gained wide acceptance or not, the textual evidence suggests that certain moral trends had emerged and struggled for acceptance in the Islamic context. We have already alluded to the fact that interaction between moral and functional considerations often leads to the modifications and reconstruction of doctrine. This in turn leads to a process in which moral or functional considerations struggle for acceptance. Pragmatic considerations or experiences might challenge a moral stand, and either lead to the reformation of the moral principle or to the emergence of a functionalist perspective. In other words, although one might start off with a near-absolute principled position, various challenges could lead to either the emergence of a new moral rule or to the emphasizing of functionalist tendencies. For instance, one of the early reports attributed to the Prophet states that the Prophet commanded his troops "not to kill women, children, or the elderly, not to cut down ripe trees, burn buildings, or kill cattle or sheep except to eat." The Prophet also said, "Do not burn palm trees and do not flood vegetation. Do not pillage or betray."[68] This early report conveys the sense that the mentioned prohibitions are moral imperatives. In fact, the report seems to play a corrective role; it educates as to the basic morality that must guide a Muslim at war. Consequently, many jurists hold that livestock, cattle, or any other being may not be killed even if the purpose of the killing is to weaken or frustrate the enemy. Furthermore, even if Muslims will not be able to take possession of the animals, destroying the animals is not permissible. In fact, the Hanbali jurist Ibn Qudama asserts that the intentional destruction of any creature not involved in combat is a form of corruption on the earth.[69] Yet, other jurists disagree and argue that the above-mentioned report must be interpreted to mean that it is permissible only if it will weaken the enemy or only if there is no realistic hope that Muslims will be able to take possession of the animals. The tone of the discussion conveys the sense that these jurists considered the moral imperative specified in the report above to be unrealistic or unworkable. Interestingly, however, some jurists tried to strike a balance between the principle and pragmatic interests by arguing that if the animal in question is of the type that might someday migrate to the lands of Islam, then killing such an animal is not permissible. Therefore, for example, it is not permissible to kill bees or pigeons because someday they might migrate to Muslim territory.[70] This logic is obviously strained. It is not very realistic to expect that any haphazard swarm of bees might eventually find their way to Muslim territory. But perhaps this logic indicates a shift back from functional considerations to a moral principle. Nevertheless, the context, Muslim jurists have balanced practical interests against various imperatives. Importantly, however, one clearly discerns various trends and attempts to create moral absolutist parameters within which the balancing and negotiative process may take place. One suspects that the various moral trends correlated with specific socio-historical contexts as Muslim jurists continued to creatively negotiate their realities. Importantly, Muslim juristic discourses were neither purely functional nor moral. Even more, they were far from dogmatic or essentialist in nature.

In order to better understand the processes and nature of the juristic discourses, it is important to study the details of the juristic linguistic practice within various historical contexts. By linguistic practice, I mean the details and particulars of juristic expression as it relates to the prevailing precedents in a certain legal culture, sociopolitical practices of society at large, and the normative demands placed upon and made by the jurists. If one focuses on the detailed modes of expression of the juristic debates, one can start to understand the negotiative and balancing processes engaged in by the legal system. I do not pretend to present here a thorough or even an adequate review of the linguistic practice of Muslim jurists on the rule of killing at war. Nonetheless, it is clear that essentialist positions on the nature of Islamic international law are without foundation. Muslim jurists have not focused only on promoting the interests of Muslims during the conduct of war. While it is fair to assume that Muslim jurists consider the welfare of Muslims to be the ultimate good, this does not necessarily mean that such a good can be pursued without normative constraints. Muslim jurists attempt to balance between moral imperatives and functional concerns even if this means that the material good of Muslims is not always given first order priority. The fact that under certain extreme circumstances, the material welfare of Muslims might ascend to the status of a first-order priority and might sacrifice particular moral constraints, does not mean that Muslim jurists were not interested in moral standards. It only means that for Muslim jurists, negotiating morality has also meant bargaining with reality. Every moral constraint, like every generalization, could founder on some very hard facts. It has not been my goal here to delineate the exact boundaries that separate the moral from the functional in Muslim juristic discourses, but rather to challenge the simplistic generalizations about Islamic law and its treatments on war. In order to understand the exact nature of the negotiative process, and the balance struck between functionality and morality, more scholars need to turn their attention to the particulars of the juristic linguistic practice.

Notes

I would like to thank my assistant, Anver Emon, for his invaluable help, and as always, to express my gratitude to Grace, my wife. I am especially indebted to Professor Hossein Modarressi of Princeton University for his invaluable insights and inspiration.

1. Several works address the challenges that war or political questions pose to legal systems. See Geoffrey Best, *War and Law Since 1945* (Oxford: Oxford University Press, 1994); Ron Christenson, *Political Trials: Gordian Knots in the Law,* 2d ed. (New Brunswick, N.J.: Transaction Publishers, 1999; Otto Kirchheimer, *Political Justice: The Use of Legal Procedure for Political Ends.* Princeton: Princeton University Press, 1961); Arthur J. Sabin, *In Calmer Times: The Supreme Court and Red Monday* (Philadelphia: University of Pennsylvania Press, 1999); Michael J. Glennon, *Constitutional Diplomacy* (Princeton, N.J.: Princeton University Press, 1990).

2. Abū Isḥāq al-Firūzabādhī al-Shīrāzī, *al-Muhadhdhab fī fiqh al-Imām al-Shāfiʿī* (Cairo: Maṭbaʿat Muṣṭafā al-Bābī al-Ḥalabī, 1976), 2:291. In the course of writing this essay, I unfortunately had to rely on two different editions of *al-Muhadhdhab.* The second version is al-Shīrāzī, *al-Muhadhdhab* (Beirut: Dār al-Kutub al-ʿIlmiyya, 1995). To distinguish between the two editions in the citations below, I will include the date of publication in parentheses.

3. This essay does not pretend to present a philosophical discourse on functionalism. Functionalism is a specific philosophical doctrine and is not what is intended here. Functionalism, as a theory, looks to latent or manifest roles of social practices: for instance, the fact that a ceremony to ward off evil spirits does not in fact ward off evil spirits is irrelevant. Functionalist theory will look at the other possible functions this ceremony serves. From that perspective it is possible for one to argue that any moral rule will, in fact, serve a latent function or utility. In this essay, however, I address tendencies or inclinations. For my purposes, if a jurist asserts that a rule is articulated as a matter of principle, and that it is an absolute imperative regardless of the ultimate benefits or harms that might accrue, we can assert that this rule exhibits a moral tendency even if there is a latent social benefit to be obtained from the rule. On the other hand, if the rule is articulated with a view to the material benefit that will accrue from it, we can assert that this rule exhibits a functional tendency. My point is simply that both tendencies can be observed in Islamic legal discourses.

4. A recent example of this type of work is Paul Fergosi, *Jihad in the West: Muslim Conquest from the Seventh to the Twenty-first Centuries* (Amherst, Mass.: Prometheus Books, 1998).

5. For example, jurists might assert that as a matter of principle non-Muslims must be invited to Islam and warned before being fought. In this context, it could be argued that, as a matter of principle, everyone must have a fair opportunity to become Muslim before combat is commenced. However, later on, it is possible for the rule to become modified by asserting that non-Muslims should be invited to Islam only if there is a realistic chance that they will respond favorably, and if there is no realistic chance then non-Muslims could be surprised and attacked without warning.

6. Majid Khadduri, *War and Peace in the Law of Islam* (New York: AMS Press, 1979).

7. For instance, if we argue that a bandit who repents before being captured must be pardoned, this argument might be motivated by an assessment of moral culpability, but, functionally speaking, it could have dire social and political implications.

8. A deontological view of morality focuses on absolute moral constraints in discerning what is right. Furthermore, a deontological view does not interpret the right as that which maximizes the good; rather, a moral constraint is considered right regardless of the utilitarian consequences to which it might lead. By contrast, a teleological view tends to look to the consequences of acts in order to ascertain what is good and also right. Some theorists have argued that in a deontological view, right is prior to good, and in a teleological view, good is prior to right. Typically, utilitarian and consequentialist theories of ethics are described as teleological.

On this debate, with its numerous permutations, see Geoffrey Thomas, *An Introduction to Ethics: Five Central Problems of Moral Judgment* (London: Gerald Duckworth & Co., 1993), 179–99; Thomas Nagel, *The View from Nowhere* (Oxford: Oxford University Press, 1986), 164–88; Susan Wolf, "Moral Saints," in *Ethics,* ed. Peter Singer (Oxford: Oxford University Press, 1994), 345–61; R. M. Hare, "Ontology in Ethics," in *Essays in Ethical Theory* (Oxford: Clarendon Press, 1989), 82–98.

9. A few studies deal with ethics and Islamic theology. See A. Kevin Reinhart, *Before Revelation: The Boundaries of Muslim Moral Thought* (Albany: State University of New York Press, 1995); Oliver Leaman, *An Introduction to Medieval Islamic Philosophy* (Cambridge: Cambridge University Press, 1985), 123–65; George F. Hourani, *Reason and Tradition in Islamic Ethics* (Cambridge: Cambridge University Press, 1985), 15–66.

10. Debates on the ontology of ethics are exceedingly complex and largely inaccessible to nonspecialists. To engage these debates adequately is bound to drown this essay in a sea of subtle distinctions that will distract the reader away from the main point of this chapter.

11. For instance, a case where telling the truth would result in the loss of millions of lives. See A. Donagan, *The Theory of Morality* (Chicago: University of Chicago Press, 1977), 206–7; Charles Fried, *Right and Wrong* (Cambridge: Harvard University Press, 1978), 10.

12. For instance, it does not seem possible to commit to the maximization of utility without a deontological belief in the duty of the good.

13. By institution, I mean the existence of organized means by which to meet social needs or purposes. For a discussion on this issue, see Marcus G. Singer, "Institutional Ethics," in *Ethics,* ed. A. Phillips Griffiths (Cambridge: Cambridge University Press, 1993), 223–45.

14. For example, that to allow an individual the autonomy of deciding whether to lie to a court would result in the crumbling of the legal system.

15. See Khaled Abou El Fadl, "The Common and Islamic Law of Duress," *Arab Law Quarterly* 2 (1991): 121–59.

16. Jurists who made this argument assumed that rape is not possible without a degree of desire. Therefore, due to evidentiary considerations, rape is never justified.

17. I must confess that it is difficult for me to understand how a normative constraint that is predicated on simple self-interest could be moral at all. Furthermore, I admit that I tend to see functional approaches to morality as opportunistic and as hopelessly ambiguous. Nevertheless, this is the not the issue dealt with here.

18. Manṣūr al-Buhūtī, *Kashshāf al-qināʿ*, ed. Hilāl Muṣṭafā Hilāl (Beirut: Dār al-Fikr, 1982), 5:108; Abū Muḥammad b. Muḥammad Ibn Qudāma, *al-Mughnī* (Beirut: Dār al-Kutub al-ʿIlmiyya, n.d.), 10:515–16; al-Shīrāzī, *al-Muhadhdhab* (1976), 2:338; Abū Zakariyyā al-Nawawī, *al-Majmūʿ sharḥ al-Muhadhdhab* (Beirut: Dār al-Fikr, n.d.), 19:453; Abū al-Qāsim al-Muḥaqqiq al-Ḥillī, *Sharāʾiʿ al-Islām fī masāʾil al-ḥalāl wa al-ḥarām* (Beirut: Dār al-Aḍwā', 1983), 1:308; Fakhr al-Muḥaqqiqīn al-Ḥillī, *Īḍāḥ al-Fawāʾid* (Qum: Mu'assasat Ismāʿīliyyān, 1387 A.H.), 1:352; ʿAbd al-ʿAzīz b. al-Barrāj al-Ṭarabulsī, *al-Muhadhdhab* (Tehran: Mu'assasat al-Nashr al-Islāmī, 1406 A.H.), 1:311.

19. Of course, one can claim that this rule is consequentialist because Muslim jurists expected reciprocity. However, Muslim jurists argued that the obligation is not affected by whether non-Muslims afford Muslims reciprocity or not.

20. A proper theory of ethics would be able to articulate the proper conditions under which moral constraints ought to be asserted or compromised, but this is not the focus of this chapter.

21. Abū al-Ḥasan al-Māwardī, *al-Aḥkām al-sulṭāniyya wa-l-wilāyāt al-dīniyya* (Beirut: Dār al-Kutub al-ʿIlmiyya, 1985), 75–77; Muḥammad b. Ḥusayn al-Farra Abū Yaʿlā, *al-Aḥkām al-sulṭāniyya* (Beirut: Dār al-Kutub al-ʿIlmiyya, 1983), 55–56; Shihāb al-Dīn b. Idrīs al-Qarāfī, *al-Dhakhīra* (Beirut: Dār al-Gharb al-Islāmī, 1994), 12:9.

22. See Joel L. Kraemer, "Apostates, Rebels, and Brigands," *Israel Oriental Studies* 10 (1980): 34–73; Khaled Abou El Fadl, "*'Aḥkām al-Bughāt:* Irregular Warfare and the Law of Rebellion in Islam," in *Cross, Crescent, and Sword: The Justification and Limitation of War in Western and Islamic Tradition,* eds. James Turner Johnson and John Kelsay (Westport, Conn.: Greenwood Press, 1990), 149–76.

23. See Abou El Fadl, "*'Aḥkām al-Bughāt,*" 157–60.

24. Aḥmad b. Muḥammad al-Sāwī, *Bulghat al-sālik* (Cairo: Muṣṭafā al-Bābī, 1954), 2:414–15; Abū Zakariyyā Yaḥyā Ibn Sharaf al-Nawawī, *Rawḍat al-ṭālibīn,* ed. ʿĀdil Aḥmad ʿAbd al-Mawjūd and ʿAlī Muḥammad Maʿriḍ (Beirut: Dār al-Kutub al-ʿIlmiyya, 1992), 7:270–71; Aḥmad Shihāb al-Dīn Ibn Ḥajar al-Haytamī, *Fatḥ al-jawād sharḥ al-Irshād* (Cairo: Muṣṭafā al-Bābī, 1971), 2:294; Muḥammad al-Shirbīnī al-Khaṭīb, *Mughnī al-muḥtāj* (Cairo: Muṣṭafā al-Bābī, 1958), 4:124–25; Abū Yaḥyā Zakariyyā al-Anṣārī, *Fatḥ al-wahhāb* (Cairo: Muṣṭafā al-Bābī, 1948), 153; Sharaf al-Dīn Ismāʿīl b. Abī Bakr Ibn al-Muqrī, *Kitāb al-tamshiyya bi-sharḥ Irshād al-ghāwī fī masālik al-ḥāwī* (Cairo: Dār al-Hudā, n.d.), 3:371; al-Muqrī, *Ikhlāṣ al-nāwī,* ed. ʿAbd al-ʿAzīz ʿAṭīya Zalāṭ (Cairo: Lajnat Iḥyāʿ al-Turāth al-Islāmī, 1989), 4:127. Sulaymān al-Jamāl adds that what the rebels destroy during

the course of their rebellion cannot be described as allowed or not allowed. It is merely a mistake that should be forgiven (*Hāshiyat al-Jamāl* [Beirut: Dar Iḥyā' al-Turāth al-'Arabī, n.d.], 5:113, 116). Kamāl al-Dīn Muḥammad Ibn al-Humām, *Sharh fatḥ al-qadīr,* ed. 'Abd al-Razzāq Ghālib (Beirut: Dār al-Kutub al-'Ilmiyya, 1995), 6:97; Muḥammad b. 'Umar al-Dimashqī Ibn 'Ābidīn, *Ḥāshiyat radd al-muḥtār,* ed. 'Ādil Aḥmad Mu'awwad (Beirut: Dār al-Kutub al-'Ilmiyya, 1994), 6:416; Shams al-Dīn Muḥammad b. Aḥmad al-Anṣārī al-Ramlī, *Fatāwā al-Ramlī* (printed in the margin of Ibn Ḥajar's *al-Fatāwā al-kubrā al-fiqhiyya*) (Beirut: Dār al-Kutub al-'Ilmiyya, 1983), 4:19; al-Ramlī, *Ghāyat al-bayān* (Cairo: Muṣṭafā al-Bābī, n.d.), 405; al-Ramlī, *Nihāyat al-muḥtāj ilā sharḥ al-Minhāj* (Cairo: Muṣṭafā al-Bābī, 1968), 7:402, 403–4.

25. Ibn Qudāma, *al-Mughnī,* 10:67, 70; Abū 'Abd Allāh Muḥammad Ibn Qayyim al-Jawziyya, *Aḥkām ahl al-dhimma,* ed. Ṣubḥī Ṣāliḥ (Beirut: Dār al-'Ilm li-l-Malāyīn, 1983), 2:469–70.

26. For instance, see al-Ramlī, *Nihāyat,* 7:402.

27. For instance, see Taqī al-Dīn Ibn Taymiyya, *Minhāj al-sunna al-nabawiyya* (Beirut: al-Maktaba al-'Ilmiyya, n.d.), 2:243–46. Additionally, there is a vast literature that cautions against becoming involved in *fitan.* For instance, see Abū 'Abd Allāh Nu'aym b. Ḥammād, *Kitāb al-fitan,* ed. Suhayl Zakar (Beirut: Dār al-Fikr, 1993), 78–99, 103–9; Abū 'Abd Allāh al-Bukhārī, *Saḥīḥ al-Bukhārī* (Cairo: Dār Iḥyā' al-Turāth al-'Arabī, n.d.), 4:221–33; 'Abd Allāh Ibn Abī Shayba, *al-Muṣannaf fī al-aḥādīth wa-l-āthār,* ed. Sa'īd Muḥammad al-Laḥḥām (Beirut: Dār al-Fikr, 1989), 8:590–649.

28. Muḥammad Ibn Ibrāhīm al-Wazīr, *al-'Awāṣim wa-l-qawāṣim* (Beirut: Mu'assasat al-Risāla, 1992), 8:75, 165; Abū 'Abd Allāh Muḥammad Ibn Mufliḥ, *Kitāb al-furū'* (Beirut: 'Ālam al-Kutub, 1985), 6:160; al-Nawawī, *Sharḥ Saḥīḥ Muslim,* ed. Khalīl al-Mīṣ (Beirut: Dār al-Qalam, n.d.), 12:470–71; Shihāb al-Dīn Ibn Ḥajar al-'Asqalānī, *Fatḥ al-bārī bi-sharḥ al-Bukhārī* (Beirut: Dār al-Fikr, 1993), 14:498; Muḥammad Ibn Khalīfa al-'Ābī, *Sharḥ Saḥīḥ Muslim,* (Beirut: Dār al-Kutub al-'Ilmiyya, 1994), 6:529, 554, 563–65; Abū 'Abd Allāh Fakhr al-Dīn al-Rāzī, *al-Tafsīr al-kabīr* (Beirut: Dār al-Kutub al-'Ilmiyya, 1990), 28:109.

29. See James Turner Johnson, *Can Modern War Be Just?* (New Haven, Conn.: Yale University Press, 1984), 20–21.

30. Ibn Qudāma, *al-Mughnī,* 10:67, 70; Aḥmad b. Muḥammad Ibn Ḥajar al-Haytamī, *Tuḥfat al-muḥtāj bi-sharḥ al-Minhāj* (Beirut: Dār Ṣādir, 1972), 3:70; al-Ramlī, *Nihāyat,* 7:405; al-Shirbīnī, *Mughnī,* 4:126; Ibn Muqrī, *Ikhlāṣ,* 4:126.

31. Ibn Qudāma, *al-Mughnī,* 10:67, 70; Ibn Ḥajar al-Haytamī, *Tuḥfat,* 3:70; al-Ramlī, *Nihāyat,* 7:405; al-Shirbīnī, *Mughnī,* 4:126; Ibn Muqrī, *Ikhlāṣ,* 4:126. See Abou El Fadl, "'*Aḥkām al-Bughāt,*" 160.

32. See Abū al-Ḥasan al-Māwardī, *Kitāb qitāl ahl al-bāghy min al-Ḥāwī al-kabīr,* ed. Ibrāhīm b. 'Alī Ṣandaqī (Cairo: Maṭba'at al-Madanī, n.d.), 141, 166–67.

33. See Abū al-Ḥasan 'Alī b. 'Alī al-Mas'ūdī, *Murūj al-dhahab,* ed. Muḥammad 'Abd al-Ḥamīd (Cairo: Kitāb al-Taḥrīr, 1966), 1:609; Abū Muḥammad Aḥmad Ibn

Ā'tham, *al-Futūḥ* (Beirut: Dār al-Kutub al-'Ilmiyya, 1986), 2:281, 284. Abū al-Faraj 'Abd al-Raḥmān Ibn al-Jawzī reports that it was 'Ali who told his family to kill and burn Ibn Muljam (*al-Muntaẓam fī ta'rīkh al-umam*, ed. Muḥammad 'Abd al-Qādir 'Aṭā' and Muṣṭafā 'Abd al-Qādir 'Aṭā' [Beirut: Dār al-Kutub al-'Ilmiyya, 1992], 5:175). For conflicting reports on 'Ali's conduct, particularly in the Battle of Siffin, see Abū Bakr Aḥmad b. 'Alī al-Bayhaqī, *Ma'rifat al-sunan wa al-āthār*, ed. Sayyid Kaṣrāwī Ḥusayn (Beirut: Dār al-Kutub al-'Ilmiyya, 1991), 6:283.

34. See Fred Donner, "The Sources of Islamic Conceptions of War," in *Just War and Jihad: Historical and Theoretical Perspectives on War and Peace in Western and Islamic Traditions*, ed. John Kelsay and James Turner Johnson (Westport, Conn.: Greenwood Press, 1991).

35. See John Kelsay, *Islam and War* (Louisville, Ky.: John Knox Press, 1993), 36.

36. See Taqī al-Dīn Ibn Taymiyya, *al-Siyāsa al-shar'iyya fī iṣlāḥ al-rā'ī wa al-rā'iyya* (Beirut: Dār al-'Afāq, 1983), 102–6. Also see Mohammad Talaat al-Ghunaimi, *The Muslim Conception of International Law and the Western Approach* (The Hague: Martinus Nijhoff, 1968), 165–80; Khadduri, *War and Peace*, 59–66, 75–76; Rudolph Peters, *Jihad in Classical and Modern Islam* (Princeton, N.J.: Markus Wiener, 1996), 43–44. Although I use the expression religious war, I do so with much reservation. The idea of a holy war (*al-ḥarb al-muqaddasa*) does not exist in Islamic law. Furthermore, in Islamic law, there is no notion of a religious as opposed to a secular war. If a war is waged to defend Islam or Muslims, or to protect one's honor or property, it is a jihad. A jihad is a war that is consistent with the dictates of religion. Whether that means the war is religious is a different matter.

37. Abū al-Walīd Ibn Rushd, *Bidāyat al-mujtahid wa-nihāyat al-muqtaṣid* (Cairo: Dār al-Fikr, n.d.), 1:279.

38. As we will see below, some jurists argue that the ruler has discretion to enter into a peace treaty with non-Muslims for ten years or even longer.

39. Abū al-Ḥasan al-Marghinānī, *al-Hidāya sharḥ al-Bidāya* (Cairo: Muṣṭafā al-Bābī, n.d.), 2:136; al-Shīrāzī, *al-Muhadhdhab* (1995), 3:273; Saḥnūn b. Sa'īd, *al-Mudawwana al-kubrā* (Beirut: Dār al-Kutub al-'Ilmiyya, 1994), 1:496; Ibn Rushd, *Bidāya*, 1:282, 284.

40. See Muhammad Hamidullah, *Muslim Conduct of State*, 7th ed. (Lahore: Muhammad Ashraf, 1977), 186–87, on the treatment of *ahl al-dhimma* if they rebel against a Muslim ruler.

41. Muḥammad Aḥmad al-Sarakhsī, *Sharḥ kitāb al-Siyar al-kabīr* (Beirut: Dār al-Kutub al-'Ilmiyya, 1997), 4:186.

42. Ibn Rushd, *Bidāya*, 1:281.

43. Ibn Taymiyya, *al-Siyāsa*, 106.

44. See Ibn Rushd, *Bidāya*, 1:279.

45. See James Johnson, "Historical Roots and Sources of the Just War Tradition in Western Culture," in *Just War and Jihad*, ed. Kelsay and Johnson, 3–30.

46. See al-Shīrāzī, *al-Muhadhdhab* (1995), 3:281–82.

47. Ibid., 290–91.

48. See, for instance, al-Sarakhsī, *Sharḥ,* 3:125, 128, 200, 205; Saḥnūn, *al-Mudawwana,* 1:501.

49. Al-Sarakhsī, *Sharḥ,* 4:297–303.

50. James Turner Johnson, *The Holy War Idea in Western and Islamic Traditions* (University Park: Pennsylvania State University Press, 1997), 122.

51. Al-Sarakhsī, *Sharḥ,* 3:126, 5:368. This tendency is not exclusively Hanafi. For instance, some Shafi'is argued that the reason children and women are protected is because they are of potential use to Muslims. See the discussion in al-Shīrāzī, *al-Muhadhdhab* (1995), 3:282.

52. Johnson, *Holy War Idea,* 123.

53. Johnson, *Holy War Idea,* 119; Kelsay, *Islam and War,* 62–63.

54. Al-Marghinānī, *Hidāya,* 2:137; al-Sarakhsī, *Sharḥ,* 4:186–88, 196; al-Shīrāzī, *al-Muhadhdhab* (1995), 3:277–78.

55. Ibn Qudāma, *al-Mughnī,* 10:542.

56. For example, see al-Qarāfī, *al-Dhakhīra,* 3:399.

57. For instance, see al-Sarakhsī, who reports that some have argued that if hermits are socially active, and if they provide ideological support to the unbelievers, they may be killed (*Sharḥ,* 4:196–97).

58. Ibn Rushd, *Bidāya,* 1:279; Saḥnūn, *al-Mudawwana,* 1:499; al-Qarāfī, *al-Dhakhīra,* 3:399.

59. Al-Sarakhsī, *Sharḥ,* 4:198.

60. Al-Marghinānī, *Hidāya,* 2:159. See also Ibn Rushd, *Bidāya,* 1:295; al-Shīrāzī, *al-Muhadhdhab* (1995), 3:310.

61. See al-Marghinānī, *Hidāya,* 2:160–61.

62. See Ibn Rushd, *Bidāya,* 1:279–80.

63. Al-Sarakhsī, *Sharḥ,* 3:127; al-Shīrāzī, *al-Muhadhdhab* (1995), 3:282; al-Marghinānī, *Hidāya,* 2:137.

64. Muslim jurists often quote a tradition attributed to the Prophet in which the Prophet prohibits *mithla,* or the use of torture or mutilation. See al-Sarakhsī, *Sharḥ,* 3:127; al-Shīrāzī, *al-Muhadhdhab* (1995), 3:282.

65. Al-Qarāfī, *al-Dhakhīra,* 3:408.

66. For instance, Ibn Qudama, the Hanbali jurist, states that prisoners of war may not be executed with fire. He admits that the first Caliph Abu Bakr ordered his military commander Khalid b. al-Walid in the wars of apostasy to execute some prisoners by burning them. But Ibn Qudama intimates that this historical precedent has no legal value by commenting, "but today, I know of no disagreement [regarding the prohibition against execution by fire]" (Ibn Qudāma, *al-Mughnī,* 10:502). It is significant that although there is an admission that the historical record of authoritative individuals such as the first Caliph is mixed, the jurists still constructed a strict prohibition against the use of fire.

67. Ibn Rushd, *Bidāya,* 1:281–22. On the use of weapons of indiscriminate destruction see al-Marghinānī, *Hidāya,* 2:136–37; Saḥnūn, *al-Mudawwana,* 1:501; al-Shīrāzī, *al-Muhadhdhab* (1995), 3:278–79; Hamidullah, *Muslim Conduct,* 205–8.

68. This report is also attributed to Abu Bakr, the first Caliph (Ibn Qudāma, *al-Mughnī,* 10:507).

69. Ibn Qudāma, *al-Mughnī,* 10:506.

70. See, for the Prophet's report and the various positions, al-Qarāfī, *al-Dhakhīra,* 3:398, 409; al-Shīrāzī, *al-Muhadhdhab* (1976), 2:301. Some jurists asserted that bees have a special protected status (Ibn Qudāma, *al-Mughnī,* 10:506).

71. Khadduri, *War and Peace,* 219–20; al-Shīrāzī, *al-Muhadhdhab* (1976), 2:333.

72. See Hamidullah, *Muslim Conduct,* 265–66.

73. For example, al-Qarāfī, *al-Dhakhīra,* 3:449.

74. Abū al-'Abbās Taqī al-Dīn Aḥmad Ibn Taymiyya, *al-Fatāwā al-kubrā,* ed. Muḥammad 'Abd al-Qawī 'Aṭā' and Muṣṭafā 'Abd al-Qawī 'Aṭā' (Cairo: Dār al-Rayyān li-l-Turāth, 1988), 29:140–41.

Six

Saving and Taking Life in War

Three Modern Muslim Views

Sohail H. Hashmi

A curious inversion of focus is evident in modern Islamic discussions of war when compared with the medieval literature. Most medieval writers began with a consensus on the grounds for war (*jus ad bellum*), which held jihad to be both a war of defense as well as a war for the expansion of a *pax Islamica*. They focused in their writings much more on concerns of legitimate means in warfare (*jus in bello*). Modern writers, on the other hand, concentrate heavily on *jus ad bellum* while devoting very little attention to *jus in bello*. A number of explanations may account for this emphasis.

First, modern writers are generally so fixated upon reinterpreting the grounds for jihad in light of modern sensibilities on wars of religion that discussion of proper conduct in jihad becomes marginalized. Virtually all works produced during the past century are to some degree responses to western apprehensions of jihad.

Second, most Muslims would agree that international norms of behavior in wartime conform to Islamic injunctions on humane behavior toward the enemy.[1] Moreover, inasmuch as modern Muslim jurists have contributed to the evolution of international humanitarian law and Muslim states have acceded to the United Nations Charter, the Geneva Conventions, and related protocols, as well as other international agreements, one could argue both that Islamic values have contributed implicitly if not explicitly to the evolution of international humanitarian law, and that most Muslims hold incompatible features of the medieval Islamic theory to be obsolete.[2] Indeed, some Muslim writers have argued that the antecedents for the western just war tradition's concerns with proportionality and discrimination in war, which in turn contributed to the rise of humanitarian law, lie in Islamic conceptions of jihad.[3]

Third, free discussion by Muslim authors of such controversial subjects as the morality of torture, rape, terrorism, assassination, guerrilla insurgency, and weapons of mass destruction, or the punishment of violators of Islamic principles, is seriously limited by the repressive political atmosphere in which many work.

The paucity of Muslim discussion of *jus in bello* poses some serious problems for students of the Islamic ethics of saving and taking life in war, for it is within *jus in bello* that most of the moral concerns on this topic are raised. This chapter will focus on the works of three modern writers who have addressed both *jus ad bellum* and *jus in bello* issues. Abu al-Aʿla Mawdudi (d. 1979), the founder of the most important Islamic party in the Indian subcontinent, the Jamaʿat-i Islami, began *al-Jihād fī al-Islām* (Jihad in Islam) in 1926 as a series of articles in the Urdu-language newspaper *al-Jamʿīyat*.[4] The complete work was first published in 1930 to wide acclaim from Indian Muslim intellectuals.[5] Mawdudi would continue to address topics relating to jihad in his subsequent works, most notably in his voluminous Qur'anic commentary, *Tafhīm al-Qur'ān* (Understanding the Qur'an), published between 1950 and 1973.[6] Muhammad Hamidullah, professor of Islamic law and history at Osmania University in Hyderabad, India, and later at the Sorbonne, published *The Muslim Conduct of State* in 1941–42 as a series of articles in the journal *Islamic Culture*.[7] It was one of the earliest works on Islamic international law published in a western language and thus provided an introduction to the subject to many non-Muslim as well as Muslim students. Hamidullah continued to revise the text, publishing in 1977 the seventh edition.[8] Wahba al-Zuhayli, professor of Islamic jurisprudence at the University of Damascus, first published *Āthār al-ḥarb fī al-fiqh al-islāmī: Dirāsa muqārana* (The effects of war on Islamic jurisprudence: A comparative study) in 1963, with the third edition appearing in 1981.[9] In addition, al-Zuhayli published in 1981 a shorter work titled *al-ʿAlaqāt al-duwalīya fī al-Islām: Muqārana bi-l-qānūn al-duwalī al-ḥadīth* (International relations in Islam: A comparison with modern international law) that both summarizes some arguments in *Āthār al-ḥarb* and expands on other topics.[10]

These three authors have been selected not only because they are among the few modern writers who address comprehensively and systematically the whole theory of jihad, but also because they are among the few modern writers who evaluate critically the relevance of various aspects of the medieval theory to modern norms and circumstances. Because their works are pioneering and innovative, they have significantly influenced generations of students and are well known beyond their native cultural context. Mawdudi's work, for example, was summarized in Arabic and appeared alongside articles on jihad written by two leaders of the Muslim

Brotherhood, Hasan al-Banna' and Sayyid Qutb.[11] Mawdudi's influence is particularly apparent in the works of the latter.[12]

These three authors are also significant in that they represent the general direction of Islamic thinking on issues of war and peace. Despite differing cultural backgrounds, their works bear some remarkable similarities in both methodology and substance.

First, all three authors' works are primarily exegeses of authoritative texts. Hamidullah and al-Zuhayli, as specialists in sharia, feel compelled to address the medieval juristic literature on international relations (*siyar*), highlighting its continued relevance to modern Islamic discussions. For Mawdudi, the only authoritative texts are the Qur'an and hadith, and he only infrequently mentions the *siyar*, primarily to buttress his own views.[13] The point is, though, that all three writers, like the vast majority of their colleagues, assign no Islamic value to nearly thirteen hundred years of Muslim practice or legislation.[14] Moreover, the fact that twentieth-century writers feel compelled to engage the works of theorists who wrote in the eighth through the fourteenth centuries highlights the stagnation of Islamic theory over the subsequent five centuries. Nevertheless, Hamidullah, al-Zuhayli, and of course Mawdudi do not feel bound by the conclusions of the medieval jurists (*fuqahā'*). Each assumes the need for critical reevaluation of the medieval literature, and each performs, in effect, *ijtihād* by advancing opinions based on his own reading of the Qur'an and Sunna.[15]

Second, all three realize the necessity of addressing the prevailing international legal regime. Each writes with the awareness that many aspects of the medieval Islamic theory of world order are incompatible with modern international law. Moreover, each is aware that this international law originated among European states that long considered Muslim states as unworthy of full or even partial inclusion in international society. There is thus an unmistakable apologetic tone, present to varying degrees, underlying the comparisons that each author makes between Islamic law and international law.[16]

Third, all three arrive at remarkably similar conclusions on the ethics of killing and saving life in war. We will begin by briefly considering their views on *jus ad bellum*, the legitimate grounds for war, for the very first moral calculation that occurs in war is the justification of the loss of life that inevitably follows the beginning of war. But at the level of *jus ad bellum*, the morality of saving and taking life remains at a high level of abstraction. It is only when we move to *jus in bello*, the justification for killing or protecting human beings in the midst of battle, that the moral issues become sharply focused and acquire human dimensions. Thus we will concentrate here upon five of the most salient issues within *jus in bello*, issues discussed by all three of our authors: the definition of combatants and noncombatants, the tactics and weapons which may be used against the enemy, the giving of quarter in battle, the treatment of prisoners of war, and the suspension of normal restrictions on killing in cases of necessity.

The Justification for War

Medieval Muslim writers devoted remarkably little attention to the philosophical question, Why do human beings kill each other through war?[17] In the medieval juristic literature on jihad in particular, war is treated as a mundane, universal aspect of human existence, and as such, something that Islamic law must necessarily include within its purview. Sunni jurists distinguished wars against unbelievers from wars against other Muslims. Wars against unbelievers were further divided into defensive fighting to repulse enemy aggression against Islamic territory or Muslim populations, and the struggle to expand the territory in which Islamic law applied (*dār al-Islām*) by reducing the territory of the infidels (*dār al-ḥarb*). Both types of conflict justified killing, although in the second type (what we may call the expansionist jihad), killing of the enemy was permitted only as the final stage in a hierarchy of options to be offered the enemy: first, that they accept Islam; second, that they accept Islamic sovereignty and agree to *dhimmī* (protected) status; third and finally, if they refuse the other two options, they are to be given fair warning and fought.[18]

Conflicts against other Muslims were discussed in the context of the Islamic state suppressing rebels, fighting apostates, or combating highway robbers and pirates—all of which fell within the state's police power to suppress *fitna* (civil discord) and *fasād* (corruption in society). Although killing was certainly permitted in dealing with each of the above categories of enemies of the state, medieval jurists emphasized the preference to avoid such extreme measures if other means to rehabilitate the offenders could be found, particularly in the case of rebels. Even though rebellion aimed at overthrowing the regime in power or secession aimed at creating a separate state were both seriously limited in medieval theory, stricter rules of engagement pertained to fighting between the state and rebels or secessionists than those governing fighting with non-Muslims, as Khaled Abou El Fadl indicates in the previous chapter.[19]

The collapse of a unitary Islamic caliphate and the lapse of the expansionist jihad reduced the medieval juristic worldview to a historical abstraction quite early in Islamic history. European imperialism and the subsequent emergence of Muslim states organized according to the territorial state model raised even more obvious and profound problems for the medieval Islamic approach to world order. The reinterpretation of jihad has figured prominently in modern Muslim attempts to accommodate to the changed international realities.

Mustansir Mir divides modern Muslim interpreters of medieval conceptions of jihad into three broad categories: the apologists, centered mainly in British India, who seek to present jihad historically (confining themselves largely to the life of the Prophet) as well as theoretically (confining themselves largely to the Qur'an) as purely defensive war; the neoclassicists, who reinterpret the Qur'an and Sunna according to their own light and deduce new formulations regarding jihad; and the modernists, whose principal motivation is to reinterpret the Qur'an and Sunna in light of modern conditions and prevailing international norms.[20]

Mir's typology is useful at a very general level for distinguishing different approaches, motivations, and even substantive conclusions on the meaning of jihad in modern times. But very few writers fit neatly into one category or the other, even in large part. For example, Mir considers Mawdudi representative of the neoclassical position, for his goal is to infuse Muslims with a proper appreciation of jihad following the "false" interpretations rendered by earlier apologists. Yet, another of Mawdudi's stated motivations closely resembles that of the very apologists he decried, namely to refute the false assertions of orientalists that Islam was spread by the sword. On the other hand, his views on the justifications and aims of jihad are hardly distinguishable from those of many modernists.

One thing that unites apologists, neoclassicists, and modernists is the very modern need to justify the resort to war. Mawdudi opens *al-Jihād fī al-Islām* by asserting that "the first principle of the law upon which human society rests is that life is sacred."[21] No social intercourse is possible without this principle, and thus all societies require governments to protect life by maintaining order and punishing offenders. But the role of religion, he writes, is to impress upon people the intrinsic value of life, so that life will be honored and safeguarded even in the absence of government.[22]

In Islam, Mawdudi argues, the importance assigned to protecting life, and the enormity of taking innocent life, is indicated in numerous Qur'anic verses and Prophetic hadiths. Yet the prohibition on shedding blood is qualified by the Qur'anic injunction that reads: "Do not slay the soul sanctified by God, except for just cause" (6:151; 25:68). Mawdudi comments in *Tafhīm al-Qur'ān* that what is meant by "just cause" is

> three cases . . . embodied in the Qur'an whereas two additional cases have been stated by the Prophet (peace be upon him). The cases mentioned in the Qur'an are the following: (1) That a man is convicted of

> deliberate homicide and thus the claim of retaliation is established against him. (2) That someone resists the establishment of the true faith so that fighting against him might become necessary. (3) That someone is guilty of spreading disorder in the Domain of Islam and strives to overthrow the Islamic order of government. The two cases mentioned in the hadith are: (1) That a person commits illegitimate sexual intercourse even after marriage. (2) That a Muslim is guilty of apostasy and rebellion against the Muslim body-politic. Except for these five reasons, slaying a human being is not permissible, regardless of whether he is a believer, a protected non-Muslim (*dhimmī*) or an ordinary unbeliever.[23]

The duty to take life in cases where it is warranted, Mawdudi concludes in *al-Jihād fī al-Islām,* is as strong as the normal obligation to save life. For if anything is more precious than life, it is the upholding of truth and justice (*ḥaqq*), which makes life meaningful.[24] As individuals may justly defend themselves against attack, even to the point of killing the attacker, so may communities defend themselves against threats to social stability, even to the point of eliminating the threat.[25] Likewise, as societies consist of recalcitrant individuals who resist the laws of the community, so humankind as a whole consists of recalcitrant societies who resist divine laws and thereby promote oppression (*ẓulm*), rebellion (*fitna*), and corruption (*fasād*).[26] Given the presence of such oppressive and unjust rulers or communities, Muslims must be constantly prepared for war.

Hamidullah opens his discussion of Islamic conceptions of war by observing that Muslims "think of war only as unavoidable, not as desired or to be sought after." He consciously omits what he terms "any philosophical or historical discussion of war," but it is clear from the structure of his book, which begins with regulations on peaceful intercourse, that he considers war as the exception to the normal state of peace between Islamic and non-Islamic states.[27]

Like Mawdudi, al-Zuhayli begins his discussion with a lengthy consideration of the Islamic approach to war and peace. He acknowledges that war is a necessary aspect of human existence, one sanctioned by the Qur'an as a means of self-defense and preserving a just society. But, he argues, war is not something natural to human beings, as Ibn Khaldun proposes in the *Muqaddima.*[28] Rather, it is contrary to human nature, which inclines toward peace, for does not the Qur'an state that "War is prescribed for you, though it be hateful to you" (2:216)?[29]

Al-Zuhayli expands this point to the international level by positing that the Qur'anic vision holds peace to be the normal and universal state of human relations. The majority of medieval Muslim jurists who held the opposite view, he avers, arrived at their conclusion through strained interpretations of the Qur'an and Sunna. For example, in order to justify their conception of jihad as an ongoing war to incorporate *dār al-ḥarb* into *dār al-Islām,* the majority held some 124 Qur'anic verses to have been abrogated by a single verse, the "verse of the sword" (9:5). This was clearly a misapplication of the concept of abrogation, al-Zuhayli argues. For abrogation requires some conflict between verses, and such is not the case with regard to the Qur'anic revelation regarding war. All the verses on fighting were revealed in the context of those who had persecuted and attacked the Muslims before they were ordered to be fought.[30]

What then do Mawdudi, Hamidullah, and al-Zuhayli consider to be legitimate grounds for war? Here again all three authors are in general agreement, although their specific classifications vary.

Mawdudi continues his discussion by dividing legitimate wars into two types. The first is "defensive" war (*mudāfiʿāna jang*), which, he argues, is clearly enjoined by the Qur'an. But his reading of the Qur'an leads him to invoke the modern terminology of rights. Defensive war is justified in Islam, he writes, whenever hostile forces threaten the human rights (*insānī ḥuqūq*) of Muslims:

> The Judicious Qur'an enjoins patience and forebearance in all matters, but it does not enjoin tolerating any attempts to wipe out the Islamic faith or the imposition upon Muslims of any other political order. It has forcefully commanded that if anyone attempts to seize your human rights, commits oppression, expels you from legitimately occupied land, deprives you of your faith and conscience, attempts to thwart you from your religious life, disrupts your social life with the aim of forcing you away from Islam, then in response you should never show weakness and you should devote your utmost strength to repel this oppression.[31]

As he wrote this passage, Mawdudi was aware that prominent Muslim leaders, most notably the nineteenth-century reformer Sayyid Ahmad Khan, had declared that jihad was unnecessary against an enemy, such as the British, who may deprive Muslims of sovereignty but do not interfere with Muslim religious life.[32] Mawdudi responds by arguing that defensive war is necessary whenever any threat exists against the Islamic state or territories, not just when an enemy prevents the performance of religious duties. The threat may originate from within the Muslim body politic in the form of hypocrites, rebels, or ordinary criminals.[33] Moreover, if the Muslims of a particular area are unable to defend themselves successfully against external attack or persecution, then it is obligatory (*farḍ ʿayn*) for all Muslims in all lands to assist them.[34]

The second type of legitimate war, Mawdudi suggests, is what he terms "reformative" war (*muṣliḥāna jang*). This type of war derives, he believes, from Islam's two inseparable goals, the first being to "command the right" (*amr bi-l-maʿrūf*), that is, to invite people to accept the truth of Islam's "religious" message. This appeal can in no way be pursued through coercion, and Mawdudi expatiates at length on the falsehood of Muslim and non-Muslim claims to the contrary.

"Commanding the right" is linked, however, to "forbidding the wrong" (*nahy ʿan al-munkar*), and it is this goal—Islam's "moral/political" mission to establish a just social order—that is the basis for reformative war. The second mission can and most often must be pursued through coercive means because unjust and oppressive regimes are rarely overthrown except through forceful resistance.[35]

The moral duty to enforce God's laws in this world is established, Mawdudi argues, in the Prophet's interpretation of "commanding the right and forbidding the wrong." In the Meccan period of his mission, the Prophet's weakness in the face of his enemies prevented him from resisting oppression and injury by resort to arms. In this period, commanding the right and forbidding the wrong were synonymous in terms of the means employed: verbal suasion. But when in Medina the Prophet acquired the means to resist forcefully, he fought not only in response to persecution, but also to establish an Islamic order. In Medina, according to Mawdudi, "commanding the right" diverged from "forbidding the wrong." The former obligation remained one of peacefully preaching the Islamic faith, whereas the latter became one of "cleansing the entire world of strife and corruption [*fitna* and *fasād*], whether the world consented to it or not."[36]

Mawdudi acknowledges the historical linkage between war and the spread of Islam, at least in the initial expansion of the seventh and eighth centuries.[37] Yet his lengthy discussion is vague on the moral import for modern Muslims of this history. He suggests that Islam does not oppose independent national states.[38] But because he situates the ethical basis for the expansionist jihad in the Qur'anic injunction to forbid the wrong, we can only conclude that Mawdudi sees in theory no prospect of this jihad ending as long as human beings remain true to his rather bleak assessment of their nature. In reality, however, Mawdudi and the Jamaʿat-i Islami put the reformative jihad very much on hold while they concentrated almost exclusively on defensive jihad in places like Kashmir and Afghanistan.[39]

Hamidullah's discussion parallels much of Mawdudi's. He categorizes lawful wars into defensive, which may include preventive strikes;

sympathetic, by which he means intervention of the Islamic state on behalf of persecuted and oppressed Muslims living under non-Muslim jurisdiction; punitive, which includes wars against rebels, brigands, and apostates, or non-Muslims who have violated treaties; and idealistic, which is his term for expansionist jihad. Hamidullah emphasizes that this last type of war is permissible only when peaceful means of propagating Islam have been foreclosed by a foreign power. Idealistic war emerges in Hamidullah's account as a sort of *mission civilisatrice,* bringing Islam's higher principles of justice and equality to corrupt societies and thereby opening them up to the preaching of Islam, not to coercion of faith. This was the basis for the jihad waged by the Prophet and the rightly-guided caliphs, suggests Hamidullah, but it is unclear from his discussion what relevance he attaches to this type of war in modern times.[40]

Al-Zuhayli outlines three types of legitimate war: war against those who block the preaching of Islam, or against those who foment internal dissension and conflict; war in defense of persecuted individuals or communities (Al-Zuhayli compares this type of war to cases of legitimate intervention, especially humanitarian intervention, allowed under international law); and war to repel aggression against oneself and one's country.[41] Although he holds that these grounds for war are not incompatible with principles of international law allowing resort to arms to repel aggression or oppression, al-Zuhayli also acknowledges that the purposes of jihad may not be reduced to categories employed in international law. Jihad cannot be classified as either "defensive" or "aggressive" war if defense is understood as merely protection of one's national boundaries. Islam's call to defend the right and repel injustice and oppression cannot be limited to any geographic boundaries. Jihad, he concludes, is *sui generis.*[42]

Regardless of the motivations for war, Mawdudi, Hamidullah, and al-Zuhayli emphasize that war in Islam is always regulated by concerns for fighting and killing properly. Indeed, as they argue, the proper conduct of jihad has been an important concern of Islamic ethics from its origins. The Qur'an provides the basis for *jus in bello* considerations in the first verse which transformed jihad from a nonviolent struggle, as it had been in Mecca, to a defensive war incumbent upon all able-bodied Muslims: "And fight in God's cause against those who wage war against you, but do not transgress (*lā taʿtadū*), for God loves not the transgressors" (2:190). The transgression mentioned here is ambiguous; the verse could be referring to concerns of *jus ad bellum.* But throughout Islamic history, the verse has generally been interpreted as restricting the means that Muslim forces may legitimately employ in war. Indeed, until the nineteenth century, Muslim discussion of the ethics of war (*adab al-ḥarb* or *akhlāq al-ḥarb*) meant essentially acceptable strategy or tactics.

The scope of Muslim discussion of proper conduct in war includes a broad range of issues relating to the treatment of persons and their property. In this discussion we will address only two broad questions that pertain directly to the ethics of saving and taking human life: Who ought to be saved and who may be killed in war? What means ought to be used to save life and which may be used to kill?

Combatants and Noncombatants

The idea of discrimination in targets was an early and important subject in the medieval literature. As al-Zuhayli notes, it was a topic not entirely free from controversy. The majority of jurists agreed that certain categories of persons, especially women and children, should be protected from harm because the legal rationale (*ʿilla*) for killing was the "capacity to fight and harm the Muslims." In support of their position, they cited not only several Qur'anic verses on fighting, including "Fight in the way of God those who fight you . . ." (2:190), but also many Prophetic hadith admonishing Muslim armies to spare noncombatants.[43]

A minority argued, however, that the legal rationale for killing was lack of belief (*kufr*), and thus permitted the killing of all unbelievers. They based this view on the claim that the "verse of the sword," "And when the forbidden months are passed, slay the unbelievers wherever you find them" (9:5), abrogates other Qur'anic verses. In addition, the Prophetic hadith, "I have been commanded to fight the people until they say 'There is no god but God'" establishes belief and unbelief as the motivation for war.[44]

Because they accept the general reasoning of the medieval majority, Mawdudi, Hamidullah, and al-Zuhayli generally concur on the treatment of combatants and noncombatants. Al-Zuhayli concludes his discussion by arguing, in accordance with his views on the grounds for war, that the majority position was clearly correct: women, children, and others who ordinarily do not take part in the fighting should not be killed. The Qur'anic verse 2:190 is not abrogated but binding, and if we consider closely its wording, we realize that the imperative verb "fight" (*qātilū*) belongs to the category of collaborative verbs (*afʿāl al-mushārika*), verbs that connote action being done by more than one person. It must be read as "Do not fight anyone unless they fight you. Fighting is thus justified if you fight the enemy and the enemy fights you. It is not justified against anyone who does not fight the Muslims, and it is necessary [in this event] to make peace."[45]

Al-Zuhayli rejects any notion of collective responsibility for war among the enemy population. He writes that "Islamic law does not consider the entirety of the enemy population as combatants [*muḥāribūn*]. The combatants are those who prepare themselves for battle directly or indirectly, such as soldiers—either conscripts or volunteers—whether on land, the sea, or the air."[46] But al-Zuhayli's definition of combatants is not limited to soldiers actually in the field and includes the head of state, military leaders, and even military medical personnel and military postal carriers—all who direct or support the war effort and prevent the early conclusion of hostilities. All such individuals may be targeted for attack by Muslim forces.[47]

Mawdudi opens his discussion by observing that because the purpose of war in Islam is not to annihilate or excessively injure the enemy, Islam establishes two principles for the conduct of war: "In war, only that much force that is necessary to repel evil should be used, and this force should be used only against those who are engaged in fighting or at the most those who are connected to the offense. All others should be safeguarded from the effects of war. . . ."[48] These two principles are familiar to just war theorists as proportionality of means and noncombatant immunity, although Mawdudi's discussion of the latter differs in some crucial ways from the modern just war notions.

Mawdudi continues by stating that Islamic law divides enemy persons into two categories: combatants (*ahl-i qitāl*) and noncombatants (*ghayr ahl-i qitāl*). He defines combatants, in keeping with the medieval theory, as those who actually take part in fighting *or those who have the mental and physical capacity* to take part in the fighting, that is, all adult males. All adult males, Mawdudi concludes, may be killed, whether they are actually taking part in the fighting or not.[49] How Mawdudi reconciles this view with his position that prisoners of war may not be killed is unclear. Perhaps he means to say that enemy soldiers in rout or retreating to regroup for another battle may be killed even though they are momentarily not engaged in combat.

Noncombatants are defined as those who lack the mental and physical capacity to fight, or those who ordinarily do not fight. These include, according to Mawdudi, women, children, the elderly, the sick, wounded, the blind, the insane, travelers, hermits, and religious functionaries.

Hamidullah adds to Mawdudi's list peasants, traders, merchants, contractors, and others who do not fight and are indifferent to the effects of war.[50] All of these people are protected from killing by Islamic law, unless they themselves compromise their immunity by directly participating in the fighting or by aiding enemy troops. For example, if a woman spies upon Muslim forces, or an infirm person passes military information to the enemy, they may be killed.[51]

In spite of all efforts to spare noncombatants in war, some will of course be killed. Since the time of the medieval jurists, Islamic theory has excused Muslim soldiers from culpability in such unintentional killing, what just war theory terms "double effect." As Hamidullah writes, noncombatants killed in the course of military operations where discrimination is difficult, such as night raids, are to be expected.[52] And as al-Zuhayli notes, the possibility of separating combatants from noncombatants has become nearly impossible with the advent of total war and air bombardment. The loss of life that should ordinarily have been spared is, he concludes, one of the inevitable consequences of military necessity.[53]

Permissible Tactics and Weapons

The medieval legal approach to permissible tactics and weapons demonstrates a keenly practical bent. Muslim commanders must try to avoid unnecessary killing of enemy noncombatants, but if women, children, and others who are not engaged in the hostilities are killed as a consequence of military action, the fault lies with the enemy commanders who put such persons in harm's way. In other words, the killing of enemy noncombatants at the hands of Muslim troops was self-incurred harm.[54]

In *al-ʿAlaqāt al-duwalīya,* al-Zuhayli observes that the medieval *fuqahāʾ* divided into two camps on the question of legitimate means. The first, including the Hanafis, Shafiʿis, and Hanbalis generally permitted all means required "to break the enemy's strength, whether they are stringent or lenient. But the use of severity when more lenient means are available is reprehensible, because this is unwarranted corruption. . . ." In effect, Muslim armies are "free in fighting to subdue the enemy to use any means, for example, weapons of steel [*silāḥ al-abyaḍ*] and deadly agents, even to the point of poisoning the enemy with projected incendiaries and noxious gases. . . ."[55] The Shafiʿis and Hanbalis made one exception to this general permission: None of the enemy may be killed by burning, according to the hadith: "Do not punish a creature of God with the punishment of God."[56] Hanafi jurists appear to have been the most liberal in permitting rather indiscriminate tactics, including the cutting off of the enemy's water supply, or rendering it undrinkable by poisoning it. In addition, they allowed firing enemy fortresses or inundating them with water.[57]

As for the Maliki school, al-Zuhayli writes that it did not give free latitude to overcome the enemy. Maliki jurists did not permit the firing of enemy fortresses, unless the enemy employed such means and the Muslims resorted to them in retaliation. In addition, the Malikis did not permit poisoning of the enemy, whether it was in the water, or through gases, or on arrows.[58]

Al-Zuhayli is the only writer among the three considered here who discusses in any depth the issue of permissible means and weapons. Mawdudi's primary concern is to list the acts that Islam proscribes, and we shall consider these in the section on necessity. Hamidullah does discuss "acts permitted" in war, but he does so largely by listing medieval positions on a range of issues. He concludes that "it is very difficult to give a comprehensive list of what acts are permitted. The general principle may help to a great extent that everything not prohibited is permissible."[59]

Al-Zuhayli permits, on the basis of military necessity, some tactics and weapons that undeniably will yield civilian casualties and large-scale destruction. He argues, for example, that Muslims may attack fortified locations even though they know that women, children, and possibly even Muslim hostages will likely be killed. The Muslims do not intend to kill these noncombatants, but the enemy has made their protection impossible by seeking refuge among them. This was the situation faced by the Prophet when he authorized the use of a catapult or mangonel during the siege of al-Ta'if (630 C.E.).[60]

By invoking necessity, al-Zuhayli clearly seeks to limit the recourse to such means and to proscribe completely indiscriminate and irreversible weapons. On the issue of poisons, for example, he agrees with the minority position of the Malikis that their use is prohibited.[61]

Perhaps the most salient issue confronting modern Muslim writers is the advent of weapons of mass destruction. Modern chemical weapons, one may argue, are analogous to the medieval poisons and noxious gases described and permitted by most medieval writers—although of course the analogy is strained by the lethal qualities of the modern varieties. Biological and nuclear weapons pose altogether new challenges to contemporary Muslim ethicists. To my knowledge, Mawdudi and Hamidullah have not directly addressed the implications of weapons of mass destruction for the Islamic ethics of war. Mawdudi writes only generally that the Muslims are obliged to develop and acquire all types of weapons as a deterrent to possible enemy attack. The Qur'anic verse he cites in support of this position is the one generally cited by all Muslim scholars who express an opinion on this topic: "And so prepare against them whatever force and war mounts you are able to muster, so that you might deter thereby the enemies of God" (8:60).[62]

Al-Zuhayli is one of the few Muslim scholars to address this issue, but even he does not explore the full range of moral concerns raised by such weapons. He mentions briefly that Islamic principles do not eliminate the possibility of considering these weapons as permissible, but that they "do not accord with the principles of compassion which is the basis of Islamic law, or requirements of fairness in battle."[63] Muslims may develop such weapons as a deterrent against their enemies, but they should not be used first by Muslims, for as he writes, "they cause the destruction and death of those whom it is not permissible to kill, such as those not fighting, women, and the like."[64] Their use is conceivable only if deterrence fails, and the enemy employs them first. Muslims may retaliate with such deadly force as a final and necessary recourse (*ākhir al-dawā' al-kayy*, literally "the remedy that cauterizes" the wound).[65]

Thus, for al-Zuhayli, it would seem that weapons of mass destruction do not pose qualitatively different moral concerns than conventional weapons. He, like most Muslim commentators on this subject, does not probe the moral issues raised by deterrence, including the morality of threatening to do what one considers so reprehensible, or those raised by the actual use of such weapons, such as whether mass destruction may ever be justified on the basis of reciprocity or punishment.

Quarter

One of the most important features of the Islamic ethics of war is the giving of quarter (*amān*) to enemy troops or nonbelligerents. It was an important topic in the medieval literature, so significant, al-Zuhayli notes, that it belies the claim of the jurists that Islam's international relations are predicated on war and not peace.[66] The scope of *amān* exceeded the assurance of security on the battlefield; *amān* could be granted to any foreigner originating from any territory—belligerent or not—by any adult Muslim for purposes of travel, residence, and trade within Islamic territory. The *amān* thus given was binding upon the Islamic state, according to the majority of jurists.

Our concern here though is with *amān* as an instrument for saving life in war. Muslims must always be inclined, writes Mawdudi, towards peace, even in the midst of battle. The giving of quarter to the enemy soldier is an important means of furthering this goal. If any soldier lays down his arms and requests the security of his person, Muslims must grant him quarter according to the Qur'anic verse 4:90: "Therefore if they withdraw from you and fight you not, and instead give you [assurances] of peace, then God has opened no way for you against them."[67]

A subsequent verse (4:94) refers again to offers of peace extended to Muslims: "O Believers! When you go forth in the way of God, discern [between friend and foe], and do not say to him who offers you the greeting of peace, 'You are not a believer.'" The verse is framed in general terms, but the context indicates that the allusion to "going forth in the way of God" is to jihad. Mawdudi notes in his commentary on this verse that "the greeting of peace" mentioned here served among the early Muslims as a sort of password used by sentries to distinguish between friends and potential foes among the non-Muslim Arabs. The greeting *al-salām ʿalaykum* (peace be upon you) along with the profession of faith *lā ilāha illa Allāh* (there is no god but Allah) also served as identifying signals during the confusion of battle to prevent one Muslim from accidentally killing another.[68]

Apparently, a problem arose when some Muslims disregarded these professions of faith, deeming them insincere battlefield conversions, and killed those who uttered them. Numerous hadiths are cited in the classical commentaries on this verse in which the Prophet rebukes his followers for presuming to judge the sincerity or insincerity of such declarations of faith. According to one, the Prophet asks: "Did you split open his heart and see if he was truthful or a liar?"[69]

Mawdudi writes that "the purport of the verse is that no one has the right summarily to judge those who profess to be Muslims, and assume them to be lying for fear of their lives. . . . While it is impossible to investigate a person's case properly during fighting and this may enable him to save his life by lying, it is equally possible that an innocent, true believer might be put to death by mistake. The error of letting an unbeliever go unpunished is preferable to that of killing a true believer."[70]

Quarter must therefore be granted to an enemy fighter even though the Muslims suspect him of using the profession of faith merely as a last-minute ruse to escape death. This is not *amān* properly speaking, because *amān* is extended to nonbelievers. But the underlying premise for extending quarter is the same in both cases, for as Qur'an 9:6 makes clear, the purpose of *amān* is to allow the person given security (*musta'min*) to hear the call to Islam and hopefully to embrace it. Mawdudi observes that "If they [who have been given *amān*] receive guidance and accept Islam, then that is the best outcome. But if their hearts do not open to Islam, then [Muslims] cannot kill them but must transport them safely to their own country."[71]

Hamidullah points out that it is the act of requesting security that separates the *musta'min* from ordinary prisoners of war. *Amān* may thus be extended to individuals or groups of soldiers who capitulate to the conditions offered by the Muslim commander. *Amān* may also be extended unilaterally by the Muslims, as when the Prophet declared an amnesty to the general population of Mecca upon entering the city (630 C.E.).[72]

Granting security to groups of belligerents or to the general population, al-Zuhayli observes, was restricted by medieval writers to the imam (head of state) or his representatives.[73] Given the conduct of modern war by centralized states, al-Zuhayli favors the restriction of the right to extend *amān*, even in individual cases, to state authorities. He essentially equates the medieval Islamic doctrine of *amān* to the modern practice of granting entry visas or residence permits to nationals of belligerent states. Yet he maintains some scope for individual initiative and responsibility in this area, for "Islam aspires generally toward peaceful human relations if they [the enemy] desire it. In that event, it is necessary to protect the life of an enemy by any means, including giving the right of *amān* to every individual Muslim. Necessity requires it, it is in the interest of the Muslims, and all fighters can appreciate its particular benefits."[74]

Prisoners of War

The majority opinion among medieval jurists that noncombatants should not be killed did not establish, however, the absolute immunity from harm of noncombatants. According to most jurists, all of the protected categories of persons are subject to the laws pertaining to prisoners of war. Though the majority held that they should not be executed, they could be enslaved, ransomed, or released.[75]

The most contentious issue for the medieval jurists was the fate of able-bodied, male prisoners of war, who, though momentarily incapacitated by capture, posed a potential future threat if freed. The medieval laws were based upon interpretations of two Qur'anic verses:

> When you meet the unbelievers in battle, smite at their necks; at length, when you have thoroughly subdued them, bind a bond firmly [on them]; thereafter [is the time for] either generosity or ransom, until war lays down its burdens (47:4).

A second verse dealt specifically with the fate of some seventy prisoners captured during the battle of Badr (624 C.E.):

> It is not fitting for a prophet that he should have prisoners of war until he has thoroughly subdued the land. You look for the temporal goods of this world, but God looks to the Hereafter and God is exalted in might, wise. Had it not been for a previous decree from God, a severe penalty would have reached you for what you took. But [now] enjoy what you took in war, lawful and good: But fear God, for God is oft-forgiving, most merciful (8:67–69).

The attempt to reconcile these apparently contradictory verses with each other, with other verses on war, and with the Prophet's practice yielded a number of different rulings on the treatment of prisoners. Jurists of the Hanafi school held that the second verse overruled the first and thus limited the options open to the imam to three: execution, enslavement, or release as *dhimmīs*. Some Hanafi jurists conceded that ransoming for money or exchanging prisoners for Muslims held by the enemy were options available to the imam in cases of necessity. The majority from other schools, however, held that the Muslim commander may decide according to the interests of the Muslims whether prisoners were to be executed, enslaved, ransomed, exchanged, or released. Thus, all the major schools of law held that execution of prisoners was an option available to the imam. They based this permission, writes al-Zuhayli, on the claim that the "verse of the sword" (9:5) had abrogated other rulings regarding male prisoners, on instances where the Prophet had executed prisoners, on common sense which dictates that killing belligerents is most likely to bring war to a speedy conclusion.[76] Only a minority of jurists prohibited altogether the killing of prisoners and held that this was the policy practiced by the Prophet and his companions.[77]

Mawdudi, Hamidullah, and al-Zuhayli, like most contemporary writers, reject the medieval consensus on this view while embracing the minority position. Hamidullah's presentation of this topic clearly strains to make the medieval *fiqh* accord with current international norms. He cites Ibn Rushd as recording a consensus among the companions of the Prophet that a prisoner may not be killed simply for having undertaken hostile action against Muslims. If prisoners were executed, it was for reasons other than their belligerency. Later Hamidullah qualifies slightly his assertion that Islamic law prohibits the general execution of prisoners when he notes that Abu Yusuf permitted killing if the imam deemed it in the Muslim interest. Peremptory, battlefield executions are unlikely, Hamidullah suggests, because medieval law vests the decision to kill or not to kill prisoners in the imam only, and not field commanders.[78]

In *al-Jihād fī al-Islām,* Mawdudi also categorically states that "Islam prohibits the killing of prisoners of war."[79] A full exposition of Mawdudi's reasoning behind this claim is found in *Tafhīm al-Qur'ān*. In his interpretation of Qur'an 8:67–69, Mawdudi argues that the medieval jurists had falsely interpreted the verses to sanction the general execution of prisoners. The verses can only be comprehended, he argues, if they are read in conjunction with Qur'an 47:4. Qur'an 47:4 must be the "previous decree from God" mentioned in Qur'an 8:67 and not a later revelation as assumed by many Qur'anic interpreters.[80] Thus, the real subject of the latter verse's disapproval is not the Prophet's ransoming of prisoners, but the Muslims' eagerness to collect spoils before sealing the victory over the enemy. The Qur'an's legal judgment regarding prisoners, in Mawdudi's view, is that they must be either freed or ransomed in accordance with the more general prescriptions of Qur'an 47:4.[81]

Al-Zuhayli proceeds in his argument by systematically refuting the medieval arguments permitting the killing of prisoners. First, on the claim of abrogation, al-Zuhayli argues that Qur'an 47:4 is binding and not abrogated by Qur'an 9:5 because abrogation presumes some direct conflict between verses. The two verses in question do not conflict with each other, as each deals with different aspects of fighting: the beginning of Qur'an 47:4 pertains to the time before prisoners are taken; Qur'an 9:5 deals with ongoing battle; and the end of Qur'an 47:4 focuses on the disposition of prisoners. Muslims are offered only two choices in this matter, al-Zuhayli notes, freedom or ransom.[82]

As for the Prophet's practice and military requirements, al-Zuhayli argues that the Prophet executed prisoners only in special circumstances and only when other means to prevent harm and injury to the Muslims were not available. These instances do not constitute general or binding legal precedents. They pertain to a time when the Islamic community was weak and in constant danger, as indicated by the wording of what al-Zuhayli considers to be the earlier revelation (8:67): ". . . until you have subdued the land." The second verse (47:4) was revealed later, al-Zuhayli argues, to be the binding ruling on treatment of prisoners.[83] He concludes that "killing of prisoners in Islam is closer to being prohibited than it is to being permitted. When it is permitted, it is a useful remedy in specific, special cases under extreme necessity, and not a general rule."[84]

Necessity

The language of necessity has arisen repeatedly in the course of the present discussion. The idea of necessity (*ḍarūra*) and the moral problems attached to it are familiar to Muslim theorists of war. As the well-established principle of Islamic jurisprudence states: *al-ḍarūrāt tubīḥ al-maḥẓurāt* (necessity makes permissible the prohibited). In medieval law, this principle was generally applied to cases of imminent danger to the life or physical welfare of the individual or the community, such as in the lifting of dietary restrictions when faced with starvation.[85] Applied to war, however, necessity acquired a much broader scope than imminent destruction of an individual soldier or the Muslim community as a whole. It was invoked to legitimate normally prohibited actions in situations far less dire, meaning most often—though the conditions were seldom specified—simply practical needs to attain victory or to remove exigencies such as the imminent defeat of Muslim forces in battle.

Two justifications were usually offered for the recourse to arguments of necessity: first, public welfare of the Muslim community (*maṣlaḥa mursala*) and second, reciprocity (*muqābala bi-l-mithl*) for violations of *jus in bello* perpetrated by the enemy. Al-Ghazali (d. 1111) offers in *al-Mustaṣfā fī ʿilm al-uṣūl* (Selected [topics] in the science of the sources [of jurisprudence]) one of the best-known invocations of *maṣlaḥa mursala* in the context of war: When a dangerous non-Muslim enemy that threatens to overwhelm the territory of Islam and kill all Muslims uses Muslim captives as shields, it is permissible for Muslim troops to kill the Muslim captives as collateral damage in their attack on the enemy.[86] The killing of the Muslim hostages violates a clear Qur'anic prohibition on taking innocent life, but in this case their deaths do not incur moral culpability because "(1) it is a matter of vital necessity (*ḍarūra*), (2) it is a case of clear-cut certainty (*qaṭʿiyya*), and (3) its importance is universal (*kulliya*)." Al-Ghazali's invocation of necessity in this example involves the welfare of all or nearly all Muslims facing extinction; he clearly rules out the application of the same principle when a majority, even a large majority, confronts a similar situation.[87]

We should note that al-Ghazali uses this example to illustrate a point in jurisprudence; he is not addressing Islamic injunctions on war *per se*. The rule he is illustrating is that appeals to public welfare can contradict clear injunctions in the Qur'an and Sunna only in cases of dire necessity. Other jurists who wrote specifically as interpreters of the law of war did not adhere to such a high threshold when invoking necessity in war, especially where the Qur'an and Sunna are silent or ambiguous. An instructive example comes from al-Shaybani's (d. 805) *Kitāb al-siyar al-kabīr* (Book on military campaigns): Muslim troops may flood, fire, or bombard a city, even though they know women, children, and old people are inside, even to the point that Muslim hostages inside are killed. The reason given is that "if the Muslims stopped attacking the inhabitants of the territory of war for any of the reasons [given], they would be unable to go to war at all, for there is no city in the territory of war in which there is no one at all of these you have mentioned."[88] War could be prosecuted by other, less dire methods, of course. But that does not seem to figure into al-Shaybani's argument. The legal permission for employing certain means against the enemy does not change because of any moral concerns raised by the injection of noncombatants into the hypothetical situation. It is the enemy's unwillingness or inability to safeguard noncombatants that makes the enemy responsible for their deaths.

Moreover, we should note finally that al-Ghazali as well as other medieval jurists were concerned with the welfare of the Muslims, not their foes, when considering exceptions to normal prohibitions. To continue the example from al-Shaybani: Muslim troops should avoid targeting Muslim hostages being used as shields by the enemy, and should aim "at the inhabitants of the territory of war."[89]

The principle of reciprocity was perhaps the more commonly invoked justification for necessary violations of normal prohibitions. Medieval writers found Qur'anic justification for reciprocity as a principle of *jus in bello* in such verses as "If then any one transgresses the prohibition against you, transgress you likewise against him" (2:194); "And fight the polytheists all together (*kaffatan*) as they fight you all together" (9:36–37). Both of these verses are in the context of the prohibition on fighting in the four sacred months observed by the Arabs. But by combining them with earlier Qur'anic injunctions on retaliating no worse than the original affront (16:126–27; 22:60), medieval jurists adduced the general principle that reciprocity permitted the resort to rather indiscriminate methods if the enemy had initiated their use. Unfortunately, the moral justification for such permission is developed no further than the invocation of necessity. Moreover, it disregards the fact that each of the Qur'anic verses permitting reciprocity are followed by admonitions for restraint and even forgiveness as the better moral choice.

Al-Zuhayli is one of the few contemporary scholars to grapple with the complex issue of the justification and limits of necessity in war.[90] He writes:

> In the arena of battle, the ends justify the means, according to the Islamic view. This does not mean that the desire for victory subsumes humanitarian principles, which limit [appeals to] necessity or military requirements, whether they relate to the methods of fighting and the destruction of enemy installations and military fortifications, or to issues relating to enemy persons and the seizing of their property.[91]

We saw earlier that al-Zuhayli is willing, as are Mawdudi and Hamidullah, to permit attacks upon areas where noncombatants are likely to die if military necessity requires it. So what limits on necessity do al-Zuhayli, Mawdudi, and Hamidullah posit? Hamidullah offers a list of categorical prohibitions, the majority of which enjoyed near-universal support among the medieval *fuqahā'* because they were grounded on strong Prophetic tradition and, one could argue, on fundamental principles of humanity common to most ethical systems. Mawdudi and al-Zuhayli would concur with this list: unnecessarily cruel means of killing, such as through burning alive, torture, and mutilation; killing of ambassadors or the taking of hostages as shields against enemy attack; general massacre of the enemy following surrender; killing through treachery and perfidy, such as in violating oaths or grants of *amān*.[92]

This list is not extensive, and clearly much more work needs to be done in this area by Muslim ethicists. But in war, any *a priori* list of categorical prohibitions—if it is to be plausible—can seldom be longer.

One interesting aspect of Mawdudi's, Hamidullah's, and al-Zuhayli's works is that they make no attempt to place their thought within the context of modern Muslim thought on war and peace. Their interlocutors are either long-dead: the medieval *fuqahā'*; or non-Muslim: mainly westerners concerned with Islamic law and ethics. They do not seriously engage their fellow, contemporary Muslim writers.[93]

If we were to place the three scholars within the broader context of Muslim thought, we would find that the general agreement found in comparing their ideas would extend to other contemporary interpreters. We may call this the modern scholastic consensus on the Islamic ethics of saving and taking life in war. There are certainly voices outside the mainstream, particularly those of the so-called Islamic radicals or militants analyzed by Richard Martin in the next chapter. Though they figure prominently in western media and scholarly treatments of jihad, these voices have always been marginal to the Islamic discourse and they are becoming further marginalized over time.

With regard to the grounds for war, all three emphasize the rationale of defense: defense of one's self and one's nation, defense of others suffering persecution and killing, and defense of the right to call people to God's message. All three go to great lengths to describe the early Islamic expansion as motivated by this last type of legitimate war—not by the desire to impose Islamic faith upon non-Muslims. And all three leave the import of this type of war for modern times rather ambiguous.

With regard to *jus in bello,* all three enjoin discrimination between combatants and noncombatants, and the avoidance of excessive destruction or cruel forms of military action. They all emphasize that wars should be fought with the goal of saving life as much as possible, and that killing in war is a means to repelling the original affront, not the goal itself.

Mawdudi's, Hamidullah's, and al-Zuhayli's works are also indicative of the current gaps in the Muslim literature. Some of these gaps have been evident in the preceding pages, topics such as weapons of mass destruction and the limits of military necessity. Other important topics, including terrorism, guerrilla insurgency, and accountability for violations of Islamic principles, have been absent from our discussion because the three writers—along with other Muslims—have yet to treat them systematically. There is hope though that these gaps will be increasingly filled as Muslims continue to elaborate on the Islamic ethics of war and peace.

Notes

1. In addition to the authors considered in this article, see Muhammad Abu Zahra, *Concept of War in Islam,* trans. Muhammad al-Hady and Taha Omar (Cairo: Ministry of Waqf, 1961); Yadh ben Ashoor, *Islam and International Humanitarian Law* (Geneva: International Committee of the Red Cross, 1980); and the survey of Muslim doctrine and contemporary practice by Karima Bennoune, "As-Salāmu 'Alaykum? Humanitarian Law in Islamic Jurisprudence," *Michigan Journal of International Law* 15 (winter 1994): 605–43.

2. See Ann Elizabeth Mayer, "War and Peace in the Islamic Law Tradition and International Law," in *Just War and Jihad,* ed. James Turner Johnson and John Kelsay (New York: Greenwood, 1991), 198.

3. Muhammad Hamidullah, *Muslim Conduct of State,* 7th ed. (Lahore: Sh. Muhammad Ashraf, 1961), chap. 10. Hamidullah cites Ernest Nys, *Les droits de gens et les anciens jurisconsultes espagnols* (The Hague: Martinus Nijhoff, 1914). Most recent writers making this claim rely upon Marcel Boisard, "On the Probable Influence of Islam on Western Public and International Law," *International Journal of Middle East Studies* 11 (July 1980): 429–50.

4. See Seyyed Vali Reza Nasr, *Mawdudi and the Making of Islamic Revivalism* (New York: Oxford University Press, 1996), 22–23, for the background to Mawdudi's writing of *al-Jihād fī al-Islām.*

5. From the publisher's preface to Abū al-A'lā Mawdūdī, *al-Jihād fī al-Islām* (Lahore: Idāra Tarjumān al-Qur'ān, 1988).

6. Khurshid Ahmad, foreword to Abū al-A'lā Mawdūdī, *Tafhīm al-Qur'ān (Towards Understanding the Qur'an),* trans. and ed. Zafar Ishaq Ansari (Leicester, U.K.: The Islamic Foundation, 1988), 1:xiii. See also Charles J. Adams, "Abū'l-A'lā Mawdūdī's *Tafhīm al-Qur'ān,*" in *Approaches to the History of the Interpretation of the Qur'an,* ed. Andrew Rippin (Oxford: Clarendon Press, 1988), 307–22.

7. A retrospective of Hamidullah's life and scholarship is available in *Islamic Horizons,* July/August 1999, pp. 23–45.

8. Hamidullah, *Muslim Conduct of State,* ch. 10.

9. Wahba al-Zuḥaylī, *Āthār al-ḥarb fī al-fiqh al-Islāmī: Dirāsa muqārana* (Damascus: Dār al-Fikr, 1981).

10. Wahba al-Zuḥaylī, *al-'Alāqāt al-duwalīya fī al-Islām: Muqārana bi-l-qānūn al-duwalī al-ḥadīth* (Beirut: Mu'assasat al-Risāla, 1981); a précis of al-Zuhayli's views is available in French in Wahba Moustapha Zehili, "*Dispositions internationales relatives à la guerre, justifiées au regard de l'Islam et leurs aspects humains caractéristiques,* in *Les religions et la guerre: Judaisme, Christianisme, Islam,* ed. Pierre Viaud (Paris: Cerf, 1991), 389–419.

11. Ḥasan al-Bannā', Sayyid Quṭb, and Abū al-A'lā al-Mawdūdī, *al-Jihād fī sabīl Allāh* (Cairo: Ṣawt al-Ḥaqq, 1977).

12. See for example Emmanuel Sivan, *Radical Islam: Medieval Theology and Modern Politics* (New Haven: Yale University Press, 1990), 84–86. Ibrahim Abu-Rabi' critically reappraises this view in *Intellectual Origins of Islamic Resurgence in the Modern Arab World* (Albany: State University of New York, 1996), 139.

13. On this point, with reference to Mawdudi's exegesis of the Qur'an, Charles Adams writes: "Mawdudi belongs with the large group of Muslim reformists and revivalists who consider themselves *ghayr maqallad* with respect to the medieval schools of law. Most of these people, like Mawdudi, make Qur'an and *sunna* the exclusive authorities in religion as a way of gaining more freedom for the adaptation of Muslim thought and practice to modern conditions. While in legal matters he did assign some significance to the opinions of the *fuqahā'* of previous times and believed it important for modern Muslims to acquaint themselves with their opinions, for him their views have no final validity" (Adams, "Mawdūdī's *Tafhīm al-Qur'ān,*" 314).

14. Hamidullah does mention several sources beyond the Qur'an and Prophetic Sunna as "roots and sources" of Islamic international law, including the practice of the four rightly-guided caliphs and other rulers who have not been repudiated by ulema; arbitral awards; treaties, pacts, and other conventions; internal legislation; and custom and usage. But he concludes this discussion by suggesting that only the Qur'an and Sunna form "permanent positive law," while all others are "temporary positive law," "non-positive or case law," and "suggested law" (Hamidullah, *Muslim Conduct of State,* chap. 6). His subsequent discussion of legal doctrine relies almost entirely on the corpus of medieval jurisprudence, which itself relied almost entirely on the Qur'an and precedents attributed to the Prophet and the first four caliphs.

15. Of the three, Hamidullah is most reluctant to adopt openly the goal of reinterpreting medieval theory. He writes in the preface to the third edition: "I am not writing on what, according to [the] modern average Muslim, ought to be the Muslim law, but what has always been considered to be the Muslim law" (Hamidullah, *Muslim Conduct of State,* vi–vii). The process of adducing "what has always been considered to be Muslim law" is, however, itself an interpretive process, particularly when it is coupled with Hamidullah's underlying goal, which is to argue the medieval *siyar's* essential compatibility with public international law.

16. In using the term "apologetic," I do not mean to link these three writers with the so-called apologists of the nineteenth century, mainly Indian, whose avowed goal was to refute point-by-point the charges of various orientalists regarding jihad. This is clearly not the goal of the three considered here, particularly al-Zuhayli. Their works are apologetic in the sense of advocating or defending a particular view, namely that Islamic law is as just and humane—if not more so—as public international law and other conceptions of world order. On this point see Mayer, "War and Peace in Islamic Tradition," 221n. 8.

17. Majid Khadduri has discussed briefly the few philosophical treatments of this issue in *War and Peace in the Law of Islam* (Baltimore: Johns Hopkins University Press, 1955), chap. 5.

18. This injunction is grounded in a Prophetic hadith narrated by Muslim, Abu Da'ud, and Tirmidhi. See Muḥammad ibn 'Abdallāh, Khaṭīb al-Tabrīzī, *Mishkāt al-Maṣābīḥ,* trans. Mawlana Fazlul Karim (New Delhi: Islamic Book Service, 1998), 2:389–90.

19. See also Khaled Abou El Fadl, "*'Aḥkām al-Bughāt:* Irregular Warfare and the Law of Rebellion in Islam," in *Cross, Crescent, and Sword: The Justification and*

Limitation of War in Western and Islamic Tradition, ed. James Turner Johnson and John Kelsay (New York: Greenwood, 1990), 149–76.

20. Mustansir Mir, "*Jihad* in Islam," in *The Jihad and Its Times,* ed. Hadia Dajani-Shakeel and Ronald Messier (Ann Arbor: Center for Near Eastern and North African Studies, University of Michigan, 1991), 117–22.

21. Mawdūdī, *al-Jihād fī al-Islām,* 23.

22. Ibid., 24.

23. Mawdūdī, *Tafhīm al-Qur'ān,* trans. Ansari, 2:291–92.

24. Mawdūdī, *al-Jihād fī al-Islām,* 32.

25. Ibid., 30–34.

26. Ibid., 34–36.

27. Hamidullah, *Muslim Conduct of State,* 162.

28. Ibn Khaldun, *The Muqaddimah: An Introduction to History,* trans. Franz Rosenthal (Princeton: Princeton University Press, 1980), 2:73.

29. Al-Zuḥaylī, *Āthār al-ḥarb,* 56–59.

30. Ibid., 106–20.

31. Mawdūdī, *al-Jihād fī al-Islām,* 55–56.

32. See Aziz Ahmad, *Islamic Modernism in India and Pakistan: 1857–1964* (London: Oxford University Press, 1967), 31–34.

33. Mawdūdī, *al-Jihād fī al-Islām,* 70–77.

34. Ibid., 57.

35. Ibid., 164–65.

36. Ibid.

37. Ibid., 174–75.

38. Ibid., 146.

39. See Masudul Hasan, *Sayyed Abu'l A'ala Maududi and His Thought* (Lahore: Islamic Publications, 1986, 185–96); and Seyyed Vali Reza Nasr, *The Vanguard of the Islamic Revolution: The Jama'at-i Islami of Pakistan* (Berkeley: University of California Press, 1994), 120–21.

40. Hamidullah, *Muslim Conduct of State,* 84, 172.

41. Al-Zuḥaylī, *Āthār al-ḥarb,* 93–94.

42. Ibid., 124–26; *al-'Alāqāt al-duwalīya,* 35–36.

43. Al-Zuḥaylī, *Āthār al-ḥarb,* 494–99.

44. Ibid., 498–99. This hadith is narrated by Bukhari and Muslim.

45. Ibid., 500–501.

46. Ibid., 503; *al-'Alāqāt al-duwalīya,* 70–71.

47. Al-Zuḥaylī, *Āthār al-ḥarb,* 505.

48. Mawdūdī, *al-Jihād fī al-Islām,* 217.

49. Ibid., 222–24.

50. Hamidullah, *Muslim Conduct of State,* 207.

51. Ibid.

52. Ibid., 223.

53. Al-Zuḥaylī, *Āthār al-ḥarb,* 504–6.

54. See John Kelsay, *Islam and War: A Study in Comparative Ethics* (Louisville, Ky.: Westminster/John Knox Press, 1993), 64–67.

55. Al-Zuḥaylī, *al-ʿAlāqāt al-duwalīya,* 46.

56. Ibid.

57. Hamidullah, *Muslim Conduct of State,* 225.

58. Ibid.

59. Ibid., 229.

60. Al-Zuḥaylī, *Āthār al-ḥarb,* 506–7.

61. Al-Zuḥaylī, *al-ʿAlāqāt al-duwalīya,* 50.

62. Mawdūdī, *al-Jihād fī al-Islām,* 82. Mawdudi's party, the Jamaʿat-i Islami, has not been as reticent on nuclear weapons. It has long advocated Pakistan's acquisition of nuclear weapons, particularly after India's nuclear explosion in 1974. The Jamaʿat agitated for a Pakistani test in May 1998 following India's resumption of nuclear testing. Khurshid Ahmad, a leading Jamaʿat spokesman on foreign policy, has repeatedly urged the Pakistani government not to sign the Non-proliferation Treaty without Indian compliance, and to build a nuclear deterrent to counter India's arsenal. He bases his arguments in part on the Qur'anic verse 8:60, as in his comments published in *Tarjumān al-Qur'ān,* December 1998 (transcript provided by the Jamaʿat-i Islami Pakistan).

63. Al-Zuḥaylī, *al-ʿAlāqāt al-duwalīya,* 48.

64. Al-Zuḥaylī, *Āthār al-ḥarb,* 789.

65. Author's interview with Wahba al-Zuhayli, Damascus, Syria, 2 January 1991.

66. Al-Zuḥaylī, *Āthār al-ḥarb,* 220.

67. Mawdūdī, *al-Jihād fī al-Islām,* 270–71.

68. Mawdūdī, *Tafhīm al-Qur'ān,* trans. Ansari, 2:71.

69. Abū al-Ḥasan ʿAlī ibn Aḥmad al-Wāḥidī al-Nīsābūrī, *Asbāb al-Nuzūl* (Al-Dammām: Dār al-Iṣlāḥ, 1992), 173.

70. Mawdūdī, *Tafhīm al-Qur'ān,* trans. Ansari, 2:71.

71. Mawdūdī, *al-Jihād fī al-Islām,* 273.

72. Hamidullah, *Muslim Conduct of State,* chap. 14.

73. Al-Zuḥaylī, *Āthār al-ḥarb,* 268.

74. Ibid., 264.

75. Ibid., 418–29.

76. Ibid., 429–35.

77. Ibid., 439.

78. Hamidullah, *Muslim Conduct of State,* 214–16. Al-Zuhayli writes that the majority of jurists gave the final decision on the disposition of prisoners to the *imām* as well as to his military commanders in the field. Their decision should be based on legal reasoning and not personal desire (Al-Zuḥaylī, *Āthār al-ḥarb,* 431).

79. Mawdūdī, *al-Jihād fī al-Islām,* 249.

80. Mawdudi writes in his interpretation of Qur'an 47:4: "This verse's language and context make clear that it was revealed after the command to fight had been revealed, and before fighting had actually started." It must have preceded, therefore, Qur'an 8:67–69, which by wide agreement were revealed after the first battle fought at Badr. Mawdūdī, *Tafhīm al-Qur'ān* (Lahore: Idāra Tarjumān al-Qur'ān, 1989), 5:11 (The English translation by Ansari has not yet reached this chapter).

81. Mawdūdī, *Tafhīm al-Qur'ān,* trans. Ansari, 3:169–70.

82. Al-Zuḥaylī, *Āthār al-ḥarb,* 435.

83. Ibid., 436–38.

84. Ibid., 440.

85. *Encyclopaedia of Islam,* 2d ed., s.v. "Ḍarūra."

86. Abū Ḥāmid Muḥammad al-Ghazālī, *al-Mustaṣfā fī ʿilm al-uṣūl,* ed. Muḥammad Sulaymān al-Ashqar (Beirut: Mu'assasat al-Risāla, 1997), 420–21.

87. Malcolm Kerr, *Islamic Reform: The Political and Legal Theories of Muhammad ʿAbduh and Rashid Rida* (Berkeley: University of California Press, 1966), 93–94.

88. Muḥammad ibn al-Ḥasan al-Shaybānī, *Kitāb al-siyar al-kabīr (The Islamic Law of Nations: Shaybani's Siyar),* trans. Majid Khadduri (Baltimore: Johns Hopkins University Press, 1966), 102.

89. Ibid.

90. See Wahba al-Zuḥaylī, *Naẓariyat al-ḍarūra al-sharʿīya: Muqārana maʿa al-qānūn al-waḍʿī* (Damascus: Dār al-Fikr, 1997).

91. Al-Zuḥaylī, *al-ʿAlāqāt al-duwalīya,* 45.

92. Hamidullah, *Muslim Conduct of State,* chap. 13; Mawdūdī, *al-Jihād fī al-Islām,* 224–38; al-Zuḥaylī, *Āthār al-ḥarb,* 500–507, and *al-ʿAlāqāt al-duwalīya,* 45–71.

93. Hamidullah briefly lists nineteenth- and twentieth-century Muslim works that preceded his book (pp. 30–31) and mentions English-language contributions to the field as they appear in the prefaces to the various editions of *Muslim Conduct of State.* Al-Zuhayli refers only occasionally to earlier writers with whom he agrees, most notably Muhammad ʿAbduh and Muhammad Abu Zahra.

Seven

Discourses on Jihad in the Postmodern Era

Richard C. Martin

The ethics of killing and saving life is almost exclusively linked, in Islamic discourse, to the discussion of jihad—exerting oneself in the path of God—and the discussion of jihad has primarily been the domain of jurists (*fuqahā'*). In the medieval discussions of philosophy (*falsafa*), theology (*uṣūl al-dīn, 'ilm al-kalām*), and the cultivation of proper moral character (*'ilm al-akhlāq*), there are no significant discussions based on Islamic principles of ethical values of killing and saving life, except by way of providing an example for an argument. As others in this volume have shown, theologians and philosophers were more concerned to establish the grounds for making ethical judgments and to dispute the character and source of the morally good versus the morally bad. Applied ethics related to specific acts—such as killing, maiming, or efforts to save or protect life—fell to the jurists to debate, producers of legal opinion (muftis) to research, and, in most Muslim polities, sitting judges (qadis) to apply. Thus, the range of moral attitudes found throughout Muslim societies reflects an evolving body of legal arguments drawn continually from the four sources of legal reasoning: revelation (Qur'an), Prophetic example (Sunna), scholarly consensus (*ijmā'*), and analogical reasoning (*qiyās*). The literature of applied ethics drawn from these sources consists primarily in *fiqh* manuals of each of the schools of legal opinion (sing. *madhhab*), where whole sections are found devoted to jihad, conflict with enemies, and killing.[1] Social, economic, and political developments provide the variables that color the landscape of ethical thinking in Muslim societies.

The religious grounds for going to war and for conduct in war, as framed by the doctrine of jihad in Islamic law, are therefore unique and form a distinctively Islamic concept for the comparative study of the ethics of taking and saving life. With respect to jihad, much of this volume has been devoted to explaining the classical expression of the doctrine and the legal issues in dispute surrounding it, as well as modern interpretations

This chapter was written a year prior to September 11, 2001.

required by such momentous changes for the Muslim world as colonialism and responses to modernity and the west. The Qur'an defines *jihad* as "exerting oneself in the path of God" (*jihād fī sabīl Allāh*). Thus, the ethical implications of jihad are self-evident. The larger question for this study, then, would seem to be this: what are the ethical considerations of striving in the path of God in the contemporary period, when that path traverses communities and economies of rapid technological development and political change, bringing profound social and cultural dislocations for Muslims in virtually every corner of the globe?

The last two decades of the twentieth century saw an increase in radical Muslim responses to oppression and aggression by Muslim and non-Muslim forces. The Iranian revolution, the bloody conflict over sacred space at Ayodhya, the civil war and armed Israeli intervention in Beirut, the Christian-Orthodox/Muslim confrontation in Bosnia, the heavily one-sided outcome of the Gulf War, the denial of democratic gains to the Islamic Salvation Front (FIS) in Algeria; these and numerous other places and events have provided occasions when radical Muslim (or Islamist) groups have formed and called for jihad in tones, and often in terms, that have articulated rationales for greater violence against enemies than the language of the classical sources and modern juristic definitions of jihad would seem to sanction. In this chapter, I propose to do a comparative reading of two recent radical discourses on jihad against the background of Khaled Abou El Fadl's findings regarding the rules of killing at war in the classical sources (chapter 5). Sohail H. Hashmi's analysis of three modern theories of jihad (chapter 6) will also inform the comparison I propose, for the neotraditional and radical theories are in many ways in direct competition with each other. The emergence more recently of a discourse of legitimate violence in pursuit of jihad against Muslim and non-Muslim enemies is the narrower subject of this chapter. More broadly, I am interested in how the postcolonial modern conditions of Islam have affected modern Islamic understandings of what jihad means in today's world.

A Word on Comparative Methodology

In a 1991 article titled "*Jihad* in Islam," Mustansir Mir argued that Modern Muslim constructions and understandings of jihad differ in "important ways" from the more classical constructions, especially among jurists. He went even further by claiming that a scholarly study of jihad in Islamic thought, in comparing modern with traditional perceptions, should recognize that the differences could be taken, in his words, as "symptomatic of a broad change that is taking place in the Muslim understanding of Islamic tradition and sources."[2] The more usual kind of comparison in jihad studies have been with the western just war tradition. In this case, the two most prominent categories compared between the western and Islamic traditions are the twin theological-*cum*-legal Latinisms, *jus ad bellum* (the reasons that justify going to war) and *jus in bello* (appropriate conduct toward the enemy and nonbelligerents in the pursuit of war). In the latter kind of comparison, Islamic theories of war and theories of jihad are evaluated in terms of categories that go back in western thought to St. Augustine (fifth century C.E.) and Aristotle (fourth century B.C.E.).

The difference between Mustansir Mir's historical comparison within Islamic thought and the comparisons across traditions that just war theorists have pursued calls to mind a remark Marilyn Waldman once made about comparative studies (to which she contributed so many useful insights in her published and unpublished papers). Waldman cited the comparison of a rose to a carnation with the comparison of one variety of rose to another. Both are examples of comparison that may serve some useful purpose, but the purposes in each case may be quite different.

In the case of a rose compared to a carnation—exemplifying the synchronic comparison of just war thinking in Islamicate and western societies—the purpose may be to explain from the perspective of those most familiar with roses just what a carnation is like. One presumption would be that diehard aficionados of roses can come to appreciate and even accept the beauty and value of carnations in this kind of comparison. This rose/carnation kind of comparison of just war theory with Islamic legal discourse about jihad may serve as a cross-cultural correction of ethnocentric misunderstandings of Islam. This does seem to be the aim of many recent comparative studies of jihad within the discourse of just war theological and legal thinking in the west, such as the United States Institute of Peace project led by John Kelsay and James Turner Johnson at Rutgers University in the late 1980s.[3] Through such comparative studies across religious and cultural traditions, scholars as educators can contribute to a better understanding of other religions. We also know that comparisons, even scholarly ones, can have negative purposes: to try to convince rose lovers that carnations are inferior in value to roses. Again, as Mustansir Mir, John Kelsay, and many other scholars in religious studies have remarked, western writing and scholarship on jihad and related topics in Islam often betrays an implicit, if not an explicit purpose of putting Islam "in the dock" when it comes to outbreaks of violence in contemporary clashes of civilizations and communities.[4]

However, it will not do to push the analogy of our project with the work of botanists too far. In cross-cultural, including comparative religious studies, a problem exists that botanists do not have. Terms like petal, stem, violence against the enemy, civilian or enemy, wherever they may be found in the world. One important issue debated in these competing fatwas by the Egyptian Grand Mufti, Tantawi, and by the Saudi rebel, bin Laden, is the validity of conducting jihad with non-Muslim allies, that is, of "Muslim" armies, such as the Egyptians, joining the American-led forces of Operation Desert Storm. Tantawi's fatwa argues the need to join forces with other Muslim and non-Muslim armies against Iraq in the following way. It is the duty of a Muslim ruler to adopt "every lawful measure to secure the safety of his people, their property, and their honor against any aggressor."

> If [his armed forces are] deemed inadequate, then the ruler should seek the assistance of his Muslim brothers and should consolidate all efforts to confront this danger. If the situation deteriorates, and the ruler . . . finds that the forces of his country and those who were summoned to assist are unable to deal with the situation adequately, then the Muslim country . . . has every right to seek help from Muslims and non-Muslims to repel the aggression and defend that which lawfully should be defended.[11]

Bin Laden construes the presence of non-Muslim, specifically American and European, "infidel" armies occupying the lands of the Haramayn (the sacred cities of Mecca and Medina) as the chief reason or grounds for going to war. In his 1998 fatwa, he wrote: "For over seven years the United States has been occupying the lands of Islam in the holiest places, the Arabian Peninsula, plundering its riches, dictating to its rulers, humiliating its people, terrorizing its neighbors."[12] These are interpreted as religious acts of aggression against Muslim peoples, acts that go back to and continue the Crusades. Therefore, as we have seen already in the writings of Faraj, it is a duty that devolves upon individual Muslims (*farḍ ʿayn*), not simply a communal duty, to fight those who have declared "war on God, His messenger, and Muslims."

Regarding Tantawi's and the other fatwas in support of Egypt and its Muslim allies joining Operation Desert Storm, bin Laden argues that the government tricked prominent scholars into issuing fatwas that have no basis in the Qur'an or Sunna. This is an important point regarding the hermeneutical grounds on which the ethics of killing have been debated in contemporary Islam, to which I will return briefly in the conclusion. Bin Laden goes beyond Faraj, reflecting the global discourse against Islamic radicalism that had developed in the west and in the Islamic world since the Iranian Revolution, to argue that terrorism (*irhāb*) is a legitimate and pistil, and stamen do not belong intrinsically to any one species. To say that carnations have petals, even as roses do, does not bias or intrusively affect the comparison. Indeed, such generic terminology makes scholarly comparison possible. Carnations are not offended when being spoken of by rose lovers as having petals that are "different" from rose petals. That is often not the case in comparative religious studies, where the blanket application of terms like "scripture," "fundamentalism," and "just war" across traditions is frequently contested, and often with good reason. History of religions and comparative cultural studies more generally have not developed a conceptual terminology that transcends the religious and cultural phenomena within particular traditions. This is the Heideggerian dilemma of having necessarily to view any horizon from a particular cultural place or framework. This is a problem that historians of religion have yet to resolve satisfactorily, and in some cases even to acknowledge.

The other kind of comparison, of one variety of rose with another, or more to the point, of classical determinations of jihad among jurists in the various *madhhabs* with later efforts to interpret and apply classical teachings under changing social and political circumstances, is also useful and valid in comparative religious studies. However, the purpose of such a comparison may be quite different in this case. Scholars within the tradition under consideration may be engaging in a dispute about whether ancient dogmas mean the same thing under modern circumstances. Or scholars both inside and outside the tradition may be trying to deconstruct the lame premise of modernization theory which presumes a dichotomy between a static, traditional past and a dynamic, developing modernity. In this latter type of comparison, of roses from this garden and era to roses from that garden and era, the problem of language appears on the surface to be less severe. Islamic law and theology, after all, have developed a discourse about jihad that makes perfect sense within the Islamic world view, as Majid Khadduri and others have pointed out with some clarity. Nonetheless, the point here is that Muslim and non-Muslim comparative historians of religion are still in need of a conceptual language that transcends the closed system of referentiality that characterizes the world view constructed by the language of *fiqh* and the sharia. That language and meta-reflection may come from ethics, law, ethnography, or some other scholarly discourse, such as history of religions, if the latter can develop a language that transcends the conceptual terminology of Christian historical and theological studies. But again, drawing on the example of the botanist, the method of comparing one subspecies of rose to another will not make scientific sense if the more general botanical language and taxonomies are abandoned, which of course would be unthinkable. The conceptual language one develops for one's analysis of Islamic discourses about jihad is the most fundamental contribution one can make in pursuit of the project of this book.

Given this background distinction between the two kinds of comparative studies that scholars have conducted on war and peace in Islam, I want to turn now to a specific application of the second type, the rose/rose comparison, of jihad within contemporary Islamic discourse. The remainder of this chapter is divided into three parts: first, arguments for armed jihad against modern Muslim enemies, especially apostate rulers and others who are accused by some Muslims of having turned from Islam; second, jihad against modern non-Muslim enemies; and third, jihad against modern non-Muslim world views that impinge on traditional Islamic life.

Radical Jihad against Muslim Enemies Within

In October 1981, President Anwar al-Sadat of Egypt was assassinated by a small group of Muslims with extreme views who had infiltrated a military unit that was passing in review in front of Egyptian state dignitaries. The group was led by a certain Khalid al-Islambuli who, after firing his weapon at President Sadat, fatally wounding him, was heard to shout: "I am Khalid al-Islambuli, I have killed Pharaoh, and I do not fear death."[5] The allusion to Pharaoh (*Fir'awn*) is particularly significant. In the Qur'an and Muslim tradition, as in Judaism and Christianity, Pharaoh is portrayed as an oppressive ruler who is hostile to Moses and the Israelite religion. In modern times the reference to Pharaoh has come to represent the plight of Muslims living under secular rulers, including nominal Muslim heads of state, who ignore and even oppose Islam. The ideologue of the group that claimed responsibility for the assassination of Sadat was an Egyptian electrician named 'Abd al-Salam Faraj, who wrote a treatise calling like-minded Muslims to action. His treatise, titled "The Absent [or Neglected] Duty" (*al-Farīḍa al-ghā'iba*), had circulated among Islamists who were sympathetic to his call for a jihad against the government, although not surprisingly its publication was banned by the Egyptian authorities. "The absent duty" was a reference to jihad, which in Islamic law is sometimes regarded as the sixth pillar of Islamic religious practice.

In his study of Abu l-A'la Mawdudi, Muhammad Hamidullah, and Wahba al-Zuhayli, Sohail Hashmi points out that each of these mid-twentieth-century Sunni jurists freely reinterpreted the classical texts and reconceived the grounds for going to war and proper conduct in combat in light of the modern circumstances in which Muslims were finding themselves, namely the colonial and postcolonial eras and the rise of nationalism. Those few twentieth-century jurists and intellectuals who wrote comprehensively on the ethics of war and combat exercised independent reasoning (*ijtihād*) in the use they made of Qur'an, Sunna, and the key events of combat and militia action that are usually cited by jurists in discussions of jihad. So, too, ʿAbd al-Salam Faraj and other Islamist authors have not felt bound by the interpretations of their twentieth-century predecessors. Indeed, ʿAbd al-Salam Faraj's treatise is nothing short of a diatribe against the position of the established Sunni doctrine of jihad. Whereas the modern Sunni theory generally restricts the use of force in combat to the defense of the Muslim state and the preservation of a just society, Faraj argues that armed jihad against unbelievers and unbelief is a necessary but neglected duty that falls to all Muslims. What makes this text interesting and important for this study, therefore, is the careful development of an argument for the grounds for use of deadly force in combat against one's enemies, including unjust Muslim rulers.

Al-Farīḍa al-ghā'iba was not originally presented as an external argument, meant to convince non-Muslims or Muslims with opposing views of the need for the use of force in the path of God. It is an internal argument, meant primarily to circulate among like-minded radical Islamists. That it found a sympathetic reading among Egyptians beyond the jihad movements it inspired, once it became more widely known, makes the analysis of its interpretations and arguments particularly important.[6] The contentiousness of public moral reasoning about the issues raised by the treatise is indicated by the fact that on April 15, 1982, its author, ʿAbd al-Salam Faraj, as well as Khalid al-Islambuli and three others who participated in the plot to assassinate Sadat, were hanged by the state.

Faraj's text in many ways resembles a fatwa. The formal asking of the mufti for a legal opinion on the matter (*istiftā'*) is implied, not stated in the incipit: What is the status of jihad as an instrument for bringing about Islamic reform? The text begins with a Qur'anic verse that calls Muslims back to the faith, away from backsliding: "Is the time not ripe for the hearts of those who believe to submit to Allah's reminder and to the truth which is revealed, that they become not as those who received the scripture of old but the term was prolonged for them and so their hearts were hardened, and many of them are grave sinners."[7] The author then introduces his main argument, that the present-day religious leadership, the ulema, have neglected (*ahmala*) one of God's most important duties, struggle in God's cause (*jihād fī sabīl Allāh*). He builds his case, using Qur'anic quotes, and examples from the life and sayings of the Prophet (hadith), as well as arguing historically, from the time of the nascent Muslim community (umma) to present circumstances in Egypt. Citations support the case he is trying to make. For example, he cites an interpretation by Ibn Rajab of a saying attributed to Muhammad, "I have been sent with the sword" (*bu'ithtu bi-l-sayf*). It is interpreted to mean that God sent Muhammad "to call with the sword (*dā'iyan bi-l-sayf*) humankind to acknowledge God's unicity (*tawḥīd*) after he had called with argument (*ḥujja*). Those who did not answer the call by the Qur'an, or by argument, or by textual explanation (*al-bayān*) to God's unicity should be called by the sword" (section 5).[8]

Arguing from Islamic history, Faraj claims that from time to time, beginning with the Prophet himself, it has been necessary to embark upon conquest to establish rule according to God's commands and prohibitions, in short, his revelation or sharia. Citing a hadith whose text (*matn*) carries a prediction attributed to Muhammad—that Constantinople would be conquered by Islam before Rome—Faraj argues that Constantinople fell to the Muslims eight hundred years later and that, God permitting, Rome will fall and eventually an Islamic caliphate will replace unjust worldly governments and will restore the divine and just rule of the time of the Prophet (sections 10–15). Thus the neglected duty of jihad is tantamount to a duty (*farḍ*) to reestablish an Islamic state or caliphate (*iqāmat al-khilāfa al-islāmiyya*). The radical nature of his interpretation of jihad as an urgent duty for all Muslims is borne by his conclusion to this stage of his argument: "If [such a] state (*dawla*) can not be established except through armed combat (*qitāl*) then armed combat is obligatory for us" (section 16).

'Abd al-Salam Faraj next makes a case that in the "present age" (1980s) the rule of Muslim societies is not according to what God has sent down (section 21), and more pointedly, that the rulers of this age are in apostasy from Islam (*ridda 'an al-islam*), ruling instead under the influence of various forms of anti-Islamic imperialism, namely, Crusaderism (*ṣalibiyya*), Communism (*shuyu'iyya*), or Zionism (*ṣahyuniyya*, section 25). This is a very strong charge given the fact that in Islamic jurisprudence the penalty for apostasy (believers turning away from or against Islam) is death. Following the style of jurisprudential reasoning, Faraj draws an historical parallel. He likens the rulers of the present age to the Mongols (*al-tatār*), who eventually accepted Islam externally (that is, they pronounced the twofold witness: There is no God but Allah; Muhammad is His Messenger), but who failed to rule Muslim lands according to what God had revealed and Muhammad had established in Medina. Faraj cites the fatwas of Ibn Taymiyya at length to build his case that jihad against such rule and rulers is a duty. Ibn Taymiyya had given the opinion: "Fighting the Mongols who came to the land of Syria is obligatory according to scripture and the Sunna" (section 40). The proof text cited is Qur'an 2:193: "Fight them until there is no dissension (*fitna*) and religion becomes God's."

Crucial to his argument is ʿAbd al-Salam Faraj's reply to the majority of modern Sunni jurists who hold that armed jihad in Islam is only for defense. As Sohail Hashmi notes on page 133, contemporary Sunni public intellectuals have been overly sensitive to the charge that Islam is prone to engage in religious wars, and this may be one reason why many jurists and religious writers have emphasized the defensive nature of jihad. This sensitivity to the accusation that Islam is a religion spread by the sword nonetheless reflects a longstanding dispute between Muslim and Christian theologians that dates back at least to the eighth century. The nature of this dispute is reflected in the ninth-century treatise by ʿAli ibn Rabban al-Tabari, a Nestorian Christian convert to Islam, purportedly writing from within the court of the Caliph al-Ma'mun (reg. 813–33). Al-Tabari turns on its head the Christian critique of Islam as a religion of the sword, conquering its neighbors and forcing them to convert. Citing the time of Muhammad's wars with the Meccans, al-Tabari comments:

> When he noticed that they were rejecting his order, thinking evil of him, and not entering willingly into the religion and the grace of God, he made them enter into it by force (*adkhalahum fīhi karḥan*); his claim then triumphed, and the Arabs one and all submitted to him.[9]

ʿAbd al-Salam Faraj also wants to emphasize that Muhammad exerted himself and his followers forcefully against his detractors and enemies in spreading Islam. He cites a hadith in which the Prophet is asked: "Which is the jihad in the path of God?" The Prophet's reply: "Whoever fights for the being of the Word of God (*li-takūn kālimat Allāh*) is the highest; he is in the path of God."[10] Faraj comments: "It is obligatory for Muslims to raise swords in the faces of the leaders who hide truth (*al-ḥaqq*) and manifest deceptions" (section 71). In support of this interpretation he interprets the Verse of the Sword, Qur'an 9:5: "Thus, when the sacred months have passed, slay the polytheists wherever you find them. . . ." He then cites Ibn Kathir and other classical exegetes who held that this verse abrogates 114 verses which enjoin Muslims to live in peace with infidels (sections 77–79). Those modern Muslims who claim that the duty of jihad is fulfilled by engaging in missionary activities (*daʿwa*) are answered with proof texts from the Qur'an which indicate that jihad means fighting for God's sake, that is, in the path of God and that it is an individual duty (*farḍ ʿayn*) similar to other religious duties, such as prayer and fasting (sections 84–87).

ʿAbd al-Salam Faraj ends his treatise on the necessity (*ḍarūra*) for fighting the enemies of Islam by addressing the issue of proper and permissible conduct in combat, the classical problem in just war theory of *jus in bello*. This, as other authors in this volume have demonstrated, was more a concern of the medieval jurists than it has been of modern theorists, who have been much more concerned to argue the grounds for mounting armed combat and war than proper conduct in war. As Abou El Fadl has noted on page 108:

> Classical Muslim jurists distinguish between what they call *ḥarb al-bughāh* (war against Muslims) and *ḥarb al-kuffār* (war against unbelievers). The rules that apply to fighting Muslims are different from the limitations set upon the conduct of warfare against non-Muslims. If Muslims fight other Muslims, there are binding regulations that do not necessarily apply to Muslims fighting non-Muslims or apostates.

Abou El Fadl goes on to mention that whereas for medieval jurists Muslims and Muslim property taken in combat must be released when belligerency ends, this is not necessarily the case regarding non-Muslim enemies and their property. Moreover, the more deadly means of destruction, such as mangonels and flame-throwers, are not to be used against Muslim combatants unless not to use such dire means would risk losing the war, whereas fewer such restrictions apply to war against non-Muslim combatants.

For ʿAbd al-Salam Faraj, as we have seen, jihad as combat against enemies, both within and without Islam, is an individual duty, not a duty that is sufficiently met if the community raises an army in times of threat. Against the notion that jihad is elective and of several types, that one can pursue jihad of the pen or tongue in combating infidels and hypocrites, or jihad of the soul in personal piety, Faraj takes the position that these are not disjunctive choices. They are all forms of jihad, but the true jihad is fighting (*al-qitāl*) for the sake of God. His argument is that even as God had said of another religious duty in the Qur'an: "Fasting is prescribed for you" (Qur'an 2:183), so it is also written: "Fighting is prescribed for you" (Qur'an 2:216). This means, Faraj argues, that fighting is a duty, and that it is insufficient to try to fulfill this obligation merely through missionary activity (*daʿwa*). Fighting is the essence of this duty, and it entails confrontation with the enemy and blood (*al-muwājaha wa-l-dam*, section 84). Three conditions in particular make jihad an individual duty: when a Muslim army is facing an enemy, when nonbelievers (*kuffār*) descend upon a country, and when the Imam calls upon a people to fight an enemy. The eschatological force of jihad as fighting infidels and other enemies is indicated in the passage Faraj quotes from the Qur'an (9:38–39):

> O you who have believed, what is the matter with you? When it is said to you "hasten forth in the Path of God," you become weighted to the

ground. Are you so satisfied with the life of this world that you would neglect the Hereafter? This world is a small thing in comparison to the Hereafter. If you do not hasten forth [God] will inflict upon you a painful punishment and He will substitute for you another people. You will not harm Him at all. God is powerful over all things (section 85).

In order for Muslims to achieve success in combating the enemy, ʿAbd al-Salam Faraj agrees with the medieval jurists that the other side should be called upon to accept Islam. Then, if they refuse to submit (lit. become Muslim), they may be attacked without warning (sections 119–20). Muslims should try to avoid killing or harming nonbelligerent dependents, such as women, children, or the elderly and infirm (section 122). Nonetheless, Faraj cites a hadith from the collection of *Ṣaḥīḥ Muslim* (and al-Nawawi's commentary on it) of Muslim forces attacking the most hated religious enemy, the polytheists (*mushrikūn*), in order to conclude that the rules (*aḥkām*) which apply to the fathers also apply to the children. That is, it is lawful to attack and kill the dependents of certain enemies when they cannot be distinguished in an attack on the principle enemy (section 121). The category "*mushrikūn*" has no practical value in modern sociology where it has no real referent, but for religious discourse it has enormous symbolic value, thus enabling metaphorical significance of such passages in scripture and Prophetic tradition. Interestingly, Faraj seemed only to want to establish the principle in his treatise, not to historicize it in the contemporary period.

Radical Jihad against External Enemies

Addressed more specifically to a Muslim constituency that is more suspicious of western and modernist world views are the post–Operation Desert Storm fatwas that call for radical resistance to U.S. and European aggression against Muslim peoples. Among the more radical statements on jihad in this category are the fatwas and informal tracts by the fugitive Saudi religious leader of al-Qaʿida and financier, Osama bin Laden. A famous fatwa cosigned by Osama bin Laden, Rifaʿi Taha, and several others appeared in Arabic *al-Quds al-ʿArabī* on January 23, 1998 (English translation appeared on the Web) along with other writings by and interviews with bin Laden that pertain to his views on jihad. Thus the fatwa was published over three and a half years prior to September 11, 2001.

One important characteristic of bin Laden's fatwa is that it not only argues the *jus ad bellum* case for going to war against western enemies (specifically termed "Jews and Crusaders," as we saw in the case of ʿAbd al-Salam Faraj's tract), but unlike most other fatwas on jihad in modern times, it argues the *jus in bello* case for terrorism and individual acts of morally demanded duty so long as the anti-Muslim forces are carrying arms in Muslim lands, especially in Muslim holy places. He likens American forces to a snake, which enters the house of a man and then is killed by that man. Bin Laden's argument for terrorism as a legitimate means of conduct in war is a significant development in contemporary discussions of jihad.

One of the characteristics of fatwa-writing that has been thrown into remarkable relief since 1990 is what Yvonne Haddad has called the "war of fatwas" occasioned especially by the Gulf War of 1990–91. Although differing and even conflicting interpretations by different muftis in different *madhhabs* are not surprising to students of Islamic jurisprudence, fatwas on jihad during and since the Gulf War, as we have just seen, have highlighted the sharply different interpretations of the same sources that are possible and indeed probable in the *iftā'* (fatwa writing) process. In the case of the Gulf War, as Haddad points out, "[b]oth Saudi Arabia and Iraq sought international Islamic sanctions for their policies."[13] After the invasion of Kuwait but before the outbreak of the Gulf War, Iraq convened the International Congress of Ulema in December 1990 to "undertake jihad and revolution against the Arab Muslim leaders who had joined the coalition forces under American leadership."[14] Shortly thereafter Saudi Arabia convened a counter-congress of ulema that supported 'Abd al-'Aziz ibn Baz's call for jihad against Saddam Husayn. Eventually, other grand muftis in Damascus, Cairo, and elsewhere issued fatwas on one side of the issue or the other demonstrating, in Haddad's words "the contention between the two Islamic world views that currently are vying for dominance in the Arab world."[15]

In 1991, the Grand Mufti at Dār al-Iftā' in Egypt, Muhammad Sayyid Tantawi, wrote the fifty-page fatwa referred to above. Its purpose was to establish Islamic legal grounds for President Mubarak's support for the allied forces arrayed against Iraq. The fatwa had to address two audiences: the western nations that counted on Egypt's largely moral support for Operation Desert Storm, and Muslim communities worldwide that did not. It is interesting to note that the Egyptian embassy in Washington distributed an English translation titled *Islamic Judgment on the Gulf Crisis.* This was not the first time a western government had taken an interest in Islamic fatwas pertaining to public and political issues (for example, Khomeini's fatwa on Salman Rushdie), but it does suggest that the modern *iftā'* process is one that no longer targets Muslim audiences solely. This entails, then, another attribute of the modern *iftā'* process, namely, the conscious need of some Islamic groups and nations to seek the understanding, if not the approval, of Muslims and non-Muslims abroad and to address their criticisms. On page 129 of this volume, as we have already noted, Sohail Hashmi refers to this as "reinterpreting the grounds for jihad in light of modern sensibilities on the wars of religion." Scholars, politicians, and the media are reading *and interpreting* fatwas on jihad and other topics of interest to the world community.

Jihad against Secular Modernism

Another postmodern dimension to the ethics of jihad in contemporary writing has been discussed by John Kelsay, who has studied Muslim statements published in the west about jihad during the most recent conflicts, such as in Bosnia and Chechnya. Kelsay has discovered that embedded in recent Islamic statements on the need for jihad in a world in which Muslims are increasingly under physical threat by non-Muslim governments and groups, the language of antimodernism, if not also the language of antimodernity, is prominent. The problem of modernity adds a new dimension, Kelsay's article suggests, to Islamic discourse about the ethics of killing and saving life. Here we may recall Mustansir Mir's point, cited at the beginning of this chapter, that modernity must be taken into account in interpreting contemporary understandings of jihad among jurists and intellectuals. To put the matter differently, textual scholars need to explore the seams and cracks in the historic Islamic discourse about jihad into which the concern about modernity/antimodernity has seeped. Of particular interest have been the fatwas and messages of the more radical Muslim groups, as we have seen—those that contest the opinions issued by traditional Sunni ulema authorities, such as Dār al-Iftā᾽ in Egypt. Closely related to discourses against modernity are theological arguments against the west, the U.S. in particular.

Citing the works of Max Weber, Talcott Parsons, and Richard L. Rubenstein, John Kelsay has essayed a comparison of western understandings and experiences of modernity with Islamic conceptions and critiques of modernity in the west. The context for this comparison is his discussion of the plight of Muslims in Bosnia after the Yugoslavian Wars began in 1989. Kelsay claims that "many Muslims see Bosnia in the context of the failure of modernity."[16] He sets the argument further: "The momentum of Islamic thinking about justice and war leads to an emphasis on such *jus ad bellum* concerns as right authority and just cause, and ultimately to discussion of how conceptions of the nature and destiny of human beings set a framework for discussions of war." He goes on: "In the end, Bosnia suggests that it is not just Islam but European and North American civilization that are in the dock."[17] Thus, by viewing modern Islamic discussions of justice and war through the lense of Muslim critiques of modernity, Kelsay turns the table on western condemnations of terrorism and violence as Islamic expressions of war and peace.

This is an important rhetorical move, which suggests that such fatwas and other writings on jihad as we have been discussing are written as public documents for global audiences. Or at least they have become public documents which are read and analyzed beyond the practical jurisdictions of Islamic law. Kelsay holds that post–Gulf War fatwas and critiques of modernity may be viewed and treated as dialectical arguments with and against modernist western ethical systems. So far, so good. Nonetheless there is an aspect to the writings of 'Abd al-Salam Faraj, Osama bin Laden, and other more radical theorists of jihad that must not be lost sight of. The deeply classical manner of these fatwas and writings, despite their radical tone and departure from the quietism of traditional Sunni theories of jihad, reminds us that scholars must read and interpret these texts as part of a very traditional theological genre and way of speaking and arguing, despite the ultramodern context of fatwas on the Internet. The urgency of the contemporary rhetoric does not surpass the urgency of many of the legal opinions written by Ibn Taymiyya against non-Muslim intrusions in Islamic religious practices in the fourteenth century, or the rulings for and against the controversial Sufi al-Hallaj in the tenth century, to name just two well-known cases. So, while it is true that western modernism, and modernity itself, have deeply affected how the ethics of jihad has been construed in recent decades, it is also true that such profound changes have forced Islamic rethinking of traditional problems throughout history. Nonetheless, the way in which the issues have been argued by some of the most radical thinkers and writers remains classical and traditional, relying on scripture, Prophetic tradition, and narratives from early Islamic history for making and destroying arguments. What seems to be relentlessly modern or postmodern about this literature is that it has become globalized in print and on the internet, attracting attention and commentary by non-jurist Muslims and non-Muslims across the world.

The very nature of jihad has been a very large and open issue for Muslims in the post-colonial, post–Gulf War, postmodern era. Enemies and opponents are there to contend with, but with the rapid globalization of the internet and the new porousness of traditional communal boundaries the nature of the dangerous "other" has become more difficult to define, locate, and agree upon. In *The Islamic Threat: Myth or Reality?*, John Esposito has convincingly argued that with the collapse of the so-called Second World—the Soviet Empire in 1989 and the Soviet Union in 1991—Islam has become the new Evil Empire. In this view, Islam is the new mythical foe that will feed the need the western political imagination has for a grand enemy to combat.

In *Shattering the Myth: Islam beyond Violence*, Bruce Lawrence has argued against the popular view in the west that Islam is a monolithically violent religious system that visits bloodshed on its enemies and suppresses women as a matter of course. Both Esposito and Lawrence contextualize the incidences of violence exposed in the news, and they produce a more nuanced and balanced description of Islamic societies in the modern world, where Muslims are more often than not the victims rather than the perpetrators of violence. For Esposito and Lawrence, the media bias that Islam is a violent tradition is based primarily on a western failure to understand Islam. Yet some Muslim intellectuals believe that the problem is not entirely a western one. Farid Esack asks as a modern Muslim:

> How do Muslims engage the religious other in a world that increasingly defies geographical, political, religious, and ideological boundaries? This is a world where the "enemy" is often the internal self (the Saudi, Iranian, or Sudanese regime, or the Shi'a, Qadiani, or modernists), and the asylum provider is the external other (Christian relief organizations, Amnesty International, or the non-Muslim neighbor).[18]

The task of this chapter has been more limited. The purpose has been to open a discussion of the more radical recent discourses on jihad that Islamist ideologues, using traditional juristic styles of reasoning, have employed in their writings. Of particular significance has been the rejection of the modern Sunni trend to limit armed jihad to defense of Muslim peoples and ways of life and religious expression against outside intervention and attack. The more radical Islamists, such as 'Abd al-Salam Faraj and Osama bin Laden, have returned to premodern arguments for armed jihad as a legitimate and indeed obligatory Islamic remedy for threats by internal and external enemies. Force—even deadly force—is found by some practitioners to be both legal and ethical, in dealing with internal and external enemies who threaten the commonweal of the Muslim umma. Although the ethical grounds for the use of deadly force, even against noncombatants and dependents in some circumstances, are not argued in the philosophical discourse of ethics and moral reasoning, radical Islamists have adduced well known juristic arguments from early Islam to make their case.

This paper has not been about ethical theories of killing and saving life in Islam, then, in the sense of a discussion of the grounds for making ethical decisions. Islamic ethics—the deciding of proper conduct in matters that arise in real life—is more a matter of case studies in which legal opinions are rendered, based on scripture, Prophetic tradition and historical precedent, especially from the earliest generations of Muslims. It follows, then, that not moral reasoning but hermeneutics is the real subject matter of this paper—the literary and legal art of interpreting texts, often competing interpretations of the same texts. This was made evident in consideration of the texts by Faraj and bin Laden, where the moral and legal arguments they have adduced turn on how to interpret a narrow range of texts. In this sense, the postmodern argument about jihad and the ethics of killing and saving life are rooted in a very traditional Islamic way of reasoning, the *iftā'* process of rendering nonbinding but nonetheless convincing opinions based on a range of texts that all parties accept as authoritative. This led in the months leading up to the Gulf War, as Yvonne Haddad's essay reminds us, to a war of fatwas between the Saudis and other Gulf Arabs and their allies on the one side and Iraq and its allies on the other. More recently, the harder line on jihad against enemies of Islam has been labeled the "Wahhabi" or "Salafi" interpretation which continues to challenge the more traditional interpretations of the ulema. One of the arguments of this paper is that despite the modern pretexts for deciding when and how to mount an armed jihad (for example, Serbian aggression, U.S. intervention in the Arab Holy Lands, Israeli occupation of Jerusalem, chemical and germ warfare), it is the classical texts and their traditional methods of interpretation that the more strident Islamists and their sympathetic followers have utilized. This poses a problem for their publication in international print media (Arabic and English) and the World Wide Web, because such discourses are closed to outsiders and based on privileged understandings of texts that are authoritative only for insiders. Such texts often have two or more opponents or layers of opponents: those named in the jihad text (for example, the U.S. or Allied forces in the Gulf) and those with whom the authors of the jihad text are making a textual argument (Sunni quietists, government-sponsored fatwa organizations, and the like).

Thus, the postmodern context of the present debate about jihad cannot be isolated from the premodern textual nature of that debate. This seems to suggest the interdisciplinary nature of the present study, requiring methodologies from the social sciences, humanities, jurisprudence, and even the life sciences and medicine. Something like "it takes a village" characterizes the adequate study of the ethics of killing and saving life in Islamic societies. Any single voice, such as the author of this chapter, must be heard not by itself, but alongside of and over and against the others that join this conversation. It also requires, as argued in the introduction, the need for comparison, a comparison of the texts on jihad we want to understand by strident Islamists with the texts of their opponents and the classical texts to which both groups appeal.

Notes

1. See, for example, ʻAbd al-Rahmān al-Jazīrī, *Kitāb al-fiqh ʻalā al-madhāhib al-arbaʻa,* 5 vols. (N.p.: Dār al-Irshād li-l-Ṭabāʻa wa-l-Nashr, n.d.), especially vol. 5, subsection on *al-bughāt wa-l-muḥāribūn,* 5:319–31.

2. Mustansir Mir, "*Jihad* in Islam," in *The Jihad and Its Times,* ed. Hadia Dajani-Shakeel and Ronald Messier (Ann Arbor: Center for Near Eastern and North African Studies, University of Michigan, 1991), 113.

3. James Turner Johnson and John Kelsay, eds., *Cross, Crescent, and Sword: The Justification and Limitation of War in Western and Islamic Tradition* (New York: Greenwood Press, 1990); Kelsay and Johnson, *Just War and Jihad: Historical and Theoretical Perspectives on War and Peace in Western and Islamic Traditions,* Contributions to the Study of Religion, 28 (New York: Greenwood Press, 1991); Kelsay, *Islam and War: A Study in Comparative Ethics* (Louisville, Ky.: Westminster/John Knox Press, 1993).

4. Mir, *Jihad,* 113; John Kelsay, "Bosnia and the Muslim Critique of Modernity," in *Religion and Justice in the War over Bosnia,* ed. G. Scott Davis (New York and London: Routledge, 1996), esp. pp. 120ff.

5. Gilles Kepel, *Muslim Extremism in Egypt: The Prophet and Pharaoh.* (Berkeley and Los Angeles: University of California Press, 1986), 191–93.

6. Ibid., 192–93. Here Kepel describes the popular approval that was accorded to the assassination of Sadat, who was viewed negatively by most Egyptians, in contrast to his image as a peacemaker and leader of goodwill by the western media and their readers and viewers. The most thorough analysis available in English, including a history of the availability of the Arabic text, is Johannes J. G. Jansen, *The Neglected Duty: The Creed of Sadat's Assassins and Islamic Resurgence in the Middle East* (Macmillan: New York, 1986).

7. Qur'an 67:16. Qur'an citations will follow Marmaduke Pickthall's translation (unless otherwise indicated), occasionally rendering some words and phrases into more understandable contemporary American English.

8. References to sections of the text follow those found in Jansen's translation. I have occasionally added terms in transliteration from an Arabic edition to clarify meaning for those familiar with the debate in modern Arabic.

9. ʻAli ibn Rabban al-Tabari, *The Book of Religion and Empire,* trans. A. Mingana (Manchester: Manchester University Press, 1922), 57 (Eng.), 108 (Ar.).

10. I was not able to find this hadith in the standard collections.

11. Yvonne Yazbeck Haddad, "Operation Desert Storm and the War of Fatwas," in *Islamic Legal Interpretation: Muftis and Their Fatwas,* eds. Muhammad Khalid Masud, Brinkley Messick, and David S. Powers (Cambridge, Mass.: Harvard University Press, 1996), 298.

12. Osama bin Laden et al., "Fatwa: Kill Americans Everywhere," *Al-Quds al-'Arabī,* February 23, 1998, 1, 3. See http://www.emergency.com/bladen98.htm (May 18, 2002).

13. Haddad, "Operation Desert Storm," 301.

14. Ibid.

15. Ibid.

16. Kelsay, *Islam and War,* 120.

17. Ibid.

18. Farid Esack, "Muslims Engaging the Other and the *Humanum,*" in *Sharing the Book: Religious Perspectives on the Rights and Wrongs of Proselytism,* eds. John Witte Jr. and Richard C. Martin (Maryknoll, N.Y.: Orbis Books, 1999), 227.

Euthanasia

Of the three issues dealt with in this book, Islamic sources say the least about euthanasia. Like abortion, euthanasia falls under the broad range of family matters over which Islamic law has limited jurisdiction. But the paucity of cases in the classical sources also has to do with the fact that until very recently, euthanasia was only a question of active means, of mercy killing. According to Islamic law, such an act could be described as suicide or homicide and would therefore be strongly prohibited. Medical advances have changed the picture, however, opening the door to almost endless attenuation of life through life-support machines.

Both essays in this section focus on the sort of euthanasia that utilizes passive means, "allowing nature to take its course." In the first, I argue that the classical sources' discussion of martyrdom and suicide leaves open the possibility that hastening of death may not always be wrong. Examining the place of death within Islamic theology, I find that the actual moment of death occupies a place of relative unimportance in the sources. These sources see God as determining the moment of death, virtually ruling out the possibility that active forms of euthanasia could be licit. This impression is verified through examination of literature on suicide and martyrdom, both of which condemn acts that aim to hasten death. On the other hand, the classical sources contain significant ambiguity about a martyr's (and a suicide's) intentions, ambiguity that seems to recommend passive euthanasia. Further, emphasis on God's determination of the moment of death may open the possibility for some types of active euthanasia in the modern world.

In the second essay, Birgit Krawietz argues that recent medical advances have significantly changed the context of euthanasia, taking death and dying out of the private hands of the family and thrusting it into the public sphere of the hospital. In addressing the issue of whether medically determined brain death can be an acceptable criterion of death for Muslims, she focuses on one of the key arguments behind some forms of euthanasia. Krawietz breaks down modern discussions into four types, finding, for instance, that a central principle behind modern discussions of brain death is the notion of *ḥurma,* or the sanctity of the body, and that debates about accepting this medical definition of death are often rooted in concerns not to transgress this principle. A second principle is that God, being omnipotent, could cause the merely brain-dead to return to life, and here Krawietz notes that empirical evidence is often no match for theological dogma. On the other hand, some modern writers distinguish between the concept and the criteria of death, asserting that medical criteria of death need not contradict theological conception of death. Finally, Krawietz looks at the possible ramifications of the special legal status conferred on the person in the last stages of death.

It is in the ethics of euthanasia that we see most clearly the ramifications of human action in killing and saving life. A secular ethicist who sees life as a finite quantity may promote euthanasia in order to preserve the dignity of human existence at the end of life, and to save the dying person and their family from unnecessary suffering and pain. But to a Muslim who sees death as a transition to life after death, the suffering of this world is a reminder of the freedom from suffering in the world to come. The classical sources therefore are concerned about any action that might hasten death, since suicide would eliminate the reward for a lifetime of good deeds. But Muslims in the modern world are caught in a bind, since the very medicine that would save a life might also overstep the predetermined moment of death. And, as Krawietz points out, modern medicine has already changed the context of death in this world. While the Prophet died at home, resting in the arms of his beloved wife 'A'isha, Muslims today are more likely to die in the public space of the hospital.

Finally, however, we must wonder why euthanasia is not a topic of wider public discussion among Muslim ethicists. As mentioned in Krawietz's essay, cases have occurred where persons languish for years on life-support machines with no hope of recovery, but the context of these discussions seems to be organ transplant, not euthanasia. Further, I point out that medieval sources could support a warrant for some types of euthanasia, yet it appears that there is no room for a positive defense of euthanasia among most muftis; rather, the muftis frame the question as whether a brain-dead individual is really dead. In other words, they are shifting the boundary of life and death from traditional indicators of death to modern medical ones. As in the case of abortion, such a move allows the sources to affirm that there is no life not worth living, and the value of life is contingent on God's decree alone. These are not merely theological platitudes, they also have a real effect on the form and content of ethical debates among Muslims today.

Eight

The "Good Death" in Islamic Theology and Law

Jonathan E. Brockopp

When euthanasia is discussed in texts on medical ethics, the focus is often on specific cases and involves the use of advanced technology. Respirators, pain medications, invasive surgery, and even suicide machines are the backdrop for modern discussions of death. In all these cases, it is easy to focus attention on machines and technicians, and to lose sight of the fundamental principles at stake in decisions at the end of life. In recent discussions of euthanasia, Muslims speak to this modern predicament in a near unison voice, scorning "the atheistic way of thinking" that pervades medical practice and suggesting that the lack of care in medicine is "a condemnation of modern society."[1] Yet it would be erroneous to understand these sentiments as Luddite or anti-western. Rather, the muftis seem to be concerned about the tendency of situational concerns (machines, hospitals, impending death) to override fundamental principles of Islamic theology. In the modern hospital environment, focus on these concerns can result in a utilitarian approach to saving and taking life, one that leaves little room for the primary considerations of Islamic theology: the respect owed a human person, body and soul, as a "trust" (*amāna*) from God; the place of death within the larger scheme of God's creative activity; and God's essential role as the giver and taker of life.

Like Khaled Abou El Fadl, in his essay on war (see chapter 5), I argue that Islamic law allows for utilitarian considerations in the field of medicine, but in a strictly limited fashion. That is, doctors, like commanders on the field of battle, are understood to have a certain expertise and are given substantial leeway in making pragmatic decisions. But these decisions must rest within a larger framework of rules.[2] This ethical stance explains the continued reference to classical texts of theology and law when dealing with very modern issues such as euthanasia. Even radically new conceptions of the nature of life and death do not change the value of the traditional Islamic sources in providing a context for the muftis' answers. Not surprisingly, perhaps, that answer is not an outright prohibition of euthanasia, but rather an expression of grave concern.[3]

For the muftis, it is not possible to say that euthanasia is always forbidden, as long as the act of euthanasia may be described in such a way that it does not defy the central tenets of Islamic theology. This flexibility both maintains the relevance of the classical Islamic sources and also offers due respect for technical and medical innovations. The balance of classic theology and modern medicine is exemplified in a recent discussion of euthanasia at a major medical conference.[4] In a report on this conference, Muhammad Sayyid Tantawi, the rector of al-Azhar University, is first described as taking a hard line: "[Tantawi] dismissed everything that would result in mercy killing, confirming that killing the patient who has no hope [of recovery] is not an allowable decision (*qarār mubāḥ*) according to Islamic law: not for the sake of the doctor, nor for the ease of the patient, nor for the patients themselves."[5] From this position, Tantawi moves to a larger theological explanation, mentioning both the command to preserve one's body and also the prohibition of suicide.

> Human life is a trust [from God] which [human beings] are required to preserve, along with preservation of their bodies so as not to cast themselves into perdition, according to God's word, "do not cast yourselves into perdition by your own hands" [Qur'an 2:195]. Human beings are forbidden from suicide according to His word, "do not kill yourselves, surely God is merciful to you" [Qur'an 4:29, discussed below, pp. 183–84]. The Prophet, God's peace and blessings be upon him, forbade human beings from suicide in the strongest terms, and he threatened those who would do such things with the worst of destinies both in this world and in the next. Islamic law . . . orders physicians to be concerned for the sick, and, at the end, to take pains to care for them, and for both patient and doctor to leave the result up to God—may He be praised and exalted—and for the physician not to answer the plea of the patient to end his life. For if he answers, he will prove disloyal to the trust, regardless of whether this is at the request of the patient or not.[6]

With this basis clear, Tantawi then allows that certain cases of euthanasia might be permitted, describing a substantial area of personal discretion within the parameters of the theological principles outlined above.

> Death is the separation from life, and those who can judge a separation from life are the physicians, not the religious scholars. So if the doctor believes that the patient, whose heart is beating although his brain has died, is dead, this is a matter of the physician['s professional expertise]. [If] the heart of a patient continues to beat because he is hooked up to

> a machine, and his brain is dead, there is no fault in the family requesting the removal of the machine . . . they are accepting God's decree.[7]

In this response, Tantawi makes several fine distinctions: between euthanasia as killing and as letting die; between the intention to ease pain and the intention to accept God's decree; and between actions of suicide, homicide and natural death. In this chapter, I will elaborate on the foundation of this complex position, first by addressing the meaning of the moment of death within the larger Islamic discussion of the end of life, and then by examining three central principles that inform Islamic discussions of correct action at the end of life: the prohibition of suicide; the command to martyrs not to long for death; and the declaration that every soul has its life span appointed by God. Finally, I will return to modern discussions to consider some of the ways these principles have been applied in cases of euthanasia.

The Islamic Theology of Death

Whereas western secular ethicists have defended a "right to die" out of an argument for human dignity, Islamic theology tends to see human dignity as residing in the believer's relationship to God. As Tantawi states above, human life is not inherently valuable, rather it is valuable because it is a trust (*amāna*) from God. The moment of death therefore gains its meaning from this larger scheme, and often serves only as a transitional moment in a much larger set of events. Tantawi's comments express an attitude which is embedded in the Qur'an itself, which was concerned with human attitudes toward death and life from the very beginning of its message.

> Perish humankind! How unthankful they are!
> Of what did He create them?
> Of a sperm-drop
> He created them, and determined them,
> then the way eased for them,
> then makes them to die, and buries them,
> then, when He wills, He raises them.
> No indeed! Humanity has not accomplished His bidding.
> (Qur'an 80:16-23)[8]

In this early sura, God's intimate involvement with his creation is established at the beginning of life (with the insignificant sperm-drop) and reinforced at every moment up to the end of time, from life to death and resurrection. This description of God's creative activity and the relatively passive role attributed to human beings is found throughout the Qur'an and heavily influenced theological speculation.[9] The Qur'an sets God's intimate involvement with His creation in opposition to the common pre-Islamic conception that fate determines all things and that there is no ultimate meaning to death—or to life. For instance, one group of Arabs is reported to hold the following views: "They say, 'There is nothing but our present life; we die, and we live, and nothing but Time (*dahr*) destroys us.'" To which God responds, "Of that they have no knowledge; they merely conjecture" (Qur'an 45:23).[10] Further, the Qur'an continues: "Say, 'God gives you life then makes you die, then He shall gather you to the Day of Resurrection, wherein there is no doubt, but most do not know'" (Qur'an 45:26).

The Qur'an does not merely replace old concepts of destiny with God, but sees God as a different kind of active principle in the world, as the author of life and death. The point of death is then reinforced in long passages devoted to descriptions of the day of resurrection and judgment. The following verses come from the chapter of the Qur'an (*Yā Sīn*) often recited at Muslim funerals; here, the Qur'an speaks about the unbelievers:

> And the Trumpet shall be blown; then behold, they are sliding down
> from their tombs unto their Lord.
> They say, "Alas for us! Who roused us out of our sleeping place?
> This is what the All-merciful promised, and the Envoys spoke truly."
> It was only one Cry; then behold, they are all arraigned before Us:
> "So today no soul shall be wronged anything, and you shall not be
> recompensed, except according to what you have been doing.
> See the inhabitants of Paradise today are busy in their rejoicing,
> they and their spouses, reclining upon couches in the shade;
> therein they have fruits, and they have all that they call for."
> "Peace!"—such is the greeting, from a Lord All-compassionate.
> (Qur'an 36:51–58)

In these verses, unbelievers are rudely shaken from their slumber in their graves on the day of judgment. After being duly arraigned, they see the believers enter a paradise of comfort. Even for these sinners, death is transformed from a meaningless end to a key part of a much larger cycle of God's intimate involvement in human affairs. The act of dying therefore has no intrinsic importance, but rather gains its importance due to the teleology of death, resurrection, and judgment.[11]

Following the precedent of the Qur'an, classical works on death focus much more on the events that occur to the soul after death. These books formed a popular sub-genre within classical Islamic literature, and they include works by the great theologians al-Ghazali (d. 1111) and al-Qurtubi (d. 1273),[12] as well as texts from the present day.[13] The organization of al-Ghazali's text is typical: pages 1–4 focus on creation and pre-destination; pages 4–27 deal with death itself, both as experienced by the dying individual and by others, including rules of burial, washing, and so on; pages 27–38 address the time between death and last day, including punishment in the tomb, visions of the dead, and mourning at tombs; and the majority of the text (pages 38–110) addresses the actual day of judgment, from the blowing of the trumpets to the rolling up of the scroll of heaven. Thus, both the Qur'an and classical sources view the moment of death within the larger context of the soul's life before and after the death of the body.

The teleological perspective of the classical sources restricts allowable actions in cases analogous to euthanasia. To begin with, death is explicitly an act of God. In fact, the very moment of death is defined not in terms of the ceasing of brain function or the stopping of the heart, but as the separation of the soul from the body. One classical text invokes the consensus of the learned jurists in stating: "The learned say that death is not lack of palpitations, nor the ceasing of movement, but rather the cutting of the connection of the soul from the body (*inqiṭāʿ taʿlīq al-ruḥ bi-l-badan*)."[14] By defining death in terms of a generally nonobservable phenomenon, empirical evidence is of limited value, and the role of the doctor or technician is made secondary to that of God. Further, room is left for human error in determining death and for "miraculous" recoveries. Therefore, any human action at the moment of death can only be based on limited human knowledge.

From this brief survey, it is evident not only that the moment of death is of relatively little importance in comparison with the afterlife and the day of judgment, but that the ideal human role at death is one of patient acceptance. As with pre-Islamic ideas of fate, the hour of death is fixed and cannot be resisted, but to this determinism Islam adds a teleology, as the dying believer looks forward to paradise. God's role at death is further emphasized by the definition of death as separation of soul and body—an act that only angels and a few very pious individuals can witness. It follows, then, that any human reaction beyond passivity could be interpreted as resisting God's will, a stance which could consign the soul to hellish torment.

Islamic legal texts conform to this theological picture by assigning a special status to the dying person. Much as with the Jewish notion of the *goses,* Muslims who are in their "dying illness" have reduced legal capacity.[15] In part, this reduced capacity functions to protect the family from sudden loss of property, since dying Muslims may no longer make bequests of their property, nor may they emancipate slaves. In part, the loss of mental faculties is being recognized, and even deathbed conversions are not acceptable.[16] Of particular interest is the fact that the killing of a dying person is not punishable in the same way as killing of a fully capable human being.[17] All of these legal injunctions emphasize the perception of death as a transition, and reduced legal capacity allows the believer to focus on preparing for the afterlife.

Forms of Euthanasia

There is no category for cases of euthanasia in the classical legal literature, so modern muftis, like their Jewish and Christian counterparts, turn to traditions on suicide and martyrdom for analogous cases. However, many fatwas from the late twentieth century do not make full use of these rich traditions, either equating euthanasia with suicide or simply dismissing it as "mercy killing" (*qatl al-raḥma*) as in this statement from the 1981 Islamic Code of Medical Ethics: "Mercy killing, like suicide, finds no support except in the atheistic way of thinking that believes that our life on this earth is followed by void. The claim of killing for painful, hopeless illness is also refuted, for there is no human pain that cannot be largely conquered by medication or by suitable neurosurgery."[18] But euthanasia may be more generally defined as an act that results in the death of a human being, either by hastening that death or by removing hindrances to death, for some positive purpose, usually to alleviate suffering.[19] Further, the moral quality of any given instance of euthanasia depends on several variables. Most important among these are: first, whether the act is actively done to the individual or passively accomplished;[20] second, whether the act is done with the voluntary consent of the dying individual or nonvoluntarily;[21] third, whether the action is done by the dying person or by some agent; finally, the circumstances surrounding the act.

These concerns are neither western nor modern in their origins, and two examples from Islamic texts will illustrate how these categories function. In the first, an old man is suffering after a long life that has led to poverty and destitution; when he can get no help from his neighbors, he hangs himself.[22] The man has ended his life in an active, self-inflicted manner, since he has hung himself. But although the old man has died at his own hand, the sources suggest that his act may not have been voluntary, due to his distressed state of mind. Further, since his misery was caused by a lack of compassion on the part of his neighbors, his culpability may be further reduced. In another case, parents of a severely disabled child seek permission to submit the child to a radical surgery that will almost certainly result in death.[23] Since the chances of survival are 10,000 to 1, this may be described as an active, nonvoluntary act inflicted by an outside agent. Here the purpose is relief of the parents' suffering and a concern for the human dignity of the child.

In sum, these four qualities of the act of euthanasia are reflective of four fundamental concerns in the medieval texts. The first, active versus passive means of causing death, addresses the question of an individual's perceived intervention in God's plan, since actively causing death could hasten the *ajal*, God's appointed hour of death; passive means allows God's plan to run its course. The second, voluntary versus nonvoluntary action, is attached to the key principle of *niyya*, the person's intention in undertaking an act;[24] it also raises the theological question of the extent to which persons may exercise their own will. Self-inflicted death versus other-inflicted is often not dealt with in western texts on euthanasia,[25] yet the medieval sources are concerned to establish the central question of to whom guilt and responsibility for an action accrue. Finally, the circumstances in which the action occurs may change the value of the act in some observers' eyes; correct description of these circumstances is vital for determining whether a particular act is euthanasia, suicide, or martyrdom. So despite the fact that the classical texts have no category for euthanasia, suicide and martyrdom address many of the same principles. Further, suicide and martyrdom are contested categories, and they suggest allowable actions that may in fact be classified as euthanasia, specifically in its passive forms.

The prohibition of suicide in Islam arises from the principle of respect for life. Since life is from God, only God may take life away. Thus, the classical position on suicide provides evidence against active forms of euthanasia. Both Tantawi and the Islamic Code of Medical Ethics are quoted above as equating euthanasia with suicide, and many other authorities agree. In making these strong statements, modern muftis appear to be dependant on medieval commentators, yet comparison with these medieval sources reveals an interesting rhetorical positioning. While the medieval sources present a surprising variety of stances toward suicide, modern fatwas express a nearly universal prohibition of suicide. This stance is perhaps best seen as a pastoral response, as muftis seek to prevent Muslims from any action that might result in eternal punishment. First, the verse quoted above by Tantawi and others, "Do not kill yourselves (*anfusakum*), surely God is merciful to you" (Qur'an 4:29), does not appear to refer to suicide at all, though it can be read in that fashion. Both modern and medieval sources claim that this verse is better translated as "Do not kill each other"[26]—that is, Muslims should not kill other Muslims. Abu Ja'far al-Tabari (d. 923) gives the following explanation:

> [The verse means] some of you should not kill others, since you are people of a single faith, a single creed, and a single religion. For He placed all the people of Islam together [like one individual], so as for the one of you who kills another, it is as if he had killed himself.[27]

It is worth noting, however, that while al-Tabari argues that the verse is actually referring to intra-Muslim conflict, and provides no direct evidence against suicide, he likens that conflict to a presumed prohibition of suicide. Another important Qur'an commentator, Fakhr al-Din al-Razi (d. 1209), agrees that this verse is really about intra-Muslim conflict.

> [The interpreters] are agreed that this verse is a prohibition of some [Muslims] killing others, for [the Prophet] used *anfusakum* in his statement—upon him be peace—"the Muslims are like a single person (*nafs*)." And because the Arabs used to say: "he killed us and the Lord of the Ka'ba" when he killed some of them, because the killing of some of them led to their being killed.

But al-Razi goes on at length to discuss the relationship of this verse to a prohibition of suicide. Further, anticipating modern muftis, he argues that in some cases it may be useful to treat this verse as if it really were a prohibition of suicide.

> But [the interpreters] differ concerning this exhortation as to whether it is a prohibition of suicide. Some disapprove of this and say: "As for the believer with his faith, it is not allowed to prohibit him from suicide, because he takes refuge in the fact that he does not kill himself!" This is because staying away from [suicide] in this world is obvious, due to the great suffering and powerful censure [that suicide would cause]. And staying away from it is also obvious in relation to the afterlife, where [the suicide] would be subject to a terrible chastisement. So if the [Muslim] is pure in his faith, he is already prevented from doing this and in this way the prohibition is useless.
>
> Perhaps, however, it is possible to mention this prohibition in the case of one who is convinced of [the benefits of] suicide, just as the Hindus are convinced—but such a reply is not to a believer.
>
> But even the believer, despite his status as a believer in God and the last day, may suffer so from censure and injury that death seems easier to bear than these. In fact, we see many Muslims killing themselves for such reasons as we have listed. So in this case, the prohibition is beneficial.

This is one of the few discussions of suicide in the classical sources that admits its existence among Muslims. It is also striking for its awareness of Hindu influences on social perceptions. So although al-Razi prohibits suicide, it is evident that such an act is for him neither irrational nor incomprehensible. Al-Razi concludes his discussion by returning to God's qualities of mercy and compassion, providing a theological context that includes both interpretations.

> Finally, there is another interpretive possibility, as if He had said: "Do not do that which deserves death, such as killing, apostasy and adultery." So He, the Most High, has made clear that He is merciful to His servants, and at the hour [of death] His mercy is forbidding them from all that is deserving of torment or trial.[28]

Al-Razi's commentary demonstrates that the classical sources were fully aware of possible motivations for suicide, and the tone of his discussion is strikingly compassionate toward human suffering.

The legal sources continue this ambivalence, both treating suicide differently than other deaths, but also offering little agreement on how the suicide is to be treated. Most say that there is no payment of blood money (*diya*), as would normally be required in the case of murder. However, the authorities differ on the crucial issue of whether the imam prays at the funeral of the suicide. The following commentary on Muslim's collection of hadith is typical; the commentator first quotes the hadith and then provides his explanation:

> On the authority of Jabir b. Sumara who said: "the Prophet, God's blessings and peace be upon him, came to a man who had killed himself with an arrowhead, and he did not pray over him."
>
> This hadith is a proof text for those who say there is no prayer over the suicide due to his disobedience (*li-ʿiṣyānihi*), and this is the *madhhab* of ʿUmar b. ʿAbd al-ʿAziz and al-Awzaʿi. But al-Hasan, al-Nakhaʿi, Qatada, Malik, Abu Hanifa, al-Shafiʿi and the majority of the learned scholars pray over him. They answer this hadith by saying that the Prophet, God's blessings and peace be upon him, did not pray over him personally to warn the people from doing the same act, but the companions prayed over him. And this is how the Prophet, God's blessings and peace be upon him, left it in the first place for all those who [died] in the faith. It was a warning to them against laxity in striving in their faith and against negligence.[29]

At first it may seem that there is little to be gleaned from this short passage about the meaning of suicide within Islam, since it seems to support the modern prohibition by describing suicide as disobedience and negligence. The larger circumstances that may have caused the man to take his own life play no role; rather, suicide is simply a grave sin. Other hadith seem to back this impression by elaborating extensively on the punishments that the suicide will suffer in hell, often forced to repeat their dying acts in perpetuity.[30] But the subtle distinction between the Prophet's refusal to pray at the funeral of a suicide and the general acceptance of such prayer among legal authorities helps to explain the ambivalence of the classical sources. Since suicide must include an intention to die, and intentions are matters of the heart, only God (and his chosen Prophet) can know for certain whether any death was a suicide. In the face of this lack of continuity, legal scholars always presume the best interpretation.[31] These presumptions may also help explain the surprising lack of medieval fatwas on the subject, despite the significant legal consequences of suicide.[32]

The prohibition of suicide is in contrast to Islamic teachings on martyrdom. Martyrdom is hard for many religious traditions to distinguish from suicide,[33] but in Islam the distinction is of particular importance, since the martyr is sent directly to heaven, while the suicide is banished to hell. Muslims honor the deaths of those martyrs who have given their lives for the faith, whether by dying on the pilgrimage to Mecca or while fighting in a religiously sanctioned war (jihad). The Qur'an's theology of martyrdom is built on the following two verses:

> So let them fight in the way of God who sell the present life for the world to come; and whosoever fights in the way of God and is slain, or conquers, We shall bring him a mighty wage. (Qur'an 4:74)

> And those who are slain in the way of God, He will not send their works astray.
> He will guide them, and dispose their minds aright,
> and He will admit them to Paradise, that He has made known to them. (Qur'an 47:4–6)[34]

In the first of these verses, believers are urged to risk their lives for the hope of a heavenly reward, and in the second, the work of the believers' hand in battle is likened to God's work. Both verses emphasize that by submitting themselves completely to God's guidance, warriors return to the paradisiacal state of union.

The hadith record reinforces this idea of aiming for a heavenly reward. The Prophet is said to have wished for three lives so he could lose each of them in fighting for the faith,[35] and stories abound of early Muslims throwing themselves into battle with the hope of dying "in God's path." In one such tale, a soldier who is taking a break in the midst of battle suddenly throws down his dates, and says: "Am I so eager for the good things of this world that I should sit here and finish these morsels in my hand?" He then grabs his sword and races back to the front, eventually losing his life.[36] With these words, the soldier was repeating a familiar refrain in the Qur'an: the good to be found in this world is mere chance compared to the good things which God has prepared in the world to come.

The zeal of this soldier is attractive to many modern Muslim leaders, such as Hasan al-Banna'. But in the following quotation, al-Banna' seems to blur the line between aiming for heavenly reward and aiming for death:

> Brothers! God gives the umma that is skilled in the practice of death and that knows how to die a noble death, an exalted life in this world and eternal felicity in the next. What is the fantasy that has reduced us to loving this world and hating death? If you gird yourselves for a lofty deed and yearn for death, life shall be given to you. Know, then, that death is inevitable, and that it can only happen once. If you suffer it in the way of God, it will profit you in this world and bring you reward in the next.[37]

Al-Banna's exhortation to "yearn for death" seems to be a direct contradiction of certain Prophetic hadith (discussed below), but two cases from the classical literature demonstrate just how fine a line there is between seeking God's reward as a martyr in battle and seeking death. In the first, 'Amir b. Sinan accidentally slays himself while beating an enemy with the broad side of his sword. Interestingly, the story says that the people of Medina began to lament, because they assumed that 'Amir's actions would be considered suicide. The narrator tells us:

> The people said: "his good deeds have gone to waste: he killed himself!" But I said: "O Prophet of God, they claim that 'Amir's good deeds have gone to waste" and he responded: "The one who says this lies; 'Amir will receive two rewards, since he died a martyr."[38]

So although 'Amir actively caused his own death, he did so nonvoluntarily, since his intention was only to fight an enemy. In the second case, a Muslim also actively causes his own death with his sword, but different intentions lead to different consequences. This story of a fatally wounded warrior, who falls on his own sword to hasten death, is found in many sources.[39] Each man in these examples died by his own hand, and both fought in jihad, or religiously sanctioned war. Both appeared to intend the taking of their own lives, but in the first case, the Prophet, due to his knowledge of the unseen, discovered 'Amir's real intent. So the distinction between these examples remains one of inscrutable intentions.

The extensive literature on martyrdom and suicide also reveals some significant tensions between religious precepts and popular practices.[40] The persistence of this tension suggests that extenuating circumstances, such as considerations of love or honor, may reflect a more lenient popular attitude toward suicide and therefore toward certain forms of euthanasia. One final example from the hadith literature demonstrates that even the Prophet recognized that suffering may make life unbearable:

> On the authority of Anas b. Malik, God be pleased with him; the Prophet, God's blessings and peace be upon him, said: "Do not any one of you desire death out of any need which oppresses you (*min ḍurra aṣābahu*). If there is no way out, then say: 'Oh God, revive me if life is better for me, or take me away, if passing away is better for me.' "[41]

The formulation in this prayer, in which the supplicant remains open to God's will, reinforces the impression that difference between martyrdom and suicide lies in an active intent to determine the moment of death (*ajal*).[42] But in this prayer, survival and death are seen as equivalent goods, both contingent on God's will; neither has an intrinsic value. Further, the dying person's prayer seems to have the possibility of real effect.[43] The caution of the Prophet, then, can be seen as remaining passive, and not taking an active role in influencing the moment of death.

While the classical sources are quite clear on disallowing the active, voluntary taking of one's own life, there seems to be a large area of ambiguity. On the one hand, intentions seem important, since the Prophet warned against "desiring death." But on the other hand, Hasan al-Banna' urges his followers to "yearn for death" and other martyrs seem to purposely cast themselves in harms way.[44] Further, the response of the religious scholars to the question of praying at the funeral of a suspected suicide suggests that only God can determine the true intentions of these individuals. In cases of euthanasia, these examples seem to support every case where the patient retains a passive attitude toward the working out of God's will; thus opening the door to all passive forms of euthanasia. This helps explain why Tantawi and others have ruled that in cases of brain death, patients should be allowed to die. Further, the sources would seem to support the notion that difficult decisions of life and death are better kept away from doctors and public officials, leaving room for the family of the dying to make decisions in private.[45] Finally, all these rulings come down to the central concern that Muslims not arrogate themselves to God's position as author of life and death.

The Life Span as Warrant for Euthanasia?

A number of Qur'anic verses clearly state that God determines a fixed span of life for every person. For instance, 6:2 reads: "For He is the one who created you from clay, then He appointed a span (*ajal*), and a specified span preserved with Him."[46] Interestingly, the medieval commentators say little about this verse, merely speculating on whether the verse refers to one or two spans and what these two spans might be. Early theologians made much of these verses, however, seeing the determination of the life span as one of God's essential qualities.[47] This position is hardly unique among religious traditions, but the consequences of acting in God's place are particularly severe in Islam. So the question arises, if suicide transgresses "God's bounds" in one direction, could modern life-support machines transgress it in another?

As Birgit Krawietz points out in the following chapter, this question of when life ends is a relatively new problem. But recent breakthroughs in emergency medicine have forced the issue both in terms of the resuscitation of the dead and also the prolongation of life. Massive hemorrhagic strokes, injuries to the brain, and severe infections are no longer the death sentences they once were, though patients may survive the necessary medical operations without the memory and higher cognitive functions that mark them as individuals. Further, they may not be able to survive without significant dependence on life-support machines and other technology. In many countries, these concerns have led to a wide acceptance of living wills, though these have been resisted by muftis as an intent to take life. Still, one could imagine an argument in favor of such wills, based on the very concerns expressed in the classical sources, since the modern ability to maintain bodily function almost indefinitely could cause the predetermined *ajal* never to come to pass. Such a line of argument is beyond the classical sources, though similar sorts of arguments have been employed by Jewish and Christian authorities.[48]

Finally, the traditional Islamic sources see the precise act of dying is far less important than the teleology of death. And while the life span is determined by God, the sources are much less fatalistic than they are pragmatic. Human beings, after all, used to have little or no control over the time of death, and death itself is accomplished by an action, the extraction of the soul from the body, that is not visible. Therefore, the whole question of euthanasia can only occupy a small and rather unimportant place in the teleology of the classical sources. Now that modern medicine has reached the level of possibly prolonging the life of the body past its appointed time, however, this teleology seems to be the strongest argument in favor of both passive and active forms of euthanasia. In the first case, human beings are relinquishing control over death to God, and in the second case, they are rejecting the "chance goods of this world" and recognizing that human life is not of intrinsic value. Therefore, the good death in Islamic theology and law embraces this teleology by focusing not on the pain and suffering of this world, but on God's promise of eternal life in paradise.

Notes

1. The first quotation is from the Islamic Code of Medical Ethics, endorsed by the First International Conference on Islamic Medicine (Kuwait: Islamic Organization of Medical Sciences, 1981, 65). The second is from a fatwa found on the internet at "Ask the Imam" (http://www.islamicity.com/qa/). According to this site, questions are answered by any one of the following individuals: Dr. Dani Doueiri (Beirut, Lebanon); Muhammed Musri, Islamic Center of Central Florida, Orlando; Dr. Yahia Abdul Rahman, LaRiba Bank, California; Dr. Ahmed H. Sakr, Foundation of Islamic Knowledge, California; Dr. Muzammil Siddiqui, Islamic Society of Orange County, California.

2. It does not seem right, however, to characterize this system as "rule utilitarian," since rules are derived from scripture, not from other utilitarian concerns. Rather, this system recognizes that the value of any action inheres solely in its ability to express the divine will. The same action in different situations may therefore have a divergent moral value.

3. This position is cognate to Donna Lee Bowen's description of the conservative Muslim position on abortion in chapter 3 as "more a soft 'no, but' than an adamant 'never'" (p. 51).

4. The twenty-third conference on medicine at the Ain Shams Medical College (Cairo), held February 21–24, 2000.

5. "The Rector of al-Azhar to Physicians: Concerning you and mercy killing!" reported on www.IslamOnline.net, February 25, 2000 (in Arabic).

6. "Rector of al-Azhar to Physicians."

7. Ibid.

8. The translation is from A. J. Arberry, *The Koran Interpreted* (New York: Macmillan, 1955), 2:324.

9. Many Muslim theologians adapted Greek atomistic philosophy to express this view of the world, a world in which every atom of each tree, rock, and creature was being held in place—indeed being constantly recreated—by God in every moment. For further discussion of atomism, see chapter 1.

10. This overwhelming fatalism is the same that can be seen in the work of pre-Islamic Arab poetry, where human frailty is contrasted with the cold irresistible force of time.

11. For a wide-ranging discussion of Qur'an and hadith accounts, see Thomas O'Shaughnessy, *Muhammad's Thoughts on Death: A Thematic Study of the Qur'anic Data* (Leiden: E. J. Brill, 1969). In the following chapter, Birgit Krawietz argues somewhat differently, demonstrating that the moment of death is important from an Islamic legal perspective.

12. Al-Ghazali's book is *Kitāb al-durra al-fākhira fī kashf 'ulūm al-ākhira*, translated by Jane Smith as *The Precious Pearl* (Missoula, Mont.: Scholars Press, 1979). Al-Qurtubi's book is *al-Tadhkira fī awāl al-mawta wa-umūr al-ākhira*, ed.

Ṭāhā 'Abd al-Ra'ūf Sa'd (Cairo: Dār Iḥyā' al-Kutub al-'Arabiyya, n.d). See also Muḥammad b. Ṭulūn al-Ṣāliḥī (d. 935/1345), *al-Taḥrīr al-marsakh fī awāl al-barzakh,* ed. Abū 'Abd al-Raḥmān al-Miṣrī al-Atharī (Tanta: Dār al-Ṣaḥābah li-l-Turāth, 1991). Other sources are listed in Smith, *Precious Pearl,* 3.

13. Ibn Abi Dunya (d. 281) is the earliest author of the genre, as far as I am aware (see his *Kitāb al-Muḥtaḍarīn,* ed. Muḥammad Khayr Ramaḍān Yūsuf [Beirut: Dar Ibn Ḥazm, 1997]) and one of the most recent is 'Abd al-Ḥayy al-Faramāwī, *al-Mawt fī l-fikri l-Islāmī* (Cairo: Dar al-I'tiṣām, 1991). Al-Faramāwī is professor of *tafsīr* and Qur'an at al-Azhar University in Cairo.

14. Al-Ṣāliḥī, *Taḥrir al-marsakh,* 16. See also Smith, *Precious Pearl,* 11, for her introductory remarks. For modern discussions of euthanasia and the moment of death, see the sources cited in Krawietz, *Die Ḥurma* (Berlin: Duncker and Humblot, 1991), 111–13.

These descriptions may be seen as the direct corollary of ensoulment at the beginning of life. Al-Ghazali states: "The soul in [the fetus] is lifeless, but its essential Malakūtī nature keeps the body from decomposing. Then God, may He be exalted, breathes into it His spirit, rendering to it its secret essence that had been taken and hidden for a time in one of the treasurehouses of the Throne" (Smith, *Precious Pearl,* 21). Bowen discusses this passage further on page 56.

15. Hiroyuki Yanagihashi, "The Doctrinal Development of "*Maraḍ al-Mawt,*" in *Islamic Law and Society* 5 (1998): 326–58. For some additional early references, see my *Early Mālikī Law* (Leiden: E. J. Brill, 2000), 267 and 279. For the importance of the *goses* within Jewish discussions of euthanasia, see Louis Newman, "Woodchoppers and Respirators," and Byron Sherwin, "A View of Euthanasia," both in Louis Newman and Elliot Dorff, eds., *Contemporary Jewish Ethics and Morality* (New York: Oxford University Press, 1995).

16. The Qur'an explicitly states: "God shall not turn towards those who do evil deeds until, when one of them is visited by death, he says, 'Indeed now I repent!'" (4:22).

17. Nevertheless, both are still clearly forbidden, and modern authorities have not used this reduced penalty as a warrant for euthanasia.

18. Kuwait: Islamic Organization of Medical Sciences, 1981, 65.

19. In this way euthanasia differs from murder, which is killing for a negative purpose, and accidental killing, which does not aim at death. However, the distinctions among suicide, homicide and euthanasia are not always so obvious.

20. An example of active euthanasia is the administration of a deadly injection, while passive euthanasia might involve the removal of a respirator.

21. Nonvoluntary euthanasia might be undertaken, for instance, in the case of a traumatic accident resulting in brain death. There is also a category for "involuntary" euthanasia, that is euthanasia committed *against* the will of the person; this type of euthanasia is little discussed in religious texts and will not be addressed here.

22. This classical example is described in Rosenthal, "On Suicide in Islam," in *Journal of the American Oriental Society* 66 (1946): 249.

23. This modern example is described in Krawietz, *Die Ḥurma,* 105.

24. This distinction is one of the most important for the Islamic tradition as well as for other traditions that emphasize the importance of intention in actions. See Philippa Foot's discussion in "The Problem of Abortion and the Doctrine of Double Effect" in Joram Haber, ed., *Absolutism and Its Consequentialist Critics* (Lanham, Md.: Rowman and Littlefield, 1994), 147–57.

25. In a private communication, Joyce Kloc McClure wrote that "many ethicists use the term 'euthanasia' only to mean other-inflicted, so essays on euthanasia for them would not deal with self-inflicted death. . . . In Western texts [these are found] under the rubric of physician assisted suicide/dying." The latter sort of death is now legally acceptable in some jurisdictions of Europe and North America.

26. See Rosenthal, "Suicide," 241, for discussion of modern interpretations; to his list may be added Tantawi's own commentary, where he quotes al-Razi in part. Muḥammad Sayyid Ṭanṭawī, *Tafsīr sūra al-nisā'* (Cairo: Maṭba'a al-Sa'āda, 1977), 163–65.

27. Abū Ja'far al-Ṭabarī, *Jāmi' al-bayān 'an ta'wīl al-Qur'ān,* ed. Muḥammad Muḥammad Shākir (Cairo: Dār al-Ma'ārif, n.d.), 8:229.

28. Fakhr al-Dīn al-Rāzī, *al-Tafsīr al-kabīr* (Cairo: al-Maṭba'a al-Bāhiya al-Miṣriya, 1938), 10:82.

29. *Ṣaḥīḥ Muslim bi-sharḥ al-Nawawī* (Cairo: Maṭba'a Ḥijāzī, n.d.), 7:47.

30. See, for examples, A. J. Wensinck, *Handbook of early Muhammadan Tradition* (Leiden: E. J. Brill, 1960), 222. Rosenthal quotes the black humor of al-Khwarazmi, who was asked by man being tortured whether he could kill himself. He initially answered no, but when he discovered it was a tax collector he said "it did not make any difference . . . because a man like him would anyhow be doomed" ("Suicide," 247).

31. In private conversation in March, 2001, Dr. Najma Moosa told me of a recent case in South Africa, where a known suicide was accorded full burial rites, since her intentions at the end of life could not be fully ascertained. For medieval attitudes, see Rosenthal, "Intiḥār," in *The Encyclopedia of Islam,* new ed., 3:1246–48. Compare Marion Katz's discussion of the role of uncertainty in abortion, pages 32–34.

32. A search of over 450 fatwas in al-Wansharisi's collection (*al-Mi'yār al-mu'rib wa'l-jāmi' al-mughrib* [Rabat: Wizārat al-Awqāf wa'l-Shu'ūn al-Islāmīya, 1981], chapters on burial, transgressions, punishments and blood money) revealed no cases of suicides. See also Rosenthal, "Suicide," 252. An alternative explanation is forwarded by Rahman, who claims that "the incidence of suicide in the Muslim community is so rare as to be negligible" (Fazlur Rahman, *Health and Medicine in the Islamic Tradition: Change and Identity* [New York: Crossroad, 1987], 126).

33. For the Catholic church, see John Paul II, "Euthanasia: Declaration of the Sacred Congregation for the Doctrine of the Faith. May 5, 1980," *The Pope Speaks* 25 (winter 1980): 289–96. For Judaism, see Newman, "Woodchoppers and Respirators."

34. The translation is Arberry's. See also Qur'an 2:154; 3:157 and 169; and

9:111. Further information is found in *The Encyclopedia of Islam,* new ed. (Leiden: E. J. Brill, 1962) s.v. "Shuhadā'" especially the helpful bibliography.

35. See Bukhari (as quoted in *Fatḥ al-Bārī.* Cairo: al-Maṭba'a al-Salafiyya, n.d.) chapters 56,3 and 56,7.

36. Mālik b. Anas, *al-Muwaṭṭa',* ed. Ḥasan 'Abdallāh Sharaf (Cairo: Dār al-Rayyān, 1988), 1:301.

37. Ḥasan al-Bannā', *Five tracts of Hasan Al-Banna' (1906–1949): A Selection from the* Majmu'āt rasā'il al-Imām al-shahīd Ḥasan al-Bannā', trans. Charles Wendell (Berkeley: University of California Press, 1978). This attitude toward martyrdom seems to condone suicide bombings and other acts normally forbidden in war. Compare Richard Martin's discussion in the previous chapter.

38. Found in Bukhari, chap. 87 (*Diyāt*), para. 17 (quoted in Ibn Ḥajar, *Fatḥ al-Bārī,* 12:218). See also Rosenthal, "Suicide," 244.

39. For a list of several versions, see Rosenthal, "Suicide," 244.

40. Rosenthal raises several examples of the heroic tradition in Islam that sees certain sorts of suicide as honorable, and points out that even the Prophet considered suicide at the very beginning of his career ("Suicide," 253–54).

41. Ibn Ḥajar, *Fatḥ al-bārī,* chap. 75 (*al-Marḍā*), no. 19.

42. More evidence is found in the *hadīth qudsī:* "My servant anticipated my action by taking his soul in his own hand; therefore he will not be admitted into Paradise" (quoted in Rosenthal, "Suicide," 244).

43. Note a similar sort of claim in Judaism, where in a midrash on Proverbs, a woman withholds the prayer that was keeping her alive (Sherwin, "A View of Euthanasia," 371).

44. Rosenthal even states that in medieval texts, "'Suicide' is widely used figuratively to indicate voluntary exposure to serious danger in war or through such activities as excessive praying and fasting" ("Intiḥār," in *Encyclopedia of Islam,* 3:1247).

45. Some modern scholars, such as H'mida Ennaifer, professor of Islamic thought at the Zaitouna University, Tunis, make just such recommendations (interviewed on April 5, 2000). The specific case he referred to was one of passive euthanasia, involving a woman who was lying unresponsive in a coma for over a year.

46. See also Qur'an 3:145, 39:42, 45:26, and 63:11.

47. W. M. Watt, *Free Will and Pre-Destination in Early Islam* (London: Luzac, 1948), 66.

48. See, for example, Fred Rosner, "Euthanasia," in *Contemporary Jewish Ethics,* especially pp. 358–60.

Nine

Brain Death and Islamic Traditions

Shifting Borders of Life?

Birgit Krawietz

The notion of brain death has evolved only during the last decades. Since 1968, it has challenged traditional understandings of death all over the world. For centuries, the Islamic concept of death and dying had remained relatively stable,[1] and the determination of death was traditionally a task that fell to the immediate family of the deceased. Western civilization and modern life brought about fundamental changes that gravely affected conventional wisdom and behavior in this regard.[2] As a consequence, illnesses and dying increasingly became the responsibility of doctors and hospitals. On the one hand, Muslims do not have so many general objections to modern medical treatment as a non-Muslim observer might assume. On the other hand but not at all paradoxically, they often react fiercely and adversely when problems of death and dying are handed over to secular experts and regulated according to secular needs.[3] This chapter sees such sensibilities to be rooted in the Islamic notion of the sanctity (*ḥurma*) and dignity (*karāma*) of the human body, a cornerstone of Islamic legal thinking. Without it, various anxious reactions to modern developments cannot be properly understood.

Traditional Islamic law already pays great attention to death and dying. The reason lies not only in its general responsibility for worldly legal consequences, but also in the fact that the only way to preserve *ḥurma* and *karāma* is through the legally prescribed ritual program to bury the deceased. This program guarantees that the one stricken with a fatal illness is not deprived of any second of life by premature declarations of death. Likewise, the deceased person knows that his or her corpse will be left untouched and "handed back" to the Creator. Brain death affects both these aspects, but it is the central thesis of this chapter that the notion of brain death does not necessarily cause a total upheaval of Islamic tradition such that the border between life and death would have to be shifted and newly defined in the light of modern scientific findings. Rather, the underlying traditional *concept* of death as the departure of the soul (*rūḥ*) is upheld by the majority of scholars.[4] But while most Muslim scholars are not willing to equate death with the failure of one organ, be it the whole brain or only the brain stem, a number of them realize that brain death challenges the death *criteria* of Islamic law, the inappropriateness of which can no longer be overlooked. Two trends in Islamic legal discussions on brain death become noticeable: "if in doubt, don't," stressing *ḥurma;* and the proposing of an "intermediate state," relocating *ḥurma.*

Both these different approaches will be presented in the last part of the chapter. Without being able to predict which one will finally prevail, the necessity to redefine the Islamic legal criteria for the determination of death seems, already at this early stage of the discussion, to be inevitable.[5]

History of Brain Death and Islamic Reactions

Waves of infantile paralysis—polio (*wabā' shalal al-aṭfāl*)—in 1952 in Denmark and 1953 in the US led to the use of machines allowing artificially sustained breathing and, therefore, heartbeat. Patients were thereby given time to recover and regain these vital functions. Such means were also newly employed during the Korean War (1950–1953).[6] Due to constant improvements in the field of modern anesthetics, intensive care medicine (which actually created a new type of patient and hitherto unknown special units in hospitals), operative techniques, and immune suppressive therapies, organ transplantation constantly gained new ground from about the middle of the twentieth century onward. Since it became possible to supplant "vital" functions like heartbeat and breathing, the failure of these functions no longer had the character of a clear-cut measure of death. All of a sudden, established truths about the discernment of death lost ground. Besides, the decay of organs, which naturally sets in after a few minutes, could now be avoided by artificial means and such organs thereby be "rescued" for transplantation purposes. Before achieving worldwide recognition, the idea of brain death had emerged in France in 1959 as "coma dépassé."[7] In 1967, the South African surgeon Christiaan Barnard carried out the first successful transplantation of the heart of a "brain dead" person. Given the legally awkward situation, a so-called "Ad hoc Committee of the Harvard Medical School" consisting of medical, legal, and theological scholars proposed a definition for brain death in 1968.[8] Different nations and cultures were now called upon to react against the background of their own traditions and to reconsider their ideas about death.[9]

As for the Islamic world, organ transplantation has been discussed in Sunni fatwa literature since about the 1950s.[10] Brain death as a consequent problem has been expressly dealt with only since about the first half of the 1980s.[11] While the Islamic world can be said to be very much in favor of organ transplantation, it took Muslim scholars some time to realize the impact of the new operation techniques and their consequences for the definition of death. In 1985, a conference was held in Kuwait on the question of the beginning and end of human life.[12] Medical as well as Islamic legal scholars had been invited and produced a substantial congress volume. This chapter also draws on a forty-page study on the definition of death written by one of the former rectors of al-Azhar Jad al-Haqq ʻAli Jad al-Haqq (d. 1996). It was published in a larger collection in 1992.[13] Further, a 1997 Syrian monograph by Nada al-Daqr assembles and analyzes hitherto published material on brain death.[14] Additional information comes from scattered articles from newspapers and magazines, since the definition of death has now become an issue for a broader Islamic public. [15] As an example, consider the case of the late King Hussein of Jordan, as reported by the German magazine *Der Spiegel:*

> Already on Friday in the week before last, the physicians diagnosed the brain death of King Hussein. According to Muslim tradition, Hussein would have to be buried within 24 hours—in that case, however, without international dignitaries, who could not show up that fast in Amman. The physicians thereupon declared cardiac arrest to be the decisive criterion of death. According to the official version, the king was therefore still alive, when, on Friday, the heads of state and government were invited for the burial on Monday. Hussein's heart stopped beating on Sunday, just twenty-four hours before the burial.[16]

*Principle of Sanctity (*ḥurma*) of the Human Body, Dead or Alive*

Non-Muslim observers at times claim that Islamic law does not have the concept of human rights. Yet there may be functional equivalents embedded in traditional law itself, and I propose that it does possess certain structures to guarantee the integrity of the human body.[17] However, these structures are not founded on any likeness to God's image, ideas of natural law, or mere human decree. Instead, sanctity or integrity (*ḥurma*) and dignity (*karāma*) are rooted in divine messages communicated in Qur'an and Sunna. The principle of inviolability embraces the living and the dead likewise, although the latter have to be handled differently. The principle even seems to include plants, as we might infer from Khaled Abou El Fadl's remarks about the rules of war.[18] There is one well-known hadith in two variants: "Breaking the bone of one who is dead is like breaking it while he is living (*inna kasr ʿaẓm al-mayyit ka-kasrihi ḥayyan*);" these are words which the Prophet Muhammad used to reproach a misbehaving gravedigger.[19] There can be no doubt that encroachments on the corpse principally represent its impairment and a violation of its integrity. Islam upholds *ḥurma* and *karāma* not only up to the time of burial but also long afterwards.[20] Human life and the integrity (*salāma*) of the parts of the body are "a right shared between the Creator and His creature (*ḥaqq mushtarak bayn al-khāliq wa-l-makhlūq*) so that it cannot be disposed of by the consent of the creature (*lā yasquṭ bi-idhn al-makhlūq*)." [21] The fact that Islamic law allows under specific circumstances to cut off a hand has to be seen as a specified exception. It certainly does not mean that doing something similar to oneself or another person is allowed, since "the sanctity of one part of the human being is like the sanctity of his life (*ḥurmat ṭaraf jasad al-insān ka-ḥurmat nafsihi*)."[22] Likewise, someone in an intensive care unit "definitely has to be treated with respect, whereby the respectful treatment of the dead has to be equated to that of the living (*iḥtirām al-mayyit ka-iḥtirām al-ḥayy*)." This is all the more true "when some of the parts of his body are kept alive by machines."[23]

Like other principles, the establishment of the exact *ḥurma* rules is an ongoing task that has to be carried out along the guidelines of the sharia and applied to specific circumstances and purposes. One should realize that although *ḥurma* implies prohibition, it is much more than that. A chain of prohibitions or repugnant things also creates a secure area that may not be violated. It is no mere accident that a wife is occasionally also called *ḥurma*. Further, there is the *ḥurmat al-muṣḥaf*, the inviolability of the Qur'an codex. The two most holy places of the Islamic world (Mecca and Medina) are called *al-ḥaramān*, the two sacred areas. As a rule, the protection of the bodily integrity and the respectful treatment (*takrīm*) of the human body do not merely serve its material quality but acknowledge the superior status of the human being. The protective shield cannot be equated with the skin as a possible borderline but is already penetrated when one looks at someone else's private parts or even when one sits on somebody's grave. On the other hand, the circumcision of girls, for instance, does not represent any violation of bodily integrity according to the majority of Muslim legal scholars, who argue with hadiths recommending this practice.[24] But the fact that protected areas are not set up following western understanding does not mean that they do not exist at all. Finally, integrity is set up by a web of punishments (and also rewards) inflicted in this world and the hereafter.

By the same token the preservation of integrity and dignity is also positively constructed. This is most clearly evident in the case of the ritual program for the deceased. The necessity of carrying out this program is one of the main reasons why Muslims have always paid great attention to the phases of dying and the exact moment of death. They have to watch the phases of dying carefully so as to offer spiritual instruction and because God will no longer accept repentance (*tawba*) once one has entered the last phase of dying.[25] People have to realize when death actually sets in, because the burial should take place with the least possible delay within the next twenty-four hours. The burial program is a collective duty (*farḍ kifāya*) of the community of believers. They may not culpably postpone or neglect the washing, shrouding, and preparing of the corpse for burial. Otherwise, they commit a sin altogether.[26] The deceased should even be told what he will have to answer to the angels of the grave, Munkar and Nakir.[27] It is not only the corpse that enjoys protection but also the grave and the cemetery even long after burial.[28]

Various Islamic genres are concerned with death and related issues. Hadith manuals have chapters of their own on burials (*janā'iz*).[29] Islamic law books traditionally lay down what is nowadays called "the rights of the dead (*ḥuqūq al-mayyit*)."[30] The correct behavior during illness or accompanying a dying person is also often dealt with in both *furū'* literature and hadith works. Besides, there is a rich eschatological literature dealing with theological and spiritual aspects of death.[31] No pious Muslim may expect an easy death. The Prophet himself suffered from fierce agony.[32] A good death may not be equated with an easy one but signifies that the deceased died as a brave Muslim upholding the right creed.[33]

Traditional Signs of Death and Its Determination

Appropriate treatment of the dying and immediate Islamic burial are not the only reasons that Islamic law pays great attention to the exact moment of death. Various legal relationships also end at death.[34] Although the Qur'an itself talks about death many times, especially God's monopoly on giving and taking life,[35] it does not provide precise information on how to discern the exact moment of death. When scholars quote the Qur'an with reference to death, they quote verses that deal mainly with preliminaries of death as such, and much less with defining it.[36] Muhammad Nu'aym Yasin from the faculty of Sharia and Islamic studies at the University of Kuwait correctly states that "there is no clear-cut text (*naṣṣ*) from Qur'an or Sunna concerning this problem of ours that could be taken as a starting point for investigation." [37]

Traditional Islamic law nevertheless developed a series of so-called characteristics (*'alāmāt*) or "signs of death (*amārāt al-mawt*)" that had to be ascertained in order to prepare the dead for burial or proceed with other rituals.[38] These signs include the glazing of the eyes, stopping of breath, parting of the lips, relaxation of the feet, bending of the nose, or caving in of the temples.[39] Obviously, these and other signs were never fixed in a binding catalogue, and they vary from one author to another. There was no need to demand a fixed standard. If there was any doubt about whether the person was really dead, the body had to be left untouched until it began to smell.[40] The legal scholars' characteristics of death were largely derived from "human experience (*tajriba bashariyya*)" and not from divine sources.[41] The variety of such signs notwithstanding, there is unanimity that the departure of the soul (*rūḥ*) from the body signifies death itself.[42] Since death is a process, a "complete departure (*inqiṭāʿ tāmm*)" has to take place as indicated by "the completion of its signs (*istikmāl amārātihi*)."[43]

According to the orthodox Islamic understanding, there are four phases of human existence each of which is larger than the former one: the womb of the mother, this world (*al-dunyā*), limbo (*barzakh*)[44], and the hereafter (*al-ākhira*). After resurrection and the Day of Judgment, true Muslims will only temporarily stay in hell. How long this has to last depends on their behavior on earth: "Death is the gate or the entrance to eternal life. Life is the key to death (*miftāḥ al-mawt*). The sense in which a person deals in his life with the blessings of God decides what he may expect behind this gate." Death is therefore "only a step towards eternal life."[45] The Azhar professor of Qur'an interpretation and Qur'an studies ʿAbd al-Hayy al-Faramawi describes it as "the move from the realm of obligation and worldly occupation to the realm of recompense and punishment in the hereafter (*intiqāl min dār al-taklīf wa-l-ʿamal al-dunyawī ilā dār al-thawāb wa-l-ʿiqāb al-ukhrawī*)."[46] Talal ʿAli Turfa, another modern author, confirms the traditional understanding of the Qur'an's testimony that "the life after death is a second creation (*khalq*) and both lives (birth and resurrection) belong to the blessings of God." Turfa further relates that God gives new human bodies to human beings at the time of resurrection so that they can take part in the new creation.[47] In all four worlds, the soul and the body, with its parts and organs, have a different relation with one another.[48] It is assumed that the soul departs from the body in accordance with the exact span of life preordained by God. This likewise applies to discernable secondary causes like illness or manslaughter, or to sudden death or a stroke (*sakta*).[49] God is always the final cause of death. Life has to end in the same way as it begins, namely with the taking away of the soul after ensoulment[50] or, as al-Ashqar puts it: "Human life began with a blowing (*nafkha*) and it ends with a blowing."[51]

Doubts and Anxieties Concerning Brain Death

The doubts and anxieties that are repeatedly expressed in connection with brain death consist of four main arguments that dominate the opposition to it: reluctance to give up customary signs, be they part of the Islamic legal tradition or not; the claim of possible recovery; the necessity of protecting all life, even vegetative or unconscious life; and the disagreement of the medical scholars themselves.

The first of these objections was the subject of an article titled "Hot Debate on Organ Donation and Clinical Death—The Center of Cairo . . . a Black Market for Organ Trade" that appeared in a well-known Arabic magazine in 1997. The writer stresses that there are two fundamentally different definitions of decease (*wafāh*), the modern medical one and the sharia law definition of death. The last one implies the total departure of the soul with the consequence that the body becomes cold and decay sets in because the organs have stopped functioning.[52] According to the latter, mere brain death (*mawt al-dimāgh*) or death of the brain stem (*mawt jidhʿ al-dimāgh*) would not really be death but would have to be considered only a warning (*nadhīr*) of death and a step towards it. As long as the separation (*infiṣāl*) of the soul has not entirely taken place, the patient has to be regarded as living.[53] Before the appearance of the "sharia signs of death (*ʿalāmāt sharʿiyya*)," the harvesting of organs would have to be regarded as an encroachment on a "dying patient (*al-marīḍ al-muḥtaḍir*)" and to be criminalized as either injury or manslaughter.[54] Further, there is the longtime general custom of regarding heartbeat as an important measure of human life. In Egypt, for instance, heartbeat is still recognized as decisive for the proclamation of death.[55] However, as some Muslim writers nowadays underline, cardiac arrest (*tawaqquf al-qalb*) normally does not rank among the sharia signs of death.[56] After several cases of "organ-tourism" of Egyptians seeking help abroad, the Egyptian government decided to accept brain death; their action in turn stirred up heavy protests. Some scholars vehemently argued against "the failure of the functions of the brain stem (*tawaqquf waẓāʾif jidhʿ al-mukhkh*)" as a valid proof of death, urging that every legislation should take into consideration the social and ethical outlook of Egyptian society. Also, they insisted, the patient should not be declared dead without further medical tests.[57] From these arguments, it seems that many Muslims—although they theoretically acknowledge the nonbinding character of legal opinions not clearly based on holy texts (*nuṣūṣ*)—tend to sacralize human findings that have been integrated into Islamic legal regulations. Theoretically, only findings that have been agreed upon through the consensus of legal scholars (*ijmāʿ*) may claim certainty and thereby irreversibility, yet cardiac arrest is not universally attested among the sharia signs of death. Finally, modern life-support machines and other scientific advances have caused the traditional signs of death to seem very out of date.

The second claim against the use of brain death criteria is that a brain-dead person might still return to life. Since God may decide whatever he wishes, and his ways are inscrutable, it is not only the religious scholars who use such an argument. In fact, several Muslim medical doctors advocate this idea of recovery. For example, Dr. Safwat Hasan Lutfi, a professor of anesthetics and intensive care medicine, suggests:

> Brain dead people (*mawtā al-mukhkh*) are not really dead but are living people who lost consciousness or were victimized by accidents. There are cases where the brain died, yet afterwards, they returned to life. To deal with those [patients] as if they were dead and remove organs from them fully amounts to the crime of manslaughter.[58]

In this sense, the Saudi Arabian judge al-Khudari declares that the soul might occasionally return to the body like a heart that resumes beating after a while.[59] This argument does not seem to carry much weight either, since there is a scientific consensus—at least in western literature—to the effect that brain death is a point of no return. Muslim authors who accept the notion of brain death therefore argue that not to remove life-support machines although the patient is clinically dead is an impairment of *ḥurma*.[60] The respect for the deceased and his corpse make it necessary to stop exposing him to useless treatment. One might think that this issue of "recovery" could be clearly decided scientifically. The problem, however, is that things can hardly be falsified when the argumentation is grounded upon theological beliefs, in this case insistence on God's monopoly to revive.

A third objection against brain death is that even an unconscious, vegetative life should be protected and upheld. 'Aqil al-'Aqili claims that a brain-dead patient's acceptance of medicaments and food indicates physical life. To disregard such a life amounts to a violation of Qur'an, Sunna, and consensus (*ijmāʿ*).[61] Reference is further made to the growing of nails and hair and—as far as children are concerned—the body itself.[62] Special suspicion arose from reports about, for instance, a brain-dead woman named Farida who in that condition gave birth to a child.[63] Since al-Khudari does not accept "the decease of the brain (*al-wafāh al-dimāghiyya*)" as dying in the true sense, he consequently counts the maintaining of brain-dead people in life-support machines among the rights (*ḥuqūq*) the Islamic sharia guarantees to humankind.[64] As far as such unconscious life denotes the so-called "persistent vegetative state (*al-ḥāla al-nabātiyya al-mustamirra*)" it has to be stated that Islamic law in no way equates it with brain death itself. The patient in such a state is affected only in his cerebrum (*qishr al-mukhkh*), which means that "the centers of will and consciousness" are destroyed but not the brain stem. It is the brain stem that organizes vital functions of the body, like temperature, blood pressure, heartbeat, and breath. People in the persistent vegetative state show no consciousness and reaction whatsoever but breathe spontaneously.[65] Some people may still recall the well-known case of Karen Ann Quinlan, a coma patient widely recognized from her high school yearbook photo, which was often displayed in the media while she was in a persistent vegetative state from 1975 to 1985. Her family fought fiercely to shut down the machines that were keeping her "alive," and it was this case that turned the general public's attention—both in America and internationally—toward the problem of brain death.[66]

According to a fourth argument, the medical doctors themselves are said to be at variance. They hold conflicting opinions, for instance, on "the death of the brain stem as a possible dividing line (*al-ḥadd al-fāṣil*) between life and death." According to the medical expert Mustafa al-Dhahabi these differences hold not only from country to country but from hospital to hospital.[67] Although Muslims have traditionally very much thought of death as a process, they are now expected to come up with an arbitrary point of death.[68] An eminent sharia judge from Qatar claims that there is not and will not be a "dividing line between life and death."[69] Dr. Ahmad al-Shawaribi, assistant professor for anesthetics and intensive care medicine at Ain Shams University in Cairo, declares that brain death is "a great lie" and that there are numerous cases of false diagnosis.[70] According to him and others, a medical doctor may anyhow never be able to define exactly the hour of death, which is up to God alone.[71] This fourth objection appears generally to be the most serious one. The undeniable diversity of opinion among medical experts themselves and biologists, philosophers, and other scholars and scientists cannot be overlooked.[72] How Muslims try to come to terms with this phenomenon will be discussed in the last section of this chapter. One general awkwardness is discernible: Since life is not an end and has for centuries been understood as a mystery and an intervention of God who sends out an angel to take up the souls, Muslim legal scholars are very much averse to hand over the power of definition to secular experts who concentrate on medical or technical subtleties.

Struggle for the Power of Definition

In Qur'an 17:85 it is explicitly said: "They will question thee concerning the spirit (*al-rūḥ*). Say: 'The spirit is of the bidding of my Lord. You have been given of knowledge nothing except a little.' "[73] Although some scholars interpret this verse to indicate that death in itself is finally inscrutable to humankind, others claim the opposite. Muhammad Yasin declares that this verse should not be construed as forbidding human legal exploration, *ijtihād*, of the issue of the *rūḥ* claiming that it belongs to the hidden things (*ghaybiyyāt*).[74] Yasin nevertheless concedes that "it in fact belongs to the most difficult tasks to find out the viewpoint of the legal scholars concerning this question."[75] Another author states the need for "human *ijtihād* (in its two halves, the legal and the medical one) in the absence of a proof of the holy law (*fī ghaybat al-naṣṣ al-sharʿī*)."[76] However, the question is which of the "two halves" may claim preeminence of definition. Al-Dhahabi insists in his 1993 monograph *Organ Transplantation Between Medicine and Religion* that "these signs (*ʿalāmāt*) [of death] are derived from people's experience in those issues." For him there is, therefore, "no hindrance from the religious law's point of view to ascertaining the signs by newly invented medical means that are available nowadays." In such specialized fields, medical experts have to be "the final authority to turn to (*al-marjiʿ al-nihāʾī*)."[77] Islamic legal scholars, however, claim that they lay down the general outlines where "decisive texts (*nuṣūṣ ḥāsima*)" are lacking. They explain to the medical doctors the issue of death as the departure of the soul. Yasin further states:

> The role of the scholars (*ʿulamāʾ*) takes priority over (*sābiq*) the role of the experts (*ahl al-ikhtiṣāṣ*) and is connected with it (*lāḥiq lahu*), for they put into the hands of our brethren, the medical doctors, first of all the principles (*mabādiʾ*), definitions (*ḥudūd*), and general conditions (*shurūṭ*) to which the Muslim adheres (*yaltazim bihā*) in the practice of his [medical] specialty.[78]

Such views need not lead to any contradiction so long as the two different tasks are not confused. Western authors insist that the *concept* and the *criteria* of death should be clearly differentiated and not mixed up. The former is first of all a philosophical, cultural, or theological question. The latter, however, depend on scientific research and technical-medical means.[79] As such they have to be open to progress and revision, like the introduction of new technology—such as the electroencephalograph (EEG). Thus far, the possibility of a certain diagnostic development and diversity should not be too disturbing. Douglas Walton warns that the matter is even more complicated. The problem with brain death is that it is "a bridge concept between the concept of death and the diagnostic criteria for the determination of death, so it is hard to know where to locate it in the usual concepts/criteria dichotomy."[80] Muslim authors do not pay much attention to the dual character of the brain. They often do not clearly distinguish between the understanding of the brain as the crucial factor for the very concept of life on the one hand and its status as just one among other discernable criteria for the establishment of death on the other. A few Muslim scholars take the potentially risky step and give up the traditional distinction between the eternal soul and the brain as an organ. Ahmad Shawqi Ibrahim, for instance, declares

> that the psyche (*nafs*) and the soul (*rūḥ*) are consciousness (*wa'y*) and discernment (*idrāk*), comprehension (*'aql*) and thinking (*fikr*) . . . and all that is connected with the brain (*mukhkh*) . . . or that the brain is their only tributary stream (*rāfiduhā al-wāḥid*) . . . therefore the end of life is brain death (*nihāyat al-ḥayāh hiya mawt al-mukhkh*).[81]

Yasin also seems to fall under this rubric of at least a semi-equation of *rūḥ* and brain although he expresses himself in more cautious terms. He first of all calls for "the existence of a rational, immaterial, living creature not perceptible to the senses;" that is the soul that is behind every intentional brain activity.[82] He declares that "cognizance (*'ilm*), discernment (*idrāk*), sensory perception (*ḥiss*) and free will (*ikhtiyār*) are the most important functions of the soul (*ahamm waẓā'if al-rūḥ*)." The whole body therein serves the soul. He hastens to remark that the soul also carries but some of its functions—although on a minor scale—without the means of the body.[83] He adds later on that when the brain becomes "totally incapable of responding to the will of the soul (*li-istijābat irādat al-rūḥ*)" and when all the other organs deteriorate to the point of no return, then "the soul has departed from (*raḥalat 'an*) the body with the permission of her master and the angel of death has taken her on a new journey."[84] His theologically tinted expression and lengthy tribute to the traditional concept of death cannot conceal the fact that his theory that the soul masters the body with the help of the brain is highly provocative. Al-Daqr praises Yasin's article highly as the "strongest discussion of the understanding of brain death from the viewpoint of canonical law (*al-shar'*)."[85] To others, though, it might smack a bit of "scientific" Qur'an interpretation.

Two Choices: "If in Doubt, Don't" or the "Intermediate State"

The majority of Islamic legal scholars do not opt for a pseudoscientific and more or less concealed equation of the soul with the brain. Instead, they are aware of the temporal gap between the fading of the invisible soul and the possibility of scientifically ascertaining death. There are two fundamentally different ways in the relevant literature to deal with this gap, namely "if in doubt, don't" and proposing of an "intermediate state."

The first approach assumes that an answer has to be sought in the light of the established methodology and principles of the sharia since there are no particulars in the holy texts. The Syrian scholar al-Buti and others therefore propagate the application of the principle according to which the continuance of the former status has to be upheld unless a change can be persuasively proven (*istiṣḥāb al-aṣl*).[86] In case of doubt, the patient or victim has to be regarded as still alive unless certainty concerning his new status can be established. 'Abd al-Rahman al-Adwi, professor in the faculty of Islamic propaganda and member of the *Majma' al-Buḥūth al-Islāmiyya* (Academy of Islamic Research) in Cairo, explains: "From the sharia point of view this human being is surely alive whereas his death has to be doubted. A doubt cannot remove a certain issue. The legal scholars may not allow the physicians to encroach on a living human being with their scalpels (*mashāriṭ*)." He then asks rhetorically whether a physician can decree the clinical death of a person who has been treated by intensive-care medicine.[87] To equate mere indicators of death with death itself is a hazard (*mughāmara*) and a folly (*mujāzafa*).[88] Somebody who claims that a situation has changed must bring forward a real proof, since the rights and duties of the deceased himself, or his wife, children, other relatives, or business partners might be involved.[89] Otherwise, the traditional sharia definition of death has to be upheld because "the death of the brain (*mukhkh*) is not as certain (*mu'akkad*) or definite (*qaṭ'ī*) as the sharia death (*al-mawt al-shar'ī*) and is subject to faulty diagnosis."[90] Jad al-Haqq refers to the legal maxims that one injury may not be removed by inflicting another one (*lā yuzāl al-ḍarar bil-ḍarar*) and that warding off evil things takes precedence over ensuring positive ones (*dar' al-mafāsid muqaddam 'alā jalb al-maṣāliḥ*). Likewise, it is not allowed to grant life to someone by killing another person who is still alive.[91] Such an "if in doubt, don't" approach is less a question of whether a person is dead or alive in an ontological sense than of whether certainty can be established concerning one state or the other. Existing diagnostic diversity and uncertainty therefore fuel reservations concerning brain death. The question, however, is whether it is realistic to demand final proofs. Yasin reminds his colleagues that once established truths might be changing—even today's assumption that brain death is irreversible. He warns them not to always demand absolute certainty in order to construct legal rulings. That would amount to undue restriction:

> Someone might say: "How can it be correct that dangerous rulings (*aḥkām khaṭīra*) like [permission for] heart transplantation are built

> upon a result (*natīja*) which is founded in strong probability (*ghalabat al-ẓann*) [i.e., the assumption of brain death] although the possibility of a mistake (*khaṭaʾ*) [i.e., the ruining of human life therein] exists." The answer to this objection is that a great part of the realities of life are known only by strong probability and not by certainty and in a definite manner (*lā bi-l-qaṭʿ wa-l-yaqīn*). To confine oneself in laying down what is certain, means to shut out many potential benefits (*fīhi taʿṭīl li-kathīr min al-maṣāliḥ al-khaṭīra*).[92]

The other general approach calls for a third legal category between life and death. Normally, life and death are defined in mutually exclusive terms.[93] Although it is not claimed that somebody may be only a bit alive, traditional Islamic law did already establish a sort of third category. The legal scholars differentiated among "the continuing life (*al-ḥayāh al-mustamirra*)" even of the one who is only one breath away from death; "the lingering life (*al-ḥayāh al-mustaqirra*)" of the one who has been fatally attacked but does not die immediately and will probably die within days although he can still speak, see and move at will; and "the expiring life (*al-ḥayāh ghayr al-mustaqirra*)," which is labeled as "the movement of the fatally wounded (*ḥarakat al-madhbūḥ*)" and denotes somebody who has been fatally hurt, has not yet died, but can no longer speak, see, or move at will.

The existence of such a third category between life and death comes out in discussions of responsibility for attack on one who is already fatally wounded (*al-ishtirāk fī al-qatl al-ʿamd ʿalā al-tatābuʿ*).[94] There are various differences among the authors of the law schools, such as the Shafiʿi al-Nawawi (d. 1277), the Hanbali Ibn Qudama (d. 1233), the Hanafi Ibn ʿAbidin (d. 1888), or the Maliki al-Zarkashi (d. 1391), which cannot be dealt with here in detail.[95] Suffice it to say that in different scenarios the law manuals deal in their chapters on retaliation (*qiṣāṣ*) and blood money (*diya*) with the question of responsibility when somebody attacks a person whose life is already expiring.[96] Most jurists argue that the person who kills someone in this third state is not liable to the punishment for murder but only for infringing on a corpse—that is, liable to *taʿzīr.* Even if a person's life was expiring only because of illness, retaliation (*qiṣāṣ*) would nevertheless be necessary.[97] Al-Ashqar proposes to regard the *madhbūḥ* as "living but legally dead (*ḥayy fī ḥukm al-mayyit*);" that is, to treat him as dead concerning the removal of life-support machines and the harvesting of organs, but to treat him as living with regard to heritage and other rights.[98] Such a third legal category has not only been dealt with in chapters on the responsibility for manslaughter or injury but also in connection with the old doctrine of death sickness (*maraḍ al-mawt*) which forbids the fatally ill to undertake certain legal transactions.[99] The advocates of an intermediate legal state still have to explain in detail how this could completely excuse a medical doctor who takes out organs from someone without having to face *taʿzīr* -punishment. The future will show in how far this "return to Islamic law (*ʿawda ilā al-fiqh al-islāmī*)"[100] is taken up by more scholars and accepted by a wider Islamic public.

Regardless which of the two approaches prevails, they are both properly founded in Islamic legal traditions. The mechanisms of inner-Islamic discussions decide where the track is going. However, Muslim authors who embrace the concept of brain death hastily might fail to convince large Muslim populations from Morocco to Indonesia and hesitant Muslims in the west as well. It is most often lay people who count when it comes to the question of whether organs may be removed from a deceased relative. The physician A. S. Daar, for example, selectively highlights one of the few clearly positive statements on brain death (made in 1986 at the Third International Conference of Islamic Jurists in Amman),[101] reduces other judgements more or less to mere footnotes, and declares that "Muslims are permitted to choose between these options."[102] Even if such is the attitude taken up by state regulations in countries with ambitious organ transplant programs, such as Kuwait or Saudi Arabia, the announcements will probably not suffice to soothe anxious relatives and prospective donors. In fact, brain death certificates are already used in Oman and Saudi Arabia, among other places.[103] It is up to experts of state law, medical scholars, and anthropologists to investigate the actual situation in different Islamic countries.

At least for the time being, most Islamic legal scholars obviously feel no need to give up the traditional theological concept of death as the departure of the soul. Al-Daqr even argues that according to classical Islamic teaching, although the heart of the embryo starts beating beginning with the fourth week, the ensoulment is said to take place only after 120 days, when an angel blows the soul into the fetus.[104] With this realization that there is no necessary connection between heartbeat and quality as a human being, "Islam anticipates the west in its 'new' understanding of death by fourteen centuries."[105] In this view, it is rather the western world that has recently shifted its concept of death and narrowed down the borders of life.

Notes

I thank the contributors to this volume and especially Jonathan E. Brockopp for their discussion of a distinctively different earlier draft. Edward Badeen, Annabelle

Böttcher, Hamid Lahmer, Vardit Rispler-Chaim, and Janet Voigtmann helped me to obtain relevant source material. Christopher Melchert critically read a prior version. I am further indebted to Patricia Crone and the participants of her seminar at the Institute for Advanced Study as well as to Michael Cook.

1. Traditionally, it was not the ending of life but its exact beginning that was put into question and stirred up discussions. See particularly Marion Holmes Katz's chapter on some of these debates.

2. On the introduction of forensic medicine in Egypt see Khaled Fahmy, "The Anatomy of Justice: Forensic Medicine and Criminal Law in Nineteenth-Century Egypt," *Islamic Law and Society* 6 (1999): 224–71, quotation at 231. Cf. the case dealt with in *al-Manār* in 1910 concerning the new practice of calling a doctor to determine the precise cause of death and exclude contagious diseases as cause, in *Fatāwā al-imām Muḥammad Rashīd Riḍā,* ed. Salāḥ al-Dīn al-Munajjid (Beirut: Dār al-Kitāb al-Jadīd, 1970–71), 3:851–53.

3. For details on this particular sensibility towards human dying, death, and corpses see Birgit Krawietz, *Die Ḥurma: Schariatrechtlicher Schutz vor Eingriffen in die körperliche Unversehrtheit nach arabischen Fatwas des 20. Jahrhunderts* (Berlin: Duncker & Humblot, 1991), 91–168.

4. The Islamic theology of death is outlined in the preceding chapter.

5. This has nothing to say about the application of brain-death criteria in hospitals in the Islamic world.

6. Dr. Sharbīnī, in *Nadwat al-ḥayāh al-insāniyya: Bidāyatuhā wa-nihāyatuhā fī al-mafhūm al-islāmī* (Kuwait: Dawlat al-Kuwait, 1985), 354–55, cf. 508. On these techniques in general see Sebastian Schellong, *Künstliche Beatmung* (Stuttgart and New York: G. Fischer, 1990).

7. David Lamb, *Death, Brain Death and Ethics* (London and Sydney: Croom Helm, 1985), 4.

8. See "A Definition of Irreversible Coma: Report of the Ad Hoc Committee of the Harvard Medical School to Examine the Definition of Brain Death," *Journal of the American Medical Association* 205, no. 6 (1968): 337–40.

9. Cf. for instance Abraham Steinberg, "The Definition of Death," in *Medicine and Jewish Law,* ed. Fred Rosner (Northvale, N.J.: J. Aronson, 1990), 137–67; Yves Nordmann, *Zwischen Leben und Tod: Aspekte der jüdischen Medizinethik* (Bern: Peter Lang, 1999), 95–116.

10. It started with the discussion of cornea (*qarniyya*) transplants. See Hasan Ma'mūn, "Naql 'uyūn al-mawtā li-l-aḥyā'," fatwa of 1959, in *Al-Fatāwā al-islāmiyya min Dār al-Iftā' al-Miṣriyya,* ed. Jumhūriyyat Miṣr al-'Arabiyya: Wizārat al-Awqāf (Cairo: Dār al-Iftā' al-Miṣriyya, 1980–), 7 (1982):2552–54. See Nadā al-Daqr, *Mawt al-dimāgh: Bayn al-ṭibb wa-l-islām* (Damascus: Dār al-Fikr, 1997), 204, for a list of the fifteen most important Arabic fatwas on organ transplants between 1952 and 1990. Cf. Vardit Rispler-Chaim, *Islamic Medical Ethics in the Twentieth Century* (Leiden: E. J. Brill, 1993), 28–43; Krawietz, *Ḥurma,* 167–200. Shi'i discussions are harder to find, but see a report in *Tehran Times,* November 22, 1998, on a seminar about "Brain Death and Organ Transplant" that included religious scholars.

11. Cf. Krawietz, *Ḥurma,* 167–68.

12. Fully quoted in n. 6 above.

13. Jād al-Ḥaqq ʻAlī Jād al-Ḥaqq: "Taʻrīf al-wafāh," in his *Buḥūth wa-fatāwā islāmiyya fī qaḍāyā muʻāṣira,* 6 vols. ([Cairo:] al-Azhar al-Sharīf, al-Amāna al-ʻĀmma li-l-Lajna al-ʻUlyā li-l-Daʻwa al-Islāmiyya, 1992–95), 2:491–530.

14. See n. 10 above.

15. Organ transplantation is not the only reason why the concept of brain death arises. There are also utterances concerning the permissibility of intensive care units in modern hospitals (*al-ʻināya al-murakkaza*) as well as the topic of euthanasia (*qatl al-raḥma*). The latter, however, is scarcely addressed in this type of publication, perhaps because people still take it for granted that it is strictly forbidden. As a consequence, more statements concerning brain death are found in the frame of organ transplants, but some assessments relevant for euthanasia might also be sought here. For euthanasia see the relevant chapter in Krawietz, *Ḥurma,* 104–15.

16. *Der Spiegel* no. 7 (1999): 143. For the legal definition of death in various Muslim countries see al-Daqr, *Mawt al-dimāgh,* 229–34; A. S. Daar, "Current Practice and the Legal, Ethical, and Religious Status of Post Mortem Organ Donation in the Islamic World," in W. Land and J. B. Dossetor, ed., *Organ Replacement Therapy: Ethics, Justice, Commerce* (Berlin: Springer, 1991), 294–95.

17. For details see Krawietz, *Ḥurma,* 317–26 and *passim.*

18. See his discussion on page 119–20.

19. *Nadwa,* 477, 495. For the two versions and their reporters see *Sunan Ibn Māja,* ed. Bashshār ʻAwwād Maʻrūf (Beirut: Dār al-Jīl, 1998), 3:126–27.

20. Al-Daqr, *Mawt al-dimāgh,* 33.

21. Ibid., 31.

22. Ibid., 32.

23. Al-Khuḍarī in *al-Majalla,* no. 992, February 14–20, 1999, 4–5, quotation at 5.

24. Explained in detail in Krawietz, *Ḥurma,* 222–35; Krawietz, "Ethical Versus Medical Values According to Contemporary Islamic Law," in *Recht van de Islam* 16 (1999): 1–26, 15–18.

25. Cf. Qur'an 4:18, to which Jād al-Ḥaqq ("Taʻrīf al-wafāh," 496–97) refers.

26. ʻAbd al-Ḥalīm Maḥmūd, "Mā ra'y al-dīn fī ta'jīl dafn juthmān al-mayyit akthar min al-ḥadd al-mafrūḍ," in *Fatāwā al-imām ʻAbd al-Ḥalīm Maḥmūd,* 2 vols. (Cairo: Dār al-Maʻārif, 1979), 2:277. For the exact mode of burial see Abū al-Walīd Ibn Rushd, *The Distinguished Jurist's Primer: A Translation of Bidāyat al-Mujtahid,* 2 vols. (Reading, U.K.: Garnet, 1994–96), 1:259–82.

27. ʻAbd ar-Raḥīm b. Aḥmad al-Qāḍī, *Das Totenbuch des Islam: "Das Feuer und der Garten"—die Lehren des Propheten Mohammad über das Leben nach dem Tode* [transl. from the English] (Bern and München: Scherz, 1981), 79–80.

28. For legal discussions on tomb architecture, see Thomas Leisten, *Architektur für Tote: Bestattung in architektonischem Kontext in den Kernländern der islamischen Welt zwischen 3./9. und 6./12. Jahrhundert* (Berlin: D. Reimer, 1998), 5–25.

29. Muḥammad al-Bukhārī, *Ṣaḥīḥ al-Bukhārī: The Translation of the Meanings of Sahih al-Bukhari, Arabic-English,* 6th rev. ed., ed. Muḥammad Muhsin Khān (Lahore: Kazi Publications, 1983), 2:186–270.

30. Wahba al-Zuḥaylī, *Al-Fiqh al-islāmī wa-adillatuhu: Al-Shāmil li-l-adilla al-shar'iyya wa-l-ārā' al-madhhabiyya wa-ahamm al-naẓariyyāt al-fiqhiyya wa-taḥqīq al-aḥādīth al-nabawiyya wa-takhrījihā,* 2d ed. (Damascus: Dār al-Fikr, 1985), 2:457–543. Cf. al-Shaykh Muḥammad al-Ṣāyim, *Ijābat al-sā'ilīn 'an al-mawt wa-l-qabr wa-yawm al-dīn* (Cairo: Dār al-Bashīr, 1994), 31–33. For the Shi'a see al-Shaykh Ḥusayn Bandar al-'Āmilī, *Risāla fī al-mawt wa-l-barzakh yalīhā aḥkām tajhīz al-mayyit muṭābaqa li-fatāwā āyat Allāh al-'Uẓmā al-Sayyid Abī Qāsim al-Khū'ī quddisa sirruhu al-sharīf* (Beirut: Dār al-Rasūl al-Akram, 1996), 186–94.

31. Cf. Abū Ḥāmid al-Ghazālī, *The Remembrance of Death and the Afterlife,* trans. T. J. Winter (Cambridge: Islamic Text Society, 1989); see also discussion in the previous chapter of this volume.

32. *Al-Sīra al-nabawiyya wa-l-mu'jizāt: Khulāṣat al-bidāya wa-l-nihāya li-Ibn Kathīr,* 2 vols., ed. Muḥammad b. Aḥmad Kan'ān (Beirut: n.p., 1996), 2:299.

33. 'Abd al-Raḥīm, *Totenbuch,* 51–53; Thomas O'Shaughnessy, *Muḥammad's Thoughts on Death: A Thematic Study of the Qur'anic Data* (Leiden: E. J. Brill, 1969), 67–69.

34. Death terminates the marriage contract and begins the waiting period (*'idda*) for the widow in order to exclude a possible pregnancy (see *Encyclopedia of Islam,* new ed. [Leiden: E. J. Brill, 1962–], 3:1010–13). In case of murder, retaliation (*qiṣāṣ*) is due. If the injury had not been fatal, the attacker would have to pay only blood money (*diya;* see Jād al-Ḥaqq, "Ta'rīf al-wafāh," 501). Further, the inheritance has to be distributed (Maḥmūd Muḥammad 'Abd al-'Azīz al-Zaynī, *Al-Ḍarūra fī al-sharī'a al-islāmiyya wa-l-qānūn al-waḍ'ī, taṭbīquhā, aḥkāmuhā, āthāruhā: Dirāsa muqārina* [Alexandria: Mu'assasat al-Thaqāfa al-Jāmi'iyya, 1993], 162). For all such consequences see al-Daqr, *Mawt al-dimāgh,* 142–43; al-Wā'ī, in *Nadwa,* 483; 'Abd Allāh, in *Nadwa,* 398–99.

35. O'Shaughnessy, *Muḥammad's Thoughts on Death,* 28–39, 45–48.

36. Jād al-Ḥaqq, "Ta'rīf al-wafāh," 596, 498.

37. Yāsīn, in *Nadwa,* 403.

38. Jād al-Ḥaqq, "Ta'rīf al-wafāh," 502–6.

39. Ibid., 512; 'Aqīl b. Aḥmad al-'Aqīlī, *Ḥukm naql al-a'ḍā' ma' al-ta'qībāt al-bayyina 'alā man ta'aqqaba Ibn Taymiyya* (Jedda: Maktabat al-Ṣaḥāba, 1992), 151; 'Abd Allāh, in *Nadwa,* 396; 'Abd al-Ḥayy al-Faramāwī, *Al-Mawt fī al-fikr al-islāmī* (Cairo: Dār al-I'tiṣām, 1991), 50–51, 63.

40. Al-Wā'ī, in *Nadwa,* 476. Cf. al-Faramāwī, *Mawt,* 64.

41. Al-Ashqar, in *Nadwa,* 430.

42. *Al-Majalla,* 4–5. Jād al-Ḥaqq speaks of *mufāraqat al-rūḥ 'an al-jasad* ("Ta'rīf al-wafāh," 501). For Islamic teachings on the soul see the article "Nafs" in *The Encyclopedia of Islam,* new ed. (Leiden: E. J. Brill, 1962–), 7:880–884. For the angel of death and how he takes the soul away see 'Abd al-Raḥīm, *Totenbuch,* 34, 68–76.

43. Al-Zaynī, *Ḍarūra*, 162.

44. "Barzakh," in *The Encyclopedia of Islam,* new ed. (Leiden: E. J. Brill, 1962–), 1:1071–72. See Ragnar Eklund, *Life Between Death and Resurrection According to Islam* (Uppsala: Almquist & Wiksells Boktryckeri-A.-B.), 1941.

45. Ṭalāl 'Alī Turfa, *Al-Ṣabr fī al-islām: Ru'ya taḥlīliyya shāmila* (Beirut, 1998), 84.

46. Al-Faramāwī, *Mawt,* 15.

47. Turfa, *Ṣabr,* 85. For the relationship between body and soul see Josef van Ess, *Theologie und Gesellschaft im 2. und 3. Jahrhundert Hidschra: Eine Geschichte des religiösen Denkens im frühen Islam* (Berlin and New York: de Gruyter, 1991–97), 4:521–528.

48. Muṣṭafā Muḥammad al-Dhahabī, *Naql al-a'ḍā' bayn al-ṭibb wa-l-dīn* (Cairo: Dār al-Ḥadīth, 1993), 103. 'Abd Allah in *Nadwa,* 396 quotes Ibn al-Qayyim (d. 1350) to the effect that sleep (*nawm*) signifies a fifth category because the soul at times leaves the body.

49. Jād al-Ḥaqq, "Ta'rīf al-wafāh," 500.

50. Yāsīn, in *Nadwa,* 405.

51. Al-Ashqar, in *Nadwa,* 429.

52. "Niqāsh sākhin ḥawl al-tabarru' bi-l-a'ḍā' wa-l-mawt al-iklīnīkī: Wasaṭ al-Qāhira . . . sūq sirriyya li-tijārat al-a'ḍā'," in *al-Mujtama',* no. 1254, June 17, 1997, 20–23, quotation at 23.

53. Al-Zaynī, *Ḍarūra,* 162. In the mentioned article in *al-Mujtama'* the expressions *al-mawt al-iklīnīkī* and *mawt al-dimāgh* are used for clinical death and brain death.

54. Jād al-Ḥaqq, "Ta'rīf al-wafāh," 514.

55. Ibid., 492, 529.

56. Al-Daqr, *Mawt al-dimāgh,* 141, 178. Cf. the medical doctor Aḥmad al-Qāḍī, in *Nadwa,* 383–392.

57. "Naql al-a'ḍā' jarīmat qatl," in *al-Naba' al-Waṭanī,* May 11, 1997, 3.

58. *Al-Mujtama',* 23, where another doctor, Hamdi al-Sayyid, is quoted as saying that brain death is a point of no return. Likewise al-Daqr, *Mawt al-dimāgh,* 129, cf. 151, 160; the article "Naql al-a'ḍā' al-bashariyya fī mīzān al-islām," in *al-Aḥrār* (Cairo), April 5, 1996, 6.

59. *Al-Majalla,* 5. Cf. Jonathan Brockopp's remarks in the previous chapter on the insistence of the classical scholars on the mystery of death.

60. Krawietz, *Ḥurma,* 113–15.

61. Al-'Aqīlī, *Ḥukm naql al-a'ḍā',* 154.

62. Al-Dhahabī, *Naql al-a'ḍā',* 109.

63. 'Abd al-Bāsiṭ in *Nadwa,* 447. Cf. "Hirntote Spanierin von Kind entbunden," in *Frankfurter Allgemeine Zeitung* no. 1, January 3, 2000, 1.

64. *Al-Majalla,* 5. Al-Khudari adds that someone brain dead may under three aspects gain profits for the hereafter: continuance of good deeds set up by him, prayer on his behalf (*du'ā'*) by pious people, and the settlement of debts and unfulfilled duties.

65. Al-Daqr, *Mawt al-dimāgh,* 189–94.

66. Alexander Morgan Capron, "The Report of the President's Commission on the Uniform Determination of Death Act," in *Death: Beyond Whole-Brain Criteria,* ed. Richard M. Zaner (Dodrecht: Kluwer Academic Publishers, 1988), 147–70. Quinlan died in 1985 after ten years in the persistent vegetative state. David Randolph Smith, "Legal Issues Leading to the Notion of Neocortical Death," in Zaner, *Death,* 111–44, reference on 125.

67. Al-Dhahabī, *Naql al-aʿḍāʾ,* 109.

68. On the question whether such a point of death might be detectable see John Lachs, "The Element of Choice in Criteria of Death," in Zaner, *Death,* 233–51, esp. 233–234.

69. Al-ʿAmāwī, in *Nadwa,* 486.

70. "Su'āl bilā ijāba ḥāsima: Matā yuʿtabar al-insān mayyitan?," *Ākhir Sāʿa,* no. 3363, April 7, 1999, 38–39, quotation at 39.

71. Cf. van Ess, *Theologie und Gesellschaft,* 4:494–97.

72. Peter McCullagh, *Brain Dead, Brain Absent, Brain Donors: Human Subjects or Human Objects?* (Chichester: John Wiley & Sons, 1993), 30–31. He stresses that "brain death has been anything but a static concept since the use of the term and intensive observation of patients meeting the relevant criteria began" (66).

73. Al-Daqr, *Mawt al-dimāgh,* 107; *al-Nabaʾ al-Waṭanī,* 3. The Arabic expression runs, *Wa-yasʾalūnaka ʿan al-rūḥ. Qul al-rūḥ min amr rabbī wa-mā ūtītum min al-ʿilm illā qalīlan.* See *The Koran Interpreted,* trans. Arthur J. Arberry (1955; reprint, New York: McMillan, 1995).

74. Yāsīn, in *Nadwa,* 406.

75. Ibid., 411: *Wa-l-wāqiʿ anna istikhrāj raʾy al-fuqahāʾ fī hādhihi al-masʾala min aṣʿab al-umūr.*

76. Al-Sharbīnī, in *Nadwa,* 360.

77. Al-Dhahabī, *Naql al-aʿḍāʾ,* 106; cf. Yāsīn, in *Nadwa,* 426 and *passim;* al-Daqr, *Mawt al-dimāgh,* 177.

78. Yāsīn, in *Nadwa,* 404.

79. Douglas N. Walton, *Brain Death: Ethical Considerations* (West Lafayette, Ind.: Purdue University, 1980), 14, 51–56.

80. Walton, *Brain Death,* 53.

81. Ibrāhīm, in *Nadwa,* 376, cf. 373, 377.

82. Yāsīn, in *Nadwa,* 419.

83. Ibid., 415.

84. Ibid., 420.

85. Al-Daqr, *Mawt al-dimāgh,* 172.

86. Ibid., 160. Cf. al-Wāʿī, in *Nadwa,* 478.

87. "Naql al-aʿḍāʾ al-bashariyya fī mīzān al-Islām," in *al-Aḥrār* (Cairo), April 5, 1996, 6. Al-Dhahabī, *Naql al-aʿḍāʾ,* 2.

88. Al-ʿAqīlī, *Ḥukm naql al-aʿḍāʾ,* 135.

89. Al-Daqr, *Mawt al-dimāgh,* 13.

90. *Ākhir Sāʿa,* 39.

91. Jād al-Ḥaqq, "Ta'rīf al-wafāh," 530.

92. Yāsīn, in *Nadwa,* 422–23.

93. Al-Wā'ī, in *Nadwa,* 490.

94. Yāsīn, in *Nadwa,* 411.

95. Ibid., 146–50, with reference to relevant classical texts. Several congress participants deal with these findings; see 'Abd Allāh (398–401), Yāsīn, al-Ashqar (412–14), al-Mukhtār al-Salāmī (430–31, 436–39), al-Wā'ī (451–53), and Sharaf (480 and 489), in *Nadwa.* Cf. Jād al-Ḥaqq, "Ta'rīf al-wafāh," 502–10.

96. Al-Ashqar, in *Nadwa,* 436–38.

97. Al-Daqr, *Mawt al-dimāgh,* 144–46, 150–51.

98. Al-Ashqar, in *Nadwa,* 483–84, 439.

99. Cf. Hiroyuki Yanagihashi, "The Doctrinal Development of "*Maraḍ al-Mawt,"* in *Islamic Law and Society* 5 (1998), 326–58.

100. Al-Ashqar, in *Nadwa,* 436.

101. For details see al-Daqr, *Mawt al-dimāgh,* 174–75.

102. Daar, "Current Practice," 294.

103. See, for instance, Kingdom of Saudi-Arabia: Ministry of Health, "SCOT Protocol: Directory of the Regulations of Organ Transplantation in the Kingdom of Saudi Arabia," in *Saudi Journal of Kidney Diseases and Transplantation,* vol. 5., ed. Saudi Center for Organ Transplantation (1994) 1:37–98, app. 8: "Saudi Center for Organ Transplantation Brain-Death Documentation Form," p. 82.

104. For details see Rüdiger Lohlker, *Schari'a und Moderne: Diskussionen über Schwangerschaftsabbruch, Versicherung, und Zinsen* (Stuttgart: Steiner, 1996), 17–22.

105. Al-Daqr, *Mawt al-dimāgh,* 182.

Afterword

The Past in the Future of Islamic Ethics

A. Kevin Reinhart

The essays in this collection suggest that the ghost in the machine of Islamic ethics is Islamic law (sharia) and its legacy. But these essays also make clear that while Muslims are connecting with their rich legacy of ethical thought, they remain unsure of how it should be put to use. Some simply carry on as before; some use this legacy selectively; some seem to ignore it while still acting under its shadow; and some seek to replace the legacy of *sharīʿa* with "Islam." This variety of attitudes toward the Muslim ethical legacy ought also to lead the reader to think about the lessons of Islamic ethics for the Euro-American ethics curriculum, both in terms of understanding how Islamic ethics differs from more familiar ethical discussions and in terms of challenging our perspective of what ethics should be.

A western-schooled ethicist may be struck by the extent to which articles on the Islamic tradition, and articles on contemporary ethical controversy, point to premodern legal discourse not merely as a starting point, but as a source of authority. Most western academics would invoke Aquinas, for instance, as someone who clarified issues or who had insight into the matter or at hand, as someone who had shaped the way in which we have customarily approached an issue—rather than as an authority to be followed. The Islamic academy approaches Ibn Taymiyyah, however, rather as an eighteenth-century Catholic seminarian would have approached Aquinas—as a recognized source of authority more immediately useful even than scripture. This Islamic engagement with premodern sources is clear in all the articles (particularly those of Marion Katz, Jonathan Brockopp, Khaled Abou El Fadl), but is most clearly noted by Sohail Hashmi, who observes that, despite the fact that all three of the scholars he is studying write in the twentieth century, "all three authors' works are primarily exegeses of authoritative texts" (131). Yet even when Muslim authors engage scripture directly, bypassing medieval commentary, their views implicitly are bound to the tradition of scriptural interpretation and religious jurisprudence which they are seeming to ignore (see Hashmi's chapter, pp. 144–45). *Salafī*-type reformers assert that

Muslims ought to return anew to the authoritative scriptural texts—the Qur'an and hadith of the Prophet—and cut loose the shackles of medieval legalism through a renewal of *ijtihād* (original reasoning). Yet in reality such efforts mostly result in findings utterly consonant with the tradition they pretend to be freed from, and this is the case even when, as in the Qur'anic legislation on adultery, the scriptural bases are utterly at odds with the inherited legal tradition. This means that articles like Katz's, which might seem to be of only historical interest, are instead maps of the topography even of many contemporary ethical discussions.

This inherited tradition has a significant ascendancy, not least because of the confidence that the medieval authors have, and toward which, arguably, contemporary Muslim authors are only now finding their way. Any contemporary Muslim ethicist is sure to be confronted by this tradition, and if it is ignored he or she will be forced to justify his or her disregard. Yet it is also striking that the range of premodern authorities invoked by the contemporary Islamic academy is shockingly limited. While a medieval discussion, rich in citation, controversy, and counter-controversy, might invoke scores of legists, contemporary arguments tend to refer primarily to a handful of celebrities—al-Ghazali, for instance, and the Hanbali school is much over-represented; Ibn Taymiyya, Ibn Qudama, Ibn Qayyim al-Jawziyya have an influence in the fifteenth Islamic century (that is, late twentieth and early twenty-first Christian centuries) they never before had in Islamic history. This emphasis on the most scripturalist of schools, and arguably the most moralistic (because the least successful and thus the least involved in the actual administration of justice and policy) surely has consequences for contemporary Islamic discourse, as the flexibility and pragmatism that categorized Hanafi Ottoman experience, for example, are replaced with Hanbali theoretical rigorism.

It is important to situate the "doing" of ethics still further by calling attention to the modern authors discussed in these collected articles. It is not, to a large extent, ulema, the "clergy" of Islam, the professionally, officially religious, who are writing on the matters under consideration here. It is rather social critics (Hasan al-Banna', Osama bin Laden, Abu al-A'la Mawdudi)—trained as journalists, belletrists, watchmakers, privileged sons of the wealthy—who are producing these influential articles and books. The fact that it is non-ulema who are writing about ethics suggests a sense of suffocation from the very tradition that is being invoked. It seems to many that the ulema are too tightly tied to the premodern world to engage with the urgent issues of today. In fact, there seems to be some sense that the ulema as an establishment are in the end only mouthpieces for the government when it comes to controversial issues: Bin Baz and Tantawi, are the defenders of the Euro-American alliance with the Saudis and Egyptians, not the critics of that policy. Of course the ulema write often on more ordinary matters, but it is fair to say that ulema seem seldom to be on the cutting edge of ethical matters.

Another feature of contemporary Islamic ethical discourse on view in the preceding articles is the replacement of God and the Prophet by "Islam" as a source of authority. It has been recognized by Islamicists for nearly fifty years now that one of the most significant features of contemporary Muslim thought is the attachment to and even veneration of "Islam" in controversial debate. Thus we find that Vardit Rispler-Chaim and Donna Lee Bowen accurately represent Muslim thought when they say that "Islam requires," or "Islam accepts," or some other similar locution.

This "Islamolotry" is a move that both limits and restricts Muslim discussions of, inter alia, ethical matters. On the one hand, the idea that there is *an* "Islam" means that Ibn Taymiyya will remain the conversation partner for contemporary Sunni scholars, and Sharif al-Murtada for the Shi'a. A commitment to "Islam" means also a commitment to the idea that there is an "Islamic" solution to a problem, and that only in-house discussions can be relevant. Jad al-Haqq or Khama'ini are unlikely to take Kant as a dialog partner, or be responding to the Hastings Institute—and not just for reasons of language or exposure.

On the other hand, and paradoxically, this shift of focus to "Islam" rather than "God" or sharia can also free some Muslims to think of Islamic *principles,* rather than Islamic *rules.* Fazlur Rahman argued that the inability to discuss ethics in terms of principles rather than rules was *the* major failure of contemporary Islam.[1] Perhaps he was overly pessimistic. Now one finds even the most conservative, and even the most radically Islamist appealing to what they perceive of as general goals and principles found in authentic Islamic discourse. To say "Islam requires" can also, therefore, be rhetorically and logically a step away from the fetters of the inherited tradition, toward a general principle—inferred perhaps from scriptural sources, but by a Muslim situated not in the tenth Islamic century, but in the fifteenth.

The "situatedness" of Muslims has seldom been recognized as a legitimate determinate of ethical judgment, yet it has been and is an important fact in Islamic ethics. We are not yet at a stage in our research where we can determine exactly what role the social, political, economic, or cultural (and so on) environment had on Muslim thought,[2] but it is clear that to speak of a single Islamic perspective on an ethical question is from a scholarly point of view very dubious. Katz and Abou El Fadl make this clear for the premodern period, as Hashmi, Bowen, and Birgit Krawietz do for the modern. There appear to be a number of Islamic traditions, but we do not yet know enough to decide how the differences in Islamic norms of conduct and conduct-theory will break down: along denominational lines (Shi'i/Sunni?) or lines of rite and school-of-thought (*madhhab*) (that is, Ja'fari, Hanafi, Shafi'i-Hanbali), hermeneutic tendency (Mu'tazili-Twelver Shi'i/Salafi/Legist,[3] or regional (Andalusian–North African/Mashraq/Turkic/Persianate/Indic world, and so on). Yet it is clear from these articles and other research that variation on almost any issue can be found, and that the premodern world, variation was assumed, cultivated, and recognized.

In this, as in all comparative ethical inquiries, it appears we are still in an asymmetrical mode—perhaps for the reason that Muslims are committed exclusively to in-house discussions, but partly for other reasons. It is clear in Rispler-Chaim's discussion, for instance, that the quest is to find an Islamic equivalent of a western perspective that she finds useful and important, the "right not to be born." Yet few of these papers (and this is more a reflection of the nascent state of comparative ethics, rather than anything more malign) suggest what it is that our own contemporary ethical discourse can learn from engagement with the Islamic. "What can Euro-Americans learn from Muslims?" is a question seldom asked. What are *we* missing when we see acts as bereft of a sacramental character, a character that they have in sharia as well as in Halakhah? What does the communalist, corporatist, *gemeinschaftlich* perspective of Islamic ethics have to offer to an individualist ethics of autonomy and individual rights? The potential of Islamic legal thought to clarify or inform non-Muslim ethics is clear, for instance, in Hashmi's account of jihad-doctrine (156). Is there something to be said for a perspective that so values communal security as the precondition to the virtuous life that it *requires* the taking of human life when necessary to preserve social solidarity? This seems a stance worth considering since it challenges the individualist orientation largely taken for granted in normative academic ethics, while it captures something of the attitude of, for instance, some American death-penalty advocates. Perhaps this book will lead to the opening of that discussion.

An important feature of Islamic ethical discourse is implied in Abou El Fadl's observation that classical discussions of jihad focused on how to conduct war, rather than the justifications for war (*jus in bello* rather than *jus ad bellum*). We might ask why this would be the case. I would propose is that it is consistent with one of the most prominent features of normative Islamic ethical discourse, namely, a focus on cases rather than on general deductive rules. As he and Hashmi both point out, Islamic jurists took for granted that wars existed, and in their pragmatism they were disinclined to labor overmuch about whether the conditions for just war had preceded the hostilities. Rather, the war having begun, they were concerned to regulate its conduct. In ways that Wael Hallaq has demonstrated, the individual stipulations in treatises on jihad are likely to have arisen out of individual cases, made general by removing their situating details without sufficiently denaturing them as to reduce them to general principles.[4]

In general, Islamic ethical thought, like late medieval Latin-Christian and early modern Catholic moral theology, was case-oriented, or, to use a much misunderstood word, casuistical.[5] Those familiar with the Islamic tradition will note that, with the exception of the mystical tradition (which Katz briefly engages), and the peripatetic philosophical tradition, Islamic ethics is entirely casuistical. It considers cases, and in its normative pronouncements leaves space for the particulars of a situation to be inserted, and perhaps to modify the finding. It is in this method rather than in any substantive rule that it most directly challenges contemporary western academic ethics. Rules play little role in the process of ethical reflection, and what seem to be rules turn out on examination to be maxims, something like Dworkin's "principles" that are invoked in varying degrees, rather than in an on/off, all-or-nothing fashion.[6] With this in mind, a reading of nearly any paper in this excellent collection may require a revision of the way that many scholars think about just war, abortion, or euthanasia. In the premodern period, the *fuqahāʾ* were uncomfortable thinking in generalities; they wanted to know, first, at least the grounds for war, the activities of the enemy, their motivations for fighting, and so forth. The logic of the Islamic legacy then seems to require that ethical discussion begin with particular problems, not general rules. I could be overstating what seems to be an implicit priority, however, and it does seem to be the case that some contemporary Muslims start at least partly from general principles such as "defensive war is more acceptable than offensive war," or "the mother's life is more important than the fetus,' " or "suicide is wrong." It may be, however, that while the form of contemporary ethical discussion constrains one to enunciate general rules, the actual logic of reflection remains casuistical. Further inquiry into the implicit mode of ethical reasoning would be of interest here.

A final point for reflection pertains to the comparative ethics enterprise in general. The further one goes into a tradition, the more difficult it is to find a single "Islamic ethical tradition" (or Hindu, or Buddhist, or Jewish for that matter). Western ethicists, perfectly comfortable with the welter of "isms" and tendencies that make up their own discourse, seem often to look for a single interlocutor, a single foil, a single authoritative Muslim with whom they can engage. The authors show their expertise in part by their recognition of the variation, diversity, and dynamism of authentic Islamic ethical expression. It may be that comparative ethics will proceed most fruitfully not by comparing the *results* of ethical reflection between two traditions, but by comparing the *modes* of ethical reflection. The case-oriented, corporatist, Islamic tradition, which—at least in some versions—does not see itself as severed from the ethical heritage of the premodern period, may be a worthy contrast to western deductive, individualist, academic ethics that often asserts the importance of the Enlightenment break from medieval religion and modes of authority. While Muslims have much to learn from this tradition, the philosophy departments of Cairo University, Istanbul University, and the University of Jakarta already teach Kant and Hume. Perhaps this volume will make it slightly more likely that Ibn Taymiyya, Fakhr al-Din al-Razi, and al-Ghazali might take their rightful place in a western ethics curriculum.

Notes

1. Fazlur Rahman, "Law and Ethics in Islam," in Richard G. Hovannisian, ed., *Ethics in Islam* (Malibu, Calif.: Undena Publications, 1985), 3–15.

2. See Lawrence Rosen, *The Anthropology of Justice: Law As Culture in Islamic Society,* Lewis Henry Morgan Lectures (Cambridge: Cambridge University Press, 1989); Rosen, *Bargaining for Reality* (Chicago: University of Chicago Press, 1984); Baber Johansen, *Contingency in a Sacred Law: Legal and Ethical Norms in the Muslim fiqh*, Studies in Islamic Law and Society (Leiden: E. J. Brill, 1999), vol. 2, "Coutumes locales et coutumes universelles aux sources des règles juridiques en Droit musulman hanéfite," 163–71.

3. Mohammed M. Yunis Ali, *Medieval Islamic Pragmatics: Sunni Legal Theorists' Models of Textual Communication* (Richmond, Surrey: Curzon Press, 2000).

4. Wael B. Hallaq, "From *Fatwās* to *Furūʿ*: Growth and Change in Islamic Substantive Law," *Islamic Law and Society* 1, no. 1 (1993): 29–65.

5. D. B. MacDonald was, to my knowledge, the first to note this feature. Since he worked as an avowed Protestant in a missionary seminary, I am doubtful that he intended the term as a mere descriptive. Duncan Black MacDonald, *Development of Muslim Theology, Jurisprudence, and Constitutional Theory* (New York: Charles Scribner's Sons, 1903).

6. R. M. Dworkin, "Is Law a System of Rules?" in Dworkin, ed., *The Philosophy of Law* (Oxford: Oxford University Press, 1977), 38–65.

Glossary

ahl al-dhimma. Non-Muslims living under Muslim rule.

Al-Ahrām. The leading newspaper of Egypt.

ajal. Life span; the hour of death appointed by God.

akhlāq. Aristotelian or virtue ethics; ethics in general.

ʻalāmāt al-mawt. Legally acceptable signs of death, such as cardiac arrest.

ʻalaqa. Blood-clot; the second stage of fetal development.

ʻālim. S. of ulema; a religious authority; literally, one who knows.

amān. A safe conduct agreement; quarter.

amāna. A trust from God, in reference to the human body.

amārāt al-mawt. Legally acceptable signs of death, such as cardiac arrest.

ʻaṣabiyya. Family loyalty, as opposed to loyalty to the *umma*.

ʻazl. Contraception by withdrawal before ejaculation; *coitus interruptus.*

bughāh (s. bāghī). Rebels; Muslims who have a plausible interpretation (*ta'wīl*), have a group of supporters (*shawka*), and challenge the authority of the ruler.

casuistry. Case-based reasoning, as opposed to reasoning from principles.

coitus interruptus. Contraception by withdrawal before ejaculation; *ʻazl.*

ḍarūra. Necessity; external mitigating factors.

dār al-ḥarb. Enemy territory; literally, abode of war.

dār al-Islām. Friendly territory; literally, abode of Islam.

dār al-ṣulḥ. Enemy territory governed by a truce.

deontological. Rule-based moral thinking.

dhimmī. Non-Muslims living under Muslim rule; protected status.

diya. Blood money; monetary recompense for an infraction.

farḍ. Required; one of the five categories of legal action.

farḍ ʻayn. Individual duty, required of each Muslim individually.

farḍ kifāya. Collective duty, incumbent upon the community as a whole.

fasād. Corruption of society; sexual immorality.

fatwā (pl. fatāwā). A nonbinding legal opinion, rendered by a mufti.

fiqh. Jurisprudence; legal discourse; insight.

fitna. Civil discord.

fuqahā'. Jurists; those trained in the discipline of *fiqh*.

furūʻ. The application of the law, as opposed to its sources (*uṣūl*).

ghayla. Sexual intercourse with a lactating woman, which would result in pregnancy and injury or possibly death to the nursing child.

ghurra. Monetary recompense for the death of a fetus.

ḥadīth. A recounting of authoritative sayings or actions; words and deeds of the prophet Muhammad as collected by his companions.

ḥalāl. Allowable; licit.

Ḥanafis. The most widespread of the four Sunni schools of law, dominant in Turkey, the Eastern Mediterranean, and South Asia.

Ḥanbalis. The least widespread of the four Sunni schools of law, dominant in the Arabian peninsula.

ḥarām. Forbidden; one of the five categories of legal action.

ḥarb. War in the generic sense, not necessarily jihad.

ḥarb al-bughāh. War against Muslim rebels.

ḥarb al-kuffār. War against unbelievers.

ḥurma. Sanctity of the human body.

ʻIbādī. A minor sect of Islam, still found in some areas of North Africa.

iftā'. The giving of legal opinions (fatwas) by muftis.

ijhāḍ. Abortion.

ijmāʻ. Consensus, usually of the scholars; the third authoritative source for Islamic law, after Qur'an and Sunna.

ijtihād. The exhaustive effort of a jurist (*mujtahid*) in investigating and deducing the law in a novel or unprecedented case.

imām. The leader of prayer or of a congregation; a political leader.

IUD. Intrauterine device; a form of contraceptive.

Jamā'at-i Islāmī. The Islamic League, a political party in the Indian subcontinent.

al-Jam'īyat. The Urdu-languague newspaper of the Jama'at-i Islami.

jihād. A lawful and legitimate war against non-Muslims or, at times, Muslims; any legitimate and just struggle.

jināya. Crime; infraction.

jizya. Tax imposed upon non-Muslim subjects living under Muslim rule.

jus ad bellum. Criteria for just resort to war.

jus in bello. Criteria for just conduct of war.

kaffāra. Penance; recompense for an infraction.

karāma. Human dignity.

madhhab. School of law; group of scholars sharing a common outlook on sources and their interpretation.

makrūh. Disapproved, reprehensible; one of the five categories of legal action.

Mālikis. One of the four Sunni schools of law, dominant in North and West Africa.

mandūb. Recommended; one of the five categories of legal action.

maṣlaḥa. The principle of general societal welfare.

mawt al-dimāgh. Brain death.

mawt al-mukhkh. Brain death.

mawt jidh' al-dimāgh. Death of the brain stem.

mubāh. Allowable, indifferent; one of the five categories of legal action.

muḍgha. Cohesive lump of flesh; the third stage of fetal development.

muftī. A jurisconsult; authoritative person who renders a legal opinion (fatwa) in response to a query.

mujtahid. A jurist who performs *ijtihād* or is qualified to perform *ijtihād.*

nafs. A person; the self; the lower soul.

naṣṣ (pl. nuṣūṣ). An authoritative proof text, usually from Qur'an or Sunna.

niyya. Intention.

nuṭfa. Drop of semen; the first stage of the fetus.

qāḍī. A judge in an Islamic legal court.

qatl al-raḥma. Euthanasia; literally, mercy killing.

Qur'ān. God's revelation to the Prophet Muhammad; the most authoritative document in Islam.

rūḥ. Animating spirit; the essence of life.

Salafī. A modern politico-religious movement emphasizing reform while respecting Islamic tradition.

Shāfi'is. One of the four Sunni schools of law, dominant in Egypt and Southeast Asia.

sharī'a. Islamic law; the correct path of action as determined by God.

al-Sharq al-Awṣat. A leading Arabic-language newspaper, published in London.

Shī'is, Shī'a. A Muslim sect that differs from Sunnis in several ways, especially their veneration of the Prophet's family; Imami Shi'is are dominant in Iran and Iraq, while Zaydis dominate in Yemen.

siqṭ. Miscarriage.

siyar. International legal theory; international relations.

siyāsa. Politics; public policy concerns.

ṣūfī. One concerned with the devotional or the esoteric side of religious belief; a mystic.

Sunna. The second authoritative source for Muslims; the correct way of doing things; the Prophet's exemplary action as recorded in hadith.

Sunnī. The majority sect of Muslims, as opposed to Shi'i.

sūra. One of the 114 chapters of the Qur'an.

tafsīr. Interpretation, usually of the Qur'an.

takhalluq. Formation; the appearance of the fetus as human.

ta'wīl. A religious interpretation; a political or social cause held by rebels in opposition to ruling authority.

teleological. Goal-based moral thinking; the conviction that all actions have a divinely ordained purpose.

ulema. Religious scholars; literally, the people of knowledge.

umma. Muslim community—supercedes all other loyalties.

uṣūl al-fiqh. Theoretical literature concerning authoritative sources; literally, roots of jurisprudence.

wa'd. Female infanticide, forbidden in the Qur'an.

Ẓāhiris. A historically important school of law, emphasizing literal interpretation of the sources.

Zaydī. A subgroup of Shi'is, found in Yemen.

Bibliography

Newspaper articles and articles from encyclopedias are omitted. Arabic sources are indexed separately, beginning on page 234.

On-line Resources

islamicity.com/qa/ A searchable database of American Fatwas, hosted by IslamiCity.

omnibus.uni-freiburg.de/bruecknm/fatwa/fatwaonline.html A useful gateway to several fatwa collections.

www.guttmacher.org/sections/abortion.html International statistics on abortions

www.emergency.com/bladen98.htm Copy of Osama Bin Laden's (et al.) fatwa of February 23, 1998: "Fatwa: Kill Americans Everywhere."

www.islam-online.net/fatwa/english/searchFatwa.asp Fatwas by several important scholars; the Arabic version of the site is more extensive.

www.lib.ecu.edu/govdoc/terrorism.html#binladen A useful index of Osama bin Laden's declarations, including a copy of bin Laden's fatwa of August 23, 1996: "Declaration of War against the Americans Occupying the Land of the Two Holy Places."

European-Language Sources

Abou El Fadl, Khaled. *Conference of the Books: The Search for Beauty in Islam.* Lanham, Md.: University Press of America, 2001.

———. *Rebellion and Violence in Islamic Law.* New York: Cambridge University Press, 2001.

———. "The Common and Islamic Law of Duress." *Arab Law Quarterly* 2 (1991): 121–59.

———. "*ʿAḥkām al-Bughāt:* Irregular Warfare and the Law of Rebellion in Islam." In *Cross, Crescent, and Sword: The Justification and Limitation of War in Western and Islamic Tradition,* edited by James Turner Johnson and John Kelsay, 149–76. Westport, Conn.: Greenwood Press, 1990.

Abu-Rabi', Ibrahim. *Intellectual Origins of Islamic Resurgence in the Modern Arab World.* Albany: State University of New York, 1996.

Abu Zahra, Muhammad. *Concept of War in Islam.* Trans. Muhammad al-Hady and Taha Omar. Cairo: Ministry of Waqf, 1961.

Adams, Charles J. "Abu'l-A'la Mawdudi's *Tafhim al-Qur'an.*" In *Approaches to the History of the Interpretation of the Qur'an,* edited by Andrew Rippin. Oxford: Oxford University Press, 1988.

Ahmad, Aziz. *Islamic Modernism in India and Pakistan, 1857–1964.* London: Oxford University Press, 1967.

Arberry, A. J. *The Koran Interpreted.* New York: Macmillan, 1955.

al-Bannā', Ḥasan. *Five Tracts of Hasan Al-Banna' (1906–1949): A Selection from the Majmu'āt rasā'il al-Imām al-shahīd Ḥasan al-Bannā'.* Trans. Charles Wendell. Berkeley: University of California Press, 1978.

Ben Ashoor, Yadh. *Islam and International Humanitarian Law.* Geneva: International Committee of the Red Cross, 1980.

Bennoune, Karima. "As-Salamu 'Alaykum? Humanitarian Law in Islamic Jurisprudence." *Michigan Journal of International Law* 15 (winter 1994): 605–43.

Best, Geoffrey. *War and Law since 1945.* Oxford: Oxford University Press, 1994.

Blank, Robert, and Janna C. Merrick. *Human Reproduction, Emerging Technologies, and Conflicting Rights.* Washington, D.C.: Congressional Quarterly Press, 1995.

Boisard, Marcel. "On the Probable Influence of Islam on Western Public and International Law." *International Journal of Middle East Studies* 11 (July 1980): 429–50.

Botkin, Jeffery R. "Fetal Privacy and Confidentiality." *Hastings Center Report* 25, no. 5 (September 1995): 32–39.

Botkin, Jeffery R., and Maxwell J. Mehlman. "Wrongful Birth: Medical, Legal, and Philosophical Issues." *Journal of Law, Medicine, and Ethics* 22, no. 1 (spring 1994): 21–28.

Bowen, Donna Lee. "Islam, Abortion, and the 1994 Cairo Population Conference." *International Journal of Middle Eastern Studies,* 29, no. 2 (May 1997), 161–84.

Brockopp, Jonathan E. *Early Mālikī Law.* Leiden: E. J. Brill, 2000.

Brown, Daniel. "Islamic Ethics in Comparative Perspective." *The Muslim World* 89, no. 3 (1999): 181–92.

———. *Rethinking Tradition in Modern Islamic Thought.* Cambridge and New York : Cambridge University Press, 1996.

al-Bukhārī, Muḥammad. *Ṣaḥīḥ al-Bukhārī : The Translation of the Meanings of Sahih Al-Bukhari, Arabic-English.* 6th rev. Ed. Muḥammad Muḥsin Khān. Lahore: Kazi Publications, 1983.

Callahan, Daniel. *Abortion: Law, Choice, and Morality.* London: Macmillan, 1970.

Capron, Alexander Morgan. "The Report of the President's Commission on the Uniform Determination of Death Act." In *Death: Beyond Whole-Brain Criteria,* edited by Richard M. Zaner, 147–70. Dordrecht: Kluwer Academic Publishers, 1988.

Catechism of the Catholic Church. English trans. by United States Catholic Conference. Rome: Libreria Editrice Vaticana, Urbi et Orbi Communications, 1994.

Christenson, Ron. *Political Trials: Gordian Knots in the Law.* 2d ed. New Brunswick, N.J.: Transaction Publishers, 1999.

Conklin, Beth A., and Lynn M. Morgan. "Babies, Bodies, and the Production of Personhood in North America and a Native Amazonian Society." *Ethos* 24 (1996), 657–94.

Daar, A. S. "Current Practice and the Legal, Ethical and Religious Status of Post Mortem Organ Donation in the Islamic World." In *Organ Replacement Therapy: Ethics, Justice, Commerce,* edited by W. Land and J. B. Dossetor. Berlin: Springer, 1991.

"A Definition of Irreversible Coma: Report of the Ad Hoc Committee of the Harvard Medical School to Examine the Definition of Brain Death." *Journal of the American Medical Association* 205 (1968) 6: 337–30.

Donagan, A. *The Theory of Morality.* Chicago: University of Chicago Press, 1977.

Donner, Fred. "The Sources of Islamic Conceptions of War." In *Just War and Jihad: Historical and Theoretical Perspectives on War and Peace in Western and Islamic Traditions,* edited by John Kelsay and James Turner Johnson. Westport, Conn.: Greenwood Press, 1991.

Dorff, Elliot, and Louis Newman, ed. *Contemporary Jewish Ethics and Morality.* New York: Oxford University Press, 1995.

Ebrahim, Abul Fadl Mohsin. *Abortion, Birth Control, and Surrogate Parenting: An Islamic Perspective.* [Indianapolis]: American Trust Publications, 1989.

———. "Islamic Ethics and the Implication of Biomedical Technology: An Analysis of Some Issues Pertaining to Reproductive Control, Bioethical Parenting, and Abortion." Ph.D. diss., Temple University, 1986.

Engelhardt, H. Tristram. *The Foundations of Bioethics.* New York and Oxford: Oxford University Press, 1996.

Eklund, Ragnar. *Life Between Death and Resurrection According to Islam.* Uppsala: Almquist & Wiksells Boktryckeri-A.-B., 1941.

Esack, Farid. "Muslims Engaging the Other and the *Humanum.*" In *Sharing the Book: Religious Perspectives on the Rights and Wrongs of Proselytism,* edited by John Witte Jr. and Richard C. Martin. Maryknoll, N.Y.: Orbis Books, 1999.

Esposito, John L. *The Islamic Threat: Myth or Reality?* 3d ed. New York: Oxford University Press, 1999.

Ess, Josef van. *Theologie und Gesellschaft im 2. und 3. Jahrhundert Hidschra: Eine Geschichte des religiösen Denkens im frühen Islam.* Berlin and New York: de Gruyter, 1991–97.

Fahmy, Khaled. "The Anatomy of Justice: Forensic Medicine and Criminal Law in Nineteenth-Century Egypt." *Islamic Law and Society* 6 (1999): 224–71.

Fakhry, Majid. *Ethical Theories in Islam.* Leiden: E. J. Brill, 1994.

———. *Islamic Occasionalism.* London: Allen and Unwin, 1958.

al-Farābī, Abū Naṣr. *Al-Farabi on the Perfect State.* Trans. Richard Walzer. Oxford: Clarendon Press, 1985.

Foot, Philippa. "The Problem of Abortion and the Doctrine of Double Effect." In *Absolutism and Its Consequentialist Critics,* edited by Joram Haber. Lanham, Md.: Rowman and Littlefield, 1994, 147–57.

Forrester, Mary Gore. *Persons, Animals, and Fetuses.* Dordrecht: Kluwer Academic Publishers, 1996.

Fregosi, Paul. *Jihad in the West: Muslim Conquest from the Seventh to the Twenty-first Centuries.* Amherst, N.Y.: Prometheus Books, 1998.

Fried, Charles. *Right and Wrong.* Cambridge: Harvard University Press, 1978.

Ghanem, Isam. *Islamic Medical Jurisprudence.* London: Probsthain, 1982.

al-Ghazālī, Abū Ḥāmid. *The Remembrance of Death and the Afterlife.* Trans. T. J. Winter. Cambridge: Islamic Text Society, 1989.

al-Ghunaimi, Mohammad Talaat. *The Muslim Conception of International Law and the Western Approach.* The Hague: Martinus Nijhoff, 1968.

Giladi, Avner. *Children of Islam: Concepts of Childhood in Medieval Muslim Society.* London: Macmillan, 1992.

Glennon, Michael J. *Constitutional Diplomacy.* Princeton, N.J.: Princeton University Press, 1990.

Haddad, Yvonne Yazbeck. "Operation Desert Storm and the War of Fatwas." In *Islamic Legal Interpretation and Their Fatwas,* edited by Muhammad Khalid Masud, Brinkley Messick, and David S. Powers, 297–309. Cambridge, Mass.: Harvard University Press, 1996.

Hamidullah, Muhammad. *Muslim Conduct of State.* 7th ed. Lahore: Muhammad Ashraf, 1977.

Hare, R. M. *Essays in Ethical Theory.* Oxford: Clarendon Press, 1989.

Hasan, Masudul. *Sayyed Abu'l A'ala Maududi and His Thought.* Lahore: Islamic Publications, 1986.

Hashmi, Sohail. *Islamic Political Ethics: Civil Society, Pluralism, and Conflict.* Princeton, N.J.: Princeton University Press, 2002.

Hathout, Hassan. "The Ethics of Genetic Engineering: An Islamic Viewpoint." *Journal of the Islamic Medical Association of North America* 22, no. 3 (July 1990): 99–101.

Heyd, David. "Prenatal Diagnosis: Whose Right?" *Journal of Medical Ethics* 21, no. 5 (October 1995): 292–97.

Hoodfar, Homa. "Devices and Desires: Population Policy and Gender Roles in the Islamic Republic." *Middle East Report* 190 (September-October 1994): 11–14.

Hourani, George F. *Reason and Tradition in Islamic Ethics.* Cambridge: Cambridge University Press, 1985.

Ibn Rushd, Abū al-Walīd. *The Distinguished Jurist's Primer: A Translation of* Bidāyat al-Mujtahid. 2 vols. Reading, U.K.: Garnet, 1994–96.

Jackson, Anthony. "Wrongful Life and Wrongful Birth: The English Conception." *Journal of Legal Medicine* 17, no. 3 (September 1996): 349–81.

Jansen, Johannes J. G. *The Neglected Duty: The Creed of Sadat's Assassins and Islamic Resurgence in the Middle East.* New York: Macmillan, 1986.

Johansen, Baber, *Contingency in a Sacred Law: Legal and Ethical Norms in the Muslim Fiqh*. Leiden: E. J. Brill, 1999.

John Paul II. "Euthanasia: Declaration of the Sacred Congregation for the Doctrine of the Faith. May 5, 1980." In *On Moral Medicine: Theological Perspectives in Medical Ethics,* edited by Stephen E. Lammers and Allen Verhey, 441–44. Grand Rapids, Mich.: William B. Eerdmans, 1987. Reprinted from *The Pope Speaks* 25 (winter 1980): 259–96.

Johnson, James Turner. *The Holy War Idea in Western and Islamic Traditions.* University Park, Pa.: Pennsylvania State University Press, 1997.

———. "Historical Roots and Sources of the Just War Tradition in Western Culture." In *Just War and Jihad: Historical and Theoretical Perspectives on War and Peace in Western and Islamic Traditions,* edited by John Kelsay and James Johnson. New York: Greenwood Press, 1991.

———. *Can Modern War Be Just?* New Haven: Yale University Press, 1984.

Johnson, James Turner, and John Kelsay, eds. *Cross, Crescent, and Sword: The Justification and Limitation of War in Western and Islamic Traditions.* Contributions to the Study of Religions, 27. New York: Greenwood Press, 1990.

Jonsen, Albert R., and Toulmin, Stephen. *The Abuse of Casuistry: A History of Moral Reasoning.* Berkeley: University of California Press, 1988.

Katz, Marion Holmes. *Body of Text: The Emergence of the Sunni Law of Ritual Purity.* Albany: State University of New York Press, 2002.

Kay Kā'ūs ibn Iskandar. *A Mirror for Princes.* Trans. Reuben Levy. London: Cresset Press, 1956.

Kelsay, John. "Bosnia and the Muslim Critique of Modernity." In *Religion and Justice in the War over Bosnia,* edited by G. Scott Davis. New York and London: Routledge, 1996.

———. *Islam and War.* Louisville, Ky.: John Knox/Westminster Press, 1993.

Kelsay, John, and James Turner Johnson, eds. *Just War and Jihad: Historical and Theoretical Perspectives on War and Peace in Western and Islamic Traditions.* Contributions to the Study of Religion, 28. New York: Greenwood Press, 1991.

Kepel, Gillles. *Muslim Extremism in Egypt: The Prophet and Pharaoh.* Berkeley and Los Angeles: University of California Press, 1986.

Kerr, Malcolm. *Islamic Reform: The Political and Legal Theories of Muḥammad ʿAbduh and Rashīd Riḍā.* Berkeley: University of California Press, 1966.

Khadduri, Majid. *War and Peace in the Law of Islam.* Baltimore, Md.: Johns Hopkins University Press, 1955; reprint New York: AMS Press, 1979.

Kingdom of Saudi-Arabia, Ministry of Health. "SCOT Protocol: Directory of the Regulations of Organ Transplantation in the Kingdom of Saudi Arabia." *Saudi Journal of Kidney Diseases and Transplantation* 5 (1994), 1:37–98.

Kirchheimer, Otto. *Political Justice: The Use of Legal Procedure for Political Ends.* Princeton, N.J.: Princeton University Press, 1961.

Kohlberg, Etan. "The Position of the *Walad Zinā* in Imāmī Shīʿ ism." *Bulletin of the School of Asian and African Studies* 48, no. 2 (1985): 237–66.

Kraemer, Joel L. "Apostates, Rebels, and Brigands." *Israel Oriental Studies* 10 (1980): 34–73.

Krawietz, Birgit. "Ethical Versus Medical Values According to Contemporary Islamic Law." *Recht van de Islam* 16 (1999): 1–26.

———. "*Ḍarūra* in Modern Islamic Law: The Case of Organ Transplantation." In *Islamic Law: Theory and Practice,* edited by Robert Gleave and Eugenia Kermeli. London: I. B. Taurus, 1997.

———. *Die Ḥurma: Schariatrechtlicher Schutz vor Eingriffen in die körperliche Unversehrtheit nach arabischen Fatwas des 20. Jahrhunderts.* Berlin: Duncker & Humblot, 1991.

Lachs, John. "The Element of Choice in Criteria of Death." In *Death: Beyond Whole-Brain Criteria,* edited by Richard M. Zaner, 233–51. Dodrecht: Kluwer Academic Publishers, 1988.

Lamb, David. *Death, Brain Death, and Ethics.* London and Sydney: Croom Helm, 1985.

Lawrence, Bruce B. *Shattering the Myth: Islam beyond Violence.* Princeton, N.J.: Princeton University Press, 1998.

Leaman, Oliver. *An Introduction to Medieval Islamic Philosophy.* Cambridge: Cambridge University Press, 1985.

Leisten, Thomas. *Architektur für Tote: Bestattung in architektonischem Kontext in den Kernländern der islamischen Welt zwischen 3./9. und 6./12. Jahrhundert.* Berlin: D. Reimer, 1998.

Lohlker, Rüdiger. *Schari'a und Moderne: Diskussionen über Schwangerschaftsabbruch, Versicherung und Zinsen.* Stuttgart: Steiner, 1996.

McCullagh, Peter. *Brain Dead, Brain Absent, Brain Donors: Human Subjects or Human Objects?* Chichester: John Wiley & Sons, 1993.

Mahdi, Muhsin, and Ralph Lerner, ed. *Medieval Political Philosophy.* New York: The Free Press of Glencoe, Macmillan, 1963.

Mahmood, Tahir. *Family Planning: The Muslim Viewpoint.* New Delhi: Vikas Publishing House, 1977.

Martin, Richard C. *Defenders of Reason in Islam: Mu'tazilism from Medieval School to Modern Symbol.* Oxford: Oneworld Publications, 1997.

Masud, Muhammad Khalid, Brinkley Messick, and David Powers, eds. *Islamic Legal Interpretation: Muftis and Their Fatwas.* Cambridge, Mass.: Harvard University Press, 1996.

Mawdudi, Abu al-A'la. *Towards Understanding the Qur'an (Tafhim al-Qur'an).* Trans. and ed. Zafar Ishaq Ansari. Leicester, U.K.: The Islamic Foundation, 1988.

———. *Birth Control: Its Social, Political, Economic, Moral, and Religious Aspects.* Trans. Khurshid Ahmad and Misbahul Islam Faruqi. 3d ed. Lahore: Islamic Publications Limited, 1968.

Mayer, Ann Elizabeth. "War and Peace in the Islamic Law Tradition and International Law." In *Just War and Jihad,* edited by James Turner Johnson and John Kelsay. New York: Greenwood Press, 1991.

Messick, Brinkley. *The Calligraphic State.* Berkeley: University of California Press, 1993.

Miller, David, and Sohail Hashmi, eds. *Boundaries and Justice: Diverse Ethical Perspectives.* Princeton, N.J.: Princeton University Press, 2001.

Mir, Mustansir. "*Jihad* in Islam." In *The Jihad and Its Times,* edited by Hadia Dajani-Shakeel and Ronald Messier. Ann Arbor: Center for Near Eastern and North African Studies, University of Michigan, 1991.

Nagel, Thomas. *The View from Nowhere.* Oxford: Oxford University Press, 1986.

Nasiri, Muhammad Mekki. "A View of Family Planning in Islamic Legislation." *Islam Review* 62 (March-April, 1969): 3–4.

Nasr, Seyyed Vali Reza. *The Vanguard of the Islamic Revolution: The Jamaʿat-i Islami of Pakistan.* Berkeley: University of California Press, 1994.

Nazer, Isam, ed. *Islam and Family Planning.* Beirut: International Planned Parenthood Federation, 1974.

Neusner, Jacob, Tamara Sonn, and Jonathan Brockopp. *Judaism and Islam in Practice.* New York: Routledge, 2000.

Newman, Louis. "Woodchoppers and Respirators: The Problem of Interpretation in Contemporary Jewish Ethics." In *Contemporary Jewish Ethics and Morality,* edited by Elliot Dorff and Louis Newman, 140–60. New York: Oxford University Press, 1995.

Noonan, John. *The Morality of Abortion: Legal and Historical Perspectives.* Cambridge: Harvard University Press, 1970.

Nordmann, Yves. *Zwischen Leben und Tod: Aspekte der jüdischen Medizinethik.* Bern: Peter Lang, 1999.

Omran, Abdel Rahim. *Family Planning in the Legacy of Islam.* London: Routledge, 1992.

O'Shaughnessy, Thomas. *Muhammad's Thoughts on Death: A Thematic Study of the Qur'anic Data.* Leiden: E. J. Brill, 1969.

Outka, Gene, and John P. Reeder, ed. *Prospects for a Common Morality.* Princeton, N.J.: Princeton University Press, 1992.

Paul VI. "Respect for Life in the Womb, Address to the Medical Association of Western Flanders, April 23, 1977." In *On Moral Medicine: Theological Perspectives in Medical Ethics,* edited by Stephen E. Lammers and Allen Verhey, 396–97. Grand Rapids, Mich.: William B. Eerdmans, 1987. Reprinted from *The Pope Speaks* 22 (fall 1977): 281–82.

Pence, Gregory E. *Classic Cases in Medical Ethics.* New York: McGraw-Hill, 2000.

Peters, Rudolph. *Jihad: In Classical and Modern Islam.* Princeton, N.J.: Markus Wiener, 1996.

Pickthall, Mohammed Marmaduke. *The Meaning of the Glorious Koran.* London: New American Library, n.d.

Pines, Shlomo. *Beiträge zur islamischen Atomenlehre.* Berlin: A. Heine, 1936.

al-Qāḍī, ʿAbd ar-Raḥīm Ibn Aḥmad. *Das Totenbuch des Islam: "Das Feuer und der Garten"—die Lehren des Propheten Mohammad über das Leben nach dem Tode.* Bern and München: Scherz, 1981.

Ragab, M. Ismail. "Islam and the Unwanted Pregnancy." In *Abortion and Sterilization: Medical and Social Aspects,* edited by Jane E. Hodgson, 507–18. London: Academic Press, 1981.

Rahman, Fazlur. *Major Themes of the Qur'ān*. Minneapolis, Minn., and Chicago: Bibliotheca Islamica, 1989.

———. *Health and Medicine in the Islamic Tradition; Change and Identity.* New York: Crossroad, 1987.

———. "Law and Ethics in Islam." In *Ethics in Islam,* edited by Richard Hovannisia. Malibu, Calif.: Undena, 1985.

Reeder, John. *Killing & Saving: Abortion, Hunger, and War.* University Park: Pennsylvania State University Press, 1996.

Reinhart, A. Kevin. *Before Revelation: The Boundaries of Muslim Moral Thought.* Albany: State University of New York Press, 1995.

———. "Islamic Law as Islamic Ethics." *Journal of Religious Ethics.* 11 (1983), 186–203.

Renard, John. "Muslim Ethics: Sources, Interpretations and Challenges." *The Muslim World* 69 (1979): 163–77.

Rispler-Chaim, Vardit. *Islamic Medical Ethics in the Twentieth Century.* Leiden: E. J. Brill, 1993.

———. "Islamic Medical Ethics and the Right to Privacy." Paper presented to the first International Conference on Medical Ethics and Medical Law in Islam, Haifa, Israel, March, 2001.

Rosenthal, Franz. "On Suicide in Islam." *Journal of the American Oriental Society* 66 (1946): 239–59.

Rubin, Uri. "*Al-Walad li-l-firāsh:* on the Islamic Campaign against *zinā*'." *Studia Islamica* 78 (1994): 5–26.

Sabin, Arthur J. *In Calmer Times: The Supreme Court and Red Monday.* Philadelphia: University of Pennsylvania Press, 1999.

Samuels, Alec. "Born Too Soon and Born Imperfect: The Legal Aspects." *Medical Science and Law* 38, no. 1 (1998): 57–61.

Schellong, Sebastian. *Künstliche Beatmung.* Stuttgart and New York: G. Fischer, 1990.

Schneiderman, Lawrence J., and Nancy S. Jecker. *Wrong Medicine.* Baltimore, Md. and London: Johns Hopkins University Press, 1995.

Seedhouse, David, and Lisetta Lovett. *Practical Medical Ethics.* Chichester and New York: John Wiley, 1992.

Sharelson, Lonny. *A Chosen Death.* New York: Simon and Schuster, 1995

al-Shaybānī, Muḥammad ibn al-Ḥasan. *The Islamic Law of Nations: Shaybani's* Siyar (Kitāb al-siyar al-kabīr). Trans. Majid Khadduri. Baltimore, Md.: Johns Hopkins University Press, 1966.

Sherwin, Byron. "A View of Euthanasia." In *Contemporary Jewish Ethics and Morality,* edited by Elliot Dorff and Louis Newman, 363–81. New York: Oxford University Press, 1995.

Singer, Marcus G. "Institutional Ethics." In *Ethics,* edited by A. Phillips Griffiths. Cambridge: Cambridge University Press, 1993.

Sivan, Emmanuel. *Radical Islam: Medieval Theology and Modern Politics.* New Haven: Yale University Press, 1990.

Smith, David Randolph. "Legal Issues Leading to the Notion of Neocortical Death." In *Death: Beyond Whole-Brain Criteria,* edited by Richard M. Zaner, 111–44. Dodrecht: Kluwer Academic Publishers, 1988.

Smith, Jane Idleman, trans. *The Precious Pearl: A Translation from the Arabic with Notes of the* Kitāb al-durra al-Fākhira fī kashf 'ulūm al-ākhira *of Abū Ḥāmid Muḥammad b. Muḥammad b. Muḥammad al-Ghazālī.* Missoula, Mont.: Scholars Press, 1979.

Smith, Jane, and Yvonne Haddad. *The Islamic Understanding of Death and Resurrection.* Albany: State University of New York, 1981.

Sonbol, Amira al-Azhary. "Adoption in Islamic Society: A Historical Survey." In *Children in the Muslim Middle East,* edited by Elizabeth Warnock Fernea, 45–67. Austin: University of Texas Press, 1995.

Steinberg, Abraham. "The Definition of Death." In *Medicine and Jewish Law,* edited by Fred Rosner. Northvale, N.J.: J. Aronson, 1990.

al-Ṭabarī, 'Alī ibn Rabbān. *The Book of Religion and Empire.* Trans. A. Mingana. Manchester: Manchester University Press, 1922.

Thomas, Geoffrey. *An Introduction to Ethics: Five Central Problems of Moral Judgment.* London: Gerald Duckworth & Co., 1993.

Thomson, Judith Jarvis. "A Defense of Abortion." In *Moral Philosophy: Selected Readings,* edited by George Sher. San Diego and New York: Harcourt Brace Jovanovich, 1987.

Umri, Jalaluddin. "Suicide or Termination of Life." *Islamic Comparative Law Quarterly* 7 (1987): 136–44.

Walton, Douglas N. *Brain Death: Ethical Considerations.* West Lafayette, Ind.: Purdue University, 1980.

Watt, W. Montgomery. *The Faith and Practice of al-Ghazālī.* London: George Allen and Unwin Ltd., 1953.

———. *Free Will and Predestination in Early Islam.* London: Luzac, 1948.

Wensinck, A. J. *Handbook of Early Muhammadan Tradition.* Leiden: E. J. Brill, 1960.

———. *The Muslim Creed.* Cambridge: Cambridge University Press, 1932.

Whitefield, Adrian. "Common Law Duties to Unborn Children." *Medical Law Review* 1, no. 1 (January 1993): 28–52.

Witte, John, Jr., and Richard C. Martin, eds. *Sharing the Book: Religious Perspectives on the Rights and Wrongs of Proselytism.* Maryknoll, N.Y.: Orbis Books, 1999.

Wolf, Susan. "Moral Saints." In *Ethics,* edited by Peter Singer. Oxford: Oxford University Press, 1994.

Yanagihashi, Hiroyuki. "The Doctrinal Development of "*Maraḍ al-Mawt.*" *Islamic Law and Society* 5 (1998), 326–58.

Zehili, Wahba Moustapha. "Dispositions internationales relatives à la guerre, justifiées au regard de l'Islam et leurs aspects humains caractéristiques." In *Les religions et la guerre: Judaisme, Christianisme, Islam,* edited by Pierre Viaud. Paris: Cerf, 1991.

Arabic Sources

'Abd al-Razzāq al-Ṣan'ānī. *Al-Muṣannaf.* Beirut: al-Maktab al-Islāmī, 1983.

al-Ābī, Muḥammad Ibn Khalīfa. *Sharḥ Ṣaḥīḥ Muslim.* Beirut: Dār al-Kutub al-'Ilmiyya, 1994.

Abū Dāwud al-Sijistānī. *Sunan Abī Dāwud.* Beirut: Dār Ibn Ḥazm, 1998.

Abū Ya'lā, Muḥammad b. Ḥusayn al-Farra. *Al-Aḥkām al-sulṭāniyya.* Beirut: Dār al-Kutub al-'Ilmiyya, 1983.

al-'Āmilī, al-Shaykh Ḥusayn Bandar. *Risāla fī al-mawt wa-l-barzakh yalīhā aḥkām tajhīz al-mayyit muṭābaqa li-fatāwā Āyat Allāh al-'Uẓmā al-Sayyid Abī Qāsim al-Khū'ī quddisa sirruhu al-sharīf.* Beirut: Dār al-Rasūl al-Akram, 1996.

al-Anṣārī, Abū Yaḥyā Zakariyyā. *Fatḥ al-Wahhāb.* Cairo: Muṣṭafā al-Bābī, 1948.

al-'Aqīlī, 'Aqīl b. Aḥmad. *Ḥukm naql al-a'ḍā' ma' al-ta'qībāt al-bayyina 'alā man ta'aqqaba Ibn Taymiyya.* Jedda: Maktabat al-Ṣaḥāba, 1992.

al-Bannā', Ḥasan, Sayyid Quṭb, and Abū al-A'lā al-Mawdudi. *Al-Jihād fī sabīl Allāh.* Cairo: Ṣawt al-ḥaqq, 1977.

al-Bayhaqī, Abū Bakr Aḥmad b. 'Alī. *Ma'rifat al-sunan wa al-āthār.* Ed. Sayyid Kasrāwī Ḥusayn. Beirut: Dār al-Kutub al-'Ilmiyya, 1991.

al-Bayyūmī, Samīra Sayyid Sulaymān. *Al-Ijhāḍ wa-āthāruhu fī al-sharī'a al-islāmīya.* 1st ed. Cairo: Dār al-Ṭibā'a al-Muḥammadīya bi-l-Azhar, 1989.

al-Buhūtī, Manṣūr. *Kashshāf al-qinā'.* Ed. Hilāl Muṣṭafā Hilāl. Beirut: Dār al-Fikr, 1982.

al-Bukhārī, Abū 'Abd Allāh. *Ṣaḥīḥ al-Bukhārī.* Cairo: Dār Iḥyā' al-Turāth al-'Arabī, n.d.; also Beirut: Dār al-Fikr, 1991.

al-Daqr, Nadā Muḥammad Na'īm. *Mawt al-dimāgh bayna al-ṭibb wa-l-Islām.* Damascus: Dār al-Fikr, 1997.

[al-Dasūqī], *Ḥāshiyat al-Dasūqī 'alā l-Sharḥ al-kabīr.* Dār Iḥyā' al-Kutub al-'Arabīya, n.p., n.d.

al-Dhahabī, Muṣṭafā Muḥammad. *Naql al-a'ḍā' bayn al-ṭibb wa-l-dīn.* Cairo: Dār al-Ḥadīth, 1993.

al-Faramāwī, 'Abd al-Ḥayy. *Al-Mawt fī l-fikri l-Islāmī.* Cairo: Dar al-I'tiṣām, 1991.

al-Fatāwā al-Hindīya [1310 A.H.]. Facsimile edition. Beirut: Dār al-Ma'rifa, 1973; also *Al-Fatāwā al-'Ālamgīrīya al-ma'rūfa bi-l-Fatāwā al-Hindīya.* Cairo: Būlāq, A.H. 1310.

Fatāwā al-imām Muḥammad Rashīd Riḍā. 6 vols. Ed. Ṣalāḥ al-Dīn al-Munajjid. Beirut: Dār al-Kitāb al-Jadīd, 1970–71.

al-Fatāwā al-islāmiyya min Dār al-Iftā' al-Miṣriyya. Ed. Jumhūriyyat Miṣr al-'Arabiyya: Wizārat al-Awqāf. Cairo: Dār al-Iftā' al-Miṣriyya, 1980–.

Fatāwā al-mar'a al-muslima. Riyadh: Maktaba Ṭabariyya, 1995.

al-Ghazālī, Abū Ḥāmid. *Iḥyā' 'ulūm al-dīn.* Beirut: Dār al-Fikr, 1994.

———. *al-Mustaṣfā min 'ilm al-uṣūl.* Beirut: Dār al-Arqam ibn Abī al-Arqam, n.d.

al-Ḥaṭṭāb, Abū 'Abd Allāh Muḥammad ibn Muḥammad ibn 'Abd al-Raḥmān al-Ṭarābulusī al-Maghribī. *Mawāhib al-jalīl li-sharḥ Mukhtaṣar al-Khalīl.* Tripoli, Libya: Maktabat al-Najāh, n.d.

al-Ḥillī, Abū al-Qāsim al-Muḥaqqiq. *Sharā'i' al-Islām fī Masā'il al-ḥalāl wa-l-ḥarām*. Beirut: Dār al-Aḍwā', 1983.

al-Ḥillī, Fakhr al-Muḥaqqiqīn. *Īḍāḥ al-fawā'id*. Qum: Mu'assasat Ismā'īliyyān, A.H. 1387.

Ibn 'Ābidīn, Muḥammad b. 'Umar al-Dimashqī. *Ḥāshiyat radd al-Muḥtār*. Ed. 'Ādil Aḥmad Mu'awwad. 2d ed. [Cairo], 1966; also Beirut: Dār al-Kutub al-'Ilmiyya, 1994.

Ibn Abī Dunyā, *Kitāb al-muḥtaḍarīn*. Ed. Muḥammad Khayr Ramaḍān Yūsuf. Beirut: Dar Ibn Ḥazm, 1997.

Ibn Abī Shayba, 'Abd Allāh. *Al-Muṣannaf fī al-aḥādīth wa-l-āthār*. Ed. Sa'īd Muḥammad al-Laḥḥām. Beirut: Dār al-Fikr, 1989.

Ibn al-A'tham, Abū Muḥammad Aḥmad. *Al-Futūḥ*. Beirut: Dār al-Kutub al-'Ilmiyya, 1986.

Ibn al-Humām, Kamāl al-Dīn Muḥammad. *Sharḥ Fatḥ al-Qadīr*. Ed. 'Abd al-Razzāq Ghālib. Beirut: Dār al-Kutub al-'Ilmiyya, 1995.

Ibn al-Jawzī, Abū al-Faraj 'Abd al-Raḥmān. *Al-Muntaẓam fī ta'rīkh al-umam*. Ed. Muḥammad 'Abd al-Qādir 'Aṭā' and Muṣṭafā 'Abd al-Qādir 'Aṭā'. Beirut: Dār al-Kutub al-'Ilmiyya, 1992.

Ibn al-Muqrī, Sharaf al-Dīn Ismā'īl b. Abī Bakr. *Kitāb al-tamshiyya bi-sharḥ Irshād al-ghāwī fī masālik al-Ḥāwī*. Cairo: Dār al-Hudā, n.d.

———. *Ikhlāṣ al-nāwī*. Ed. 'Abd al-'Azīz 'Aṭīya Zalāṭ. Cairo: Lajnat Iḥyā' al-Turāth al-Islāmī, 1989.

Ibn Ḥajar al-'Asqalānī, Shihāb al-Dīn. *Fatḥ al-bārī bi-sharḥ al-Bukhārī*. Beirut: Dār al-Fikr, 1993; also Cairo: al-Maṭba'a al-salafiyya, n.d.

Ibn Ḥajar al-Haythamī, Aḥmad b. Muḥammad Shihāb al-Dīn. *Fatḥ al-jawād sharḥ al-Irshād*. Cairo: Muṣṭafā al-Bābī, 1971.

———. *Tuḥfat al-muḥtāj bi-sharḥ al-Minhāj*. Beirut: Dār Ṣādir, 1972.

Ibn Ḥammād, Abū 'Abd Allāh Nu'aym. *Kitāb al-fitan*. Ed. Suhayl Zakar. Beirut: Dār al-Fikr, 1993.

Ibn Ḥazm, *al-Muḥallā*. Beirut: Dār al-Kutub al-'Ilmiyya, [1992].

[Ibn Kathīr], *Al-Sīra al-nabawiyya wa-l-mu'jizāt : Khulāṣat al-bidāya wa-l-nihāya li-Ibn Kathīr*. 2 vols. Ed. Muḥammad b. Aḥmad Kan'ān. Beirut: n.p., 1996.

Ibn Mājā, Abū 'Abd Allāh Muḥammad, *Sunan Ibn Māja*, ed. Muḥammad Fu'ād 'Abd al-Bāqī. [Cairo]: 'Īsā al-Bābī al-Ḥalabī wa-Shurakāhu, n.d.

Ibn Mufliḥ, Abū 'Abd Allāh Muḥammad. *Kitāb al-furū'*. Beirut: 'Ālam al-Kutub, 1985.

Ibn Qayyim al-Jawziyya, Abū 'Abd Allāh Muḥammad. *Aḥkām ahl al-dhimma*. Ed. Ṣubḥī Ṣāliḥ Beirut: Dār al-'Ilm li-l-Malāyīn, 1983.

Ibn Qudāma, Abū Muḥammad b. Muḥammad. *Al-Mughnī*. Ed. Ṭāhā Muḥammad al-Zaynī. Cairo: Maktabat al-Qāhira, 1969; also Beirut: Dār al-Kutub al-'Ilmiyya, n.d.

Ibn Rushd, Abū al-Walīd. *Bidāyat al-mujtahid wa-nihāyat al-muqtaṣid*. Cairo: Dār al-Fikr, n.d.; also Cairo: n.p., 1935.

———. *al-Bayān wa-l-taḥṣīl*. Beirut: Dār al-Gharb al-Islāmī, 1985.

Ibn Taymiyya, Abū al-ʿAbbās Taqī al-Dīn Aḥmad. *Al-Fatāwā al-kubrā*. Ed. Muḥammad ʿAbd al-Qawī ʿAṭāʾ and Muṣṭafā ʿAbd al-Qawī ʿAṭāʾ. Cairo: Dār al-Rayyān li-l-Turāth, 1988.

———. *Minhāj al-sunna al-nabawiyya*. Beirut: al-Maktaba al-ʿIlmiyya, n.d.

———. *Al-Siyāsa al-sharʿiyya fī iṣlāḥ al-rāʿī wa-l-rāʿiyya*. Beirut: Dār al-ʿAfāq, 1983.

———. *Majmūʿ fatāwā shaykh al-islām Aḥmad ibn Taymīya*. 34 vols. Rabat: al-Maktab al-Taʿlīmī al-Suʿūdī fī al-Maghrib, n.d.

Jād al-Ḥaqq ʿAlī Jād al-Ḥaqq, *Buḥūth wa-fatāwā islāmiyya fī qaḍāyā muʿāṣira*. 6 vols. [Cairo:] al-Azhar al-Sharīf, al-Amāna al-ʿĀmma li-l-Lajna al-ʿUlyā li-l-Daʿwa al-Islāmiyya, 1992–95.

al-Jamāl, Sulaymān. *Ḥāshiyat al-Jamāl*. Beirut: Dar Iḥyāʾ al-Turāth al-ʿArabī, n.d.

al-Jazīrī, ʿAbd al-Raḥmān, *Kitāb al-fiqh ʿalā al-madhāhib al-arbaʿa*. 5 vols. N.p.: Dar al-Irshād li-l-Ṭabāʿa wa-l-Nashr, n.d.

al-Khaṭīb, Umm Kulthūm Yaḥyā Muṣṭafā. *Qaḍīyat taḥdīd al-nasl fī al-sharīʿa al-islāmīya*. Jidda: al-Dār al-Suʿūdīya li-l-Nashr wa-l-Tawzīʿ, 1982.

al-Luʾluʾ al-mathīn min fatāwā al-muʿawwaqīn. Riyadh: Dār al-Ṣamayʿī, 1997.

Maḥmūd, ʿAbd al-Ḥalīm, *Fatāwā al-imām ʿAbd al-Ḥalīm Maḥmūd*. 2 vols. Cairo: Dār al-Maʿārif, 1979.

Mālik b. Anas, *al-Muwaṭṭaʾ*. 2 vols. Ed. Ḥasan ʿAbdallāh Sharaf. Cairo: Dār al-Rayyān, 1988.

al-Marghinānī, Abū al-Ḥasan. *Al-Hidāya sharḥ al-Bidāya*. Cairo: Muṣṭafā al-Bābī, n.d.; also n.p., A.H. 1326.

al-Masʿūdī, Abū al-Ḥasan ʿAlī b. ʿAlī. *Murūj al-dhahab*. Ed. Muḥammad ʿAbd al-Ḥamīd. Cairo: Kitāb al-Taḥrīr, 1966.

al-Māwardī, Abū al-Ḥasan. *Al-Aḥkām al-sulṭāniyya wa-l-wilāyāt al-dīniyya*. Beirut: Dār al-Kutub al-ʿIlmiyya, 1985.

———. *Kitāb qitāl ahl al-bāghy min al-Ḥāwī al-kabīr*. Ed. Ibrāhīm b. ʿAlī Ṣandaqī. Cairo: Maṭbaʿat al-Madanī, n.d.

Mawdūdī, Abū al-Aʿlā. *Al-Jihād fī al-Islām*. Lahore: Idāra Tarjumān al-Qurʾān, 1988.

al-Mawsūʿa al-fiqhīya. 38 vols. to date. Kuwait: Wizārat al-Awqāf wa-l-Shuʾūn al-Islāmīya, 1987–.

Muslim ibn Ḥajjāj. *Ṣaḥīḥ Muslim*. Beirut: Dār Ibn Ḥazm, 1995.

Nadwat al-ḥayāh al-insāniyya: Bidāyatuhā wa-nihāyatuhā fī al-mafhūm al-Islāmī. Kuwait: Dawlat al-Kuwait, 1985.

al-Nawawī, Abū Zakariyyā Yaḥyā ibn Sharaf. *Al-Majmūʿ sharḥ al-Muhadhdhab*. Beirut: Dār al-Fikr, n.d.

———. *Rawḍat al-ṭālibīn*. Ed. ʿĀdil Aḥmad ʿAbd al-Mawjūd and ʿAlī Muḥammad Maʿriḍ. Beirut: Dār al-Kutub al-ʿIlmiyya, 1992.

———. *Sharḥ Saḥīḥ Muslim*. Ed. Khalīl al-Mīṣ. Beirut: Dār al-Qalam, n.d.; also Cairo: maṭbaʿa Ḥijāzī., n.d.

Qāḍī Zādeh, Shams al-Dīn Aḥmad. *Natāʾij al-afkār fī kashf al-rumūz wa-l-asrār*. Cairo, [A.H. 1389] 1970.

al-Qarāfī, Shihāb al-Dīn b. Idrīs. *Al-Dhakhīra*. Beirut: Dār al-Gharb al-Islāmī, 1994.

al-Qurṭubī, Abū 'Abd Allāh Muḥammad ibn Aḥmad al-Anṣārī. *Al-Jāmi' li-aḥkām al-Qur'ān*. Cairo: Dār al-Kātib al-'Arabī, 1967.

———. *Al-Tadhkira fi awāl al-mawta wa-umūr al-ākhira*. Ed. Ṭāhā 'Abd al-Ra'ūf Sa'd. Cairo: Dār Iḥyā' al-Kutub al-'Arabiyya, n.d.

al-Ramlī, Shams al-Dīn Muḥammad b. Aḥmad al-Anṣārī. *Fatāwā al-Ramlī*. Beirut: Dār al-Kutub al-'Ilmiyya, 1983 (printed in the margin of Ibn Ḥajar's *al-Fatāwā al-kubrā al-fiqhiyya*).

———. *Ghāyat al-bayān*. Cairo: Muṣṭafā al-Bābī, n.d.

———. *Nihāyat al-muḥtāj ilā sharḥ al-Minhāj*. Cairo: Muṣṭafā al-Bābī, 1968.

al-Rāzī, Fakhr al-Dīn. *Al-Tafsīr al-kabīr*. Cairo: al-Maṭba'a al-Bāhiya al-Miṣriya, 1938; also Beirut: Dār al-Kutub al-'Ilmiyya, 1990.

Ṣabrī, 'Ikrīma. *Fatwā shar'iyya ḥawla jarīmat al-ightisāb fī kūsūvū*. Jerusalem: Publications of Majlis al-fatwā al-A'lā, April 25, 1999.

Saḥnūn b. Sa'īd. *Al-Mudawwana al-kubrā*. Beirut: Dār al-Kutub al-'Ilmiyya, 1994.

al-Ṣāliḥī, Muḥammad b. Ṭulūn. *Al-Taḥrīr al-marsakh fī awāl al-barzakh*. Ed. Abū 'Abd al-Raḥmān al-Miṣrī al-Atharī. Tanta: Dār al-Ṣaḥābah li-l-Turāth, 1991.

al-Sarakhsī, Muḥammad Aḥmad. *Sharḥ kitāb al-Siyar al-kabīr*. Beirut: Dār al-Kutub al-'Ilmiyya, 1997.

———. *Kitāb Mabsūt al-Sarakhsī*. [Cairo], A.H. 1324.

al-Ṣāwī, Aḥmad b. Muḥammad. *Bulghat al-sālik*. Cairo: Muṣṭafā al-Bābī, 1954.

Shaltūt, Maḥmūd. *Al-Fatāwā: Dirāsa li-mushkilāt al-muslim al-mu'āṣir fī ḥayātihi al-yawmīya wa-'āmma*. Cairo: Dār al-Qalam, 1966

al-Shīrāzī, Abū Isḥāq al-Firūzabādhī. *Al-Muhadhdhab fī fiqh al-imām al-Shāfi'ī*. Cairo: Maṭba'at Muṣṭafā al-Bābī al-Ḥalabī, 1976; also Beirut: Dār al-Kutub al-'Ilmiyya, 1995.

al-Shirbīnī, Muḥammad al-Khaṭīb. *Mughnī al-muḥtāj*. Cairo: Muṣṭafā al-Bābī, 1958.

al-Ṭabarī, Abū Ja'far. *Jāmi' al-bayān 'an ta'wīl al-Qur'ān*. Ed. Maḥmūd Shākir. Cairo: Dār al-Ma'ārif, n.d.

Ṭanṭawī, Muḥammad Sayyid. *Tafsīr sūrat al-nisā'*. Cairo: Maṭba'a al-Sa'āda, 1977.

al-Ṭarabulsī, 'Abd al-'Azīz b. al-Barrāj. *Al-Muhadhdhab*. Tehran: Mu'assasat al-Nashr al-Islāmī, A.H. 1406.

al-Tirmidhī. *Sunan al-Tirmidhī wa-huwa-al-jāmi' al-ṣaḥīḥ* Ed. 'Abd al-Raḥmān Muḥammad 'Uthmān. Medina: Muḥammad 'Abd al-Muḥsin al-Kutubī, n.d.

Turfa, Ṭalāl 'Alī, *Al-Ṣabr fī al-islām: Ru'ya taḥlīliyya shāmila*. Beirut: n.p., 1998.

al-Wansharīsī, Abū al-'Abbās Aḥmad ibn Yaḥyā. *al-Mi'yār al-mu'rib wa-l-jāmi' al-mughrib*. Rabat: Wizārat al-Awqāf wa-l-Shu'ūn al-Islāmīya, 1981.

al-Wazīr, Muḥammad b. Ibrāhīm. *Al-'Awāṣim wa-l-qawāṣim*. Beirut: Mu'assasat al-Risāla, 1992.

Zallūm, 'Abd al-Qadīm. *Ḥukm al-shar' fī al-ijhāḍ wa-fī isti'māl ajhizat al-in'āsh al-ṭibbiyya al-ṣinā'iyya al-ḥadītha*. Baqā' al-Gharbiyya: Maktabat al-Sunna, 1997.

al-Zaynī, Maḥmūd Muḥammad ʿAbd al-ʿAzīz. *Al-Ḍarūra fī al-sharīʿa al-islāmiyya wa-l-qānūn al-waḍʿī, taṭbīquhā, aḥkāmuhā, āthāruhā: Dirāsa muqārana*. Alexandria: Mu'assasat al-Thaqāfa al-Jāmiʿiyya, 1993.

al-Zuḥayli, Wahba. *Al-ʿAlāqāt al-duwaliya fī al-Islām: Muqārana bi-l-qānūn al-duwalī al-ḥadīth*. Beirut: Mu'assasat al-Risāla, 1981.

———. *Āthār al-ḥarb fi al-fiqh al-islāmī: Dirāsa muqārana*. Beirut: Dār al-fikr, 1981.

———. *Al-Fiqh al-islāmī wa-adillatuhu*. 2 vols. 2d ed. Damascus: Dār al-Fikr, 1985.

Contributors

Khaled Abou El Fadl is acting professor at the University of California, Los Angeles School of Law, and Omar and Azmeralda Alfi Distinguished Fellow in Islamic Law. His most recent publications include *Rebellion and Violence in Islamic Law* (Cambridge University Press, 2001), *Speaking in God's Name: Islamic Law, Authority, and Women* (Oneworld Press, 2001), and *Conference of the Books: The Search for Beauty in Islam* (University Press of America, 2001).

Donna Lee Bowen is professor of political science and Near Eastern studies at Brigham Young University. She is the author of "Islam, Abortion, and the 1994 Cairo Population Conference," *International Journal of Middle East Studies* 29 (1997), 161–84, and coeditor, with Evelyn A. Early, of *Everyday Life in the Contemporary Middle East* (Indiana University Press, 1993).

Jonathan E. Brockopp has been in the religion program at Bard College from 1995 to 2003; he has accepted a position at Pennsylvania State University beginning in 2003. He is the author of *Early Maliki Law* (E. J. Brill, 2000) and coauthor (with Jacob Neusner and Tamara Sonn) of *Judaism and Islam in Practice: A Sourcebook* (Routledge, 2000). He was also guest editor for the April 1999 issue of *The Muslim World,* devoted to Islamic ethics.

Sohail H. Hashmi is associate professor of international relations at Mount Holyoke College. He is editor of *Islamic Political Ethics: Civil Society, Pluralism, and Conflict* (Princeton University Press, 2002) and coeditor, with David Miller, of *Boundaries and Justice: Diverse Ethical Perspectives* (Princeton University Press, 2001).

Marion Holmes Katz is assistant professor of Middle Eastern studies at New York University and the author of *Body of Text: The Emergence of the Sunni Law of Ritual Purity* (State University of New York Press, 2002).

Birgit Krawietz is *Privatdozent* at Tübingen University. Besides her dissertation, *Die Ḥurma* (Duncker & Humblot, 1991), she has published articles on Islamic medical ethics, Islamic law, and theology (especially on demons). Her forthcoming book *Hierarchie der Rechtsquellen im tradierten sunnitischen Islam* deals with a possible hierarchy of the sources of the Sharia.

Richard C. Martin is professor of Islamic studies at Emory University. His books include *Defenders of Reason in Islam: Mu'tazilism from Medieval Schools to Modern Symbolism* (Oneworld, 1997) and *Islamic Studies: A History of Religions Approach* (Prentice-Hall, 1977).

Gene Outka is Dwight Professor of Philosophy and Christian Ethics at Yale University. His publications include *Agape: An Ethical Analysis* (Yale University Press, 1972), and he has coedited (with John P. Reeder Jr.) and contributed to *Religion and Morality* (Doubleday Anchor, 1973) and *Prospects for a Common Morality* (Princeton University Press, 1993).

A. Kevin Reinhart is associate professor of religion at Dartmouth College. His publications include *Before Revelation: The Boundaries of Muslim Moral Knowledge* (State University of New York Press, 1994) and the entry "Ethics in the Qur'ān" in the *Encyclopedia of the Qur'ān* (E. J. Brill, 2002).

Vardit Rispler-Chaim is a senior lecturer of Islamic studies in the Department of Arabic Language and Literature at the University of Haifa. Recent publications are "Sex Change Operations," *Al-Karmil* 18–19 (1998), 165–78 (in Arabic), and "Egyptian Fatwas on Medical Ethics" (forthcoming, in Hebrew). She is also the author of *Islamic Medical Ethics in the Twentieth Century* (E. J. Brill, 1993).

Index

Index of Qur'an Citations